PRACTICAL PROJECT MANAGEMENT

PROVEN FRAMEWORK THAT GREAT PROJECT MANAGERS USE IN THE REAL WORLD

DMYTRO NIZHEBETSKYI

EDITED BY
ANDREW DAWSON

COVER DESIGN BY
VANESSA MENDOZZI

CONTENTS

PART FIVE
HOW TO START A PROJECT

PART SIX
PROJECT PLANNING PROCESS

PART SEVEN
PROJECT SCOPE OF WORK

PART EIGHT
ESTIMATION OF TASKS

PART NINE
PROJECT SCHEDULE

ABOUT THIS BOOK

There's a huge gap between the theory and practice of project management. You can spend hundreds of hours and thousands of dollars on the relevant certifications but, still, you won't know what to do with all this knowledge. You won't feel confident about what is essential for the project's success.

That's why reading Project Management Institute's **PMBOK® Guide is not the best option**. It's a great book, but it's an encyclopedia. You don't take one to solve practical problems.

In contrast, this book teaches you a practical project management approach that works in the real world. It provides you with:

- **A structured project management framework**. It will help you manage a project from start to finish with easy-to-use templates, tools, and PM software.
- Step-by-step process of **project planning.** You can scale it up and down depending on the complexity of a project.
- A proven system to **manage stakeholders and their expectations.** Learn how to engage them in a project so that they help you rather than impede your work.
- A robust **risk management** workflow that your team and stakeholders can easily understand and follow.

- A sequential process of creating a **realistic schedule**. It's also easy-to-follow step-by-step instructions that you can implement in any project management tool.
- Essential tools to manage **project scope** and **collect requirements** even if you don't have business analysis experience.
- **Case studies and examples** for tools and processes that you can relate to.
- Supporting resources that include **templates and additional materials** that you can use as a starting point on your project.

If you want to be a great project manager, you need to use this approach as the backbone for each new project. It is simple so that your team understands it. Moreover, it is scalable for different levels of the project's complexity. **What's more important - it is NOT theory in a vacuum**.

When it comes to leading real-world projects, I feel the same pains as you do because I'm still in the trenches. I've been managing software development projects for more than ten years already.

So, I wrote this book as if for myself from 10 years ago when I had just started my project management career. That's why this book will help project managers of all levels:

- If you are an **entry-level project manager**, you need to master the approach described in this book. It's all you need for the first three to five years of your career. It's much better than reading the Project Management Institute (PMI)'s *Guide to Project Management Body of Knowledge* (*PMBOK Guide*). Nevertheless, I don't go too deep into the basics: you will have to google terminology.
- If you are a **mid-level project manager**, you'll systemize your knowledge into an integrated project management approach. It may help you pass your PMI Project Management Professional exam and improve your skills.

You'll fill all the gaps in your understanding of project management.

- If you are a **senior-level project manager**, this book will serve you as a refresher. I also hope you'll find some golden nuggets from my 10 years of experience as a software project manager. In addition, it will give you a foundation for teaching junior-level project managers in your organization.

The book's structure follows real-world needs as you encounter them on a project. That's why, for example, stakeholder, scope, and risk management come first and are the biggest parts in the book: because they have the most profound impact on your project's success.

On the other hand, some parts are small. There's little value in explaining theory you'll never use. In such cases, your action plan is to find an existing solution inside your organization. Reinventing the wheel should never be your first step.

Project management is a massive profession. It requires knowledge and skills from many different areas. Unfortunately, I couldn't fit everything into one book. So, I created a free online resource to share supporting materials. You can get my templates, tools, and access to additional video lessons to help you become a great project manager. It's free of charge. Just go to my website at:

https://itpmschool.com/materials

P.S. I use one term a lot in this book and you won't find it on the internet. 'Project owners' is a collective term for all very important stakeholders on a project. Depending on the organizational structure, it includes the sponsor, client, customer, product owners, product manager, etc. So, it's everyone who has ultimate control over the project.

PART ONE
PROJECT MANAGEMENT
MINDSET

CHAPTER 1
THE MINDSET OF A GREAT PROJECT MANAGER

What makes a great project manager? I would say it's the mindset and attitude toward project management, not the hard skills or experience you have. A given skill or technique has a limited, infrequent, local application during project's lifetime. On the other hand, mindset and attitude influence every aspect of the project management approach.

ATTITUDE TOWARDS PEOPLE AND THEIR NEEDS

A great project manager understands that projects are *for* people *by* people. So, project management is mostly managing people. But not only your project team: we need to be leaders for our clients, sponsors, and all other stakeholders.

Successfully finishing a project means satisfying the needs of all these stakeholders. Sometimes a need is not directly related to the project: it can be a career goal, internal politics, gaining recognition from leadership, or simple curiosity. All of this is totally okay.

If we can finish a project successfully and someone gets a promotion, that's fine – even if they didn't contribute to that success. At least that stakeholder didn't impede the project. That's a hidden and non-monetary cost of project success. You understand that each and every person has some expectations towards the outcome of your project.

However, a project manager should never accept illegal, unethical, or unprofessional conduct.

ATTITUDE TOWARDS YOUR OWN INFLUENCE ON A PROJECT

On the other hand, a great project manager understands that their contribution to success is indirect. You don't produce tangible results towards the project's goal. You are an overhead. You need to prove your value to the project.

But what's more important: you also understand that you don't manage a project by yourself but as part of a team. Otherwise, the team won't support your decisions.

Next, a great project manager knows that their expertise is in the organization of the work, motivating people, and removing impediments from their progress. Even if you have a technical background, don't use it to influence the team's decisions. It helps you to validate those decisions and ideas but no more.

That's why a great project manager operates within the scope of work, duration of tasks, costs, risks, and committed due dates. As a result, you control the project on a higher level and in a different domain.

ATTITUDE TOWARDS MOTIVATION AND LEADERSHIP

A great project manager constantly motivates and leads the project team. You need to give them a reason to come to work beyond just picking up their paycheck. Your team will only put their heart and soul into the project if they feel they have a higher goal they want to achieve.

Finishing a project on time and within budget means nothing to your people. They want to create results and products that will make the world better. They want to be the best of the best in their professions. They want to have a fulfilling career. And your management can help them to achieve these goals.

A great project manager knows that the team's motivation and stakeholders' desire to participate are key. Project success depends on one-quarter of hard skills and three-quarters of soft skills. It is the soft skills that convince people to use your project management approach and tools.

You understand that – in project management – most of your time and effort is spent leading people.

ATTITUDE TOWARDS REAL-WORLD PROJECTS

A great project manager understands that there's a massive gap between the theory of project management and what we do in practice. You know the value of practical skills that help you get things done with real people in real organizations.

That's why you have a leadership approach that you can adapt to new people and new environments. You know how to transition from a total stranger to a leader that people love to work with. Your leadership skills work in practice, not just in theory.

Moreover, you know that the environment in which you run a project profoundly influences everything you do.

Last but not least, you understand that projects come in all shapes and sizes, and your approach should adapt accordingly. But whatever the complexity of a project, you keep your approach lightweight, repeatable, and adaptable to any environment.

This book is all about making you a great project manager. The goal is to equip you with practical skills that you can use in the real world. To start with, let me elaborate on the influence of the environment where you work.

CHAPTER 2
INFLUENCE OF ENVIRONMENT

Unrealistic examples of project management on the internet produce a false impression of how things really operate. Once I found an example of a software development project where a project manager paid for office space, supplies, and drinking water from the project budget. It seemed like this project operated as a stand-alone company.

In the real world, you don't run projects in a vacuum: there's always an environment.

You have an organization where you work. It has policies, processes, management, offices, resources, people, tools, etc. That simplifies your work because you don't need to create a working environment from scratch: this is not your area of expertise.

For sure, it comes with a price. First, you need to follow the rules and processes of this organization. Second, you need to work with people who manage and administrate the company.

But what's more important to understand is that the environment you work in has particular expertise. This is critical, so let me give you an example.

Imagine you work in a company that develops software for other firms. It means that you do projects that are similar in nature but you produce different products and services.

The company where you work already has infrastructure, equipment, processes, and people with experience doing these kinds of projects. It includes the best practices for project management as well.

But, in the real world, a company has a niche. For example, your company may specialize in the development of websites. You might be the best in this niche. However, if you start a project to develop a mobile application for iPhone here, the chances are high that you will fail because you lack the necessary skills and expertise. Project management alone won't make any difference. Also, as you understand, if you bring a construction project to this software development company, people won't even know where to start.

Yes, these are isolated examples. However, the same happens in big companies that have separate departments dedicated to different domains. Even if you have an information technology (IT) department, it doesn't mean its staff have the expertise to handle custom software development.

For this reason, big companies outsource projects to vendors who can handle them when they don't have the expertise.

IMPACT OF ENVIRONMENT ON YOUR PROJECT

You should always start by analyzing your environment.

First, don't resist it. You need to run your project respecting the policies, requirements, and stakeholders of your company.

Second, changes in processes and policies on an organizational level shouldn't be in your current project's scope (unless they are, of course!).

Third, don't reinvent the wheel. Most likely, there's a preferred way of running a project in the organization. Use this as a starting point. Introducing lots of new things in your project management approach will create resistance from both the environment and the stakeholders.

Also, if you are new to project management, don't be afraid. You don't need to handle lots of stuff beyond your area of expertise. Most likely, your company will take care of operational functions for you. Likewise, you are not on your own here. There's always someone in the organization who can help you.

For experienced project managers, it is different. First, you need to ensure that your project is not a silo. Second, you need to double down on working with subject matter experts (SMEs) in your organization. It's tempting to think that your small team can handle everything. But, most likely, you are losing opportunities to create a better product or result for your clients. You need to use the best experts at your disposal.

Last but not least, whenever you start a project, check whether your company has the required overall expertise. If no one has ever done similar projects in your organization, you have two options.

The first option is to outsource the whole project, or a part of the project, to a vendor who has the required expertise. Of course, you can't make this decision on your own. But you need to initiate this conversation with your management.

The second option is to raise a critical risk and escalate it to your management. Ensure that they know and understand its potential impact on the project's success. It will be a valid excuse for all the challenges and delays you'll face. However, you need to discuss it regularly to find ways to mitigate the impact. Don't worry. We'll talk about risk management in detail in the Part Four of this book.

CHAPTER 3
PROJECT MANAGEMENT SOFTWARE

Usually, a project manager doesn't select software for each project. It's part of your environment. It's more likely that an organization has a preferred tool that it has already procured. Or it has decided that it doesn't need dedicated software and you need to make do with spreadsheets and freeware. Sometimes you might be obliged to use the client's software.

PROJECT MANAGEMENT SOFTWARE IS AN ADVANCED CALCULATOR

I do believe that project management software saves a lot of time. But there's a catch!

All these applications are dumb. They have no intelligence. That's why you should treat each as an advanced calculator.

Project management software does what you ask it to do. So, while the picture might look great on the screen, it doesn't mean it's right.

No matter how good and expensive your software is, it is no substitute for project management knowledge. If you are not aware of the relevant concepts, the software is useless.

For example, almost all these tools have a task list on the left side. Right? Wrong! It's not just a task list: it's a work breakdown structure

(WBS) and you need to know what this means. We'll talk about this cornerstone tool in the Chapter #39.

Likewise, you see a Gantt chart on the right-hand side, and it's tempting to start moving and aligning tasks on the calendar. But it's too early! You need to allocate resources, estimate tasks, analyze dependencies, exclude vacations and holidays, and take lots of other steps before you can start working on the Gantt chart.

So, it doesn't matter how your project management software looks and what you see right in front of you on the interface. In your head, you should follow an established project management approach. Therefore, you need to understand what you should ask the software to do.

All of that doesn't sound very encouraging. So, what are the actual benefits you should expect from dedicated project management software?

BENEFITS OF PROJECT MANAGEMENT SOFTWARE

First of all, project planning is iterative. This means that you need to change your plan a lot. These changes should propagate effortlessly throughout your whole plan across all its aspects. The same happens during execution. So, if a change is requested, you need to integrate it into the entire project.

In general, PM software speeds up the planning process. Moreover, it helps you to avoid computational errors during estimating, scheduling, etc. For example, if you set up the dependencies, resources, and holidays correctly, they will adjust automatically to any change in the schedule.

Likewise, robust project management software can do some heavy computations for you on the fly. For example, it can help you with resource-leveling and program evaluation and review technique (PERT) analysis. On the other hand, manually running the same analysis is a massive waste of time.

But what's even more critical is that modern project management software allows you to collaborate on all project aspects. Everyone sees the project plan and has allocated tasks. You can communicate in the same application, share documents, report status, etc. So, you only need one tool as opposed to a bunch of other software applications and services.

However, as is always the case in real life, there's a problem. Authoritative stakeholders and executives don't have time to log into your software to find the information they need. That's why they'll ask for a high-level status report in a spreadsheet or a slide deck. So, now you need to maintain your project management software and those spreadsheets. But, of course, you want to avoid this as much as possible. So, if your project management software can substitute for any document or artifact, you should do it.

Yes, you need to sell the benefits of using one tool. You need to make it effortless for stakeholders to find what they need. And you need to educate them. Please don't assume they know all the software on the market.

TEMPLATES AND SUPPORTING MATERIALS

This brings us to another interesting topic – project management templates. I see lots of online ads that sell you a pack of a thousand templates on any imaginable project management activity. Avoid them – it doesn't work this way.

First of all, you want to have as few documents as possible. Remember that you need to maintain them and this takes your time.

Second, all templates are specific to the environment where you work. A template created in another organization won't work for your project. There's no such thing as a universal template that fits all industries, organizations, and approaches.

Keep in mind that you need to transfer information from project management software into a template. Excel won't do it for you. Instead, you'll have to copy and paste the information, match it with the template, and format the data. In the long run, you'll have to bring the updated data back to the software.

That's why I want to provide you with just a few templates that you need. You can get all of them for free from the supporting materials section of my website. For sure, you'll have to adapt a template to your project. But I've kept them as practical and straightforward as possible. So, they'll give you a great starting point to developing the templates that you can reuse.

Get access at:

https://itpmschool.com/materials

CHAPTER 4
SIZE AND COMPLEXITY OF A PROJECT

There are projects of different sizes and complexity in the real world. However, project management is always an overhead for them. Yes, project management improves chances of success. But you need to balance the effort you put in with the benefit this will bring to the project. Therefore, there are different levels of project management. Let me illustrate this using construction projects as an example because they are easy to imagine.

The first project is a kitchen renovation. It has a budget of about $10,000–$20,000 and will take several weeks. The project team will be 10 to 15 people, dealing with all supplies, delivery, and installation.

So, it's a small project. Using Microsoft (MS) Project, performing PERT analysis, or even proper risk management is overkill. Instead, you can easily plan and manage this project using a spreadsheet, email, and a cell phone.

The second project is the construction of a multistoried building. It's a $5 million project, and it will take a year to finish. Hundreds of people will work on it. Moreover, you'll need a variety of expertise: legal and procurement to secure the land, engineering for systems, construction, compliance and safety checks, and so on.

This project will obviously require a more robust approach. You'll put more effort into planning, risk management, communications, and project documentation. So, it would be wise to invest in proper project management. You'll have to create a project plan that will show how you'll use those five million dollars to achieve the project goal. It will increase the chances of the project's success.

We can take these examples one step further. Let's imagine someone's building a stadium. Most likely, it's even a group of projects. With all infrastructure, it may cost anywhere from $500 million to $1.9 billion. I can safely assume that less than 1% of project managers in the world can handle such a project.

Nevertheless, there's a role for a project manager on all of these examples. All will need a project management approach. But ask yourself this:

- Do we put a manager who built a stadium on a renovation project? No. It's overkill.
- Do we need the same skill set to build a stadium and to do home repairs? No.
- Do we need the same project management tools and techniques to manage these projects?

You get the point!

Projects vary in size and complexity. Smaller projects don't require a degree, expert knowledge, or certification. Likewise, they don't need an overcomplicated project management approach.

Moreover, there are more tiny, small, and medium projects than huge ones like building a stadium. So, it's excellent news for you if you want to start a career as a project manager. There's always a small project with which you can begin. And you don't need a specific education or certifications to get started.

Let's sum it up. A great project manager understands that their approach should be as lightweight as possible. Project management itself drains resources. It's not free of charge. Therefore, you should always start with a backbone set of processes and tools recommended by the industry and your environment. Then, you can consider adding tools, techniques, and processes as you see fit. Don't make project management complicated just because you read an article on the internet or have learned something on a course.

CHAPTER 5
A PROJECT MANAGER'S PATTERNS OF BEHAVIOR

The mindset of a great project manager transforms into a practical set of roles and responsibilities. It would be best if you learned how to fulfill them all. Nevertheless, it's an ongoing process. So, no one expects you to know it all at the start of your career. Let's break it down and see the areas you can improve.

TITLE VS. ROLE VS. RESPONSIBILITIES

You have the title – project manager. Actually, you may have the title of junior/senior project manager, delivery manager, technical project manager, IT project manager, construction project manager, etc. These titles are similar but there are some subtle differences.

Each title comes with a list of responsibilities that it is your duty to deal with. Responsibilities you see in a job description can help you understand whether you have all the required skills and knowledge. That's the level of your competency.

A role is a function or a model of behavior that you must follow. But I want you to think about the roles of a project manager specifically as daily patterns of behavior while working on a project. You need to apply the same patterns no matter what title you hold.

I believe that there are five patterns of behavior for a great project manager. These help you fulfill all your responsibilities automatically.

ROLE #1: PRESIDENT OF A SMALL COMPANY

A great project manager is never a passive executor. Instead, you should feel ownership of the project and every decision you make. So, for example:

- Project owners didn't do what was needed on time and you missed a milestone. That's your problem. You didn't communicate the priorities well.
- The job market is slow, and you can't hire people to start the project on time. You assessed your capabilities poorly and you didn't manage expectations.
- A functional manager forced you to take on an inexperienced or unsuitable specialist. That is your problem as well.

It seems like none of these are under your control. It's tempting to say, "I did everything I could." Or share responsibility for every decision with dozens of stakeholders. But you won't become a great project manager this way. Instead, you need to take the lead and ultimate responsibility for the success of your project.

The best way to model such behavior is to assume that you are responsible for everything. You should feel like the president of a small company. So you imagine yourself in the project owners' shoes. You think about their business as if it's yours, no matter what other stakeholders believe and do. Then, you implement the project as if you are spending your own money. That will help you focus on finishing the project and reaching business objectives.

But remember that this ultimate responsibility comes with limited authority. So, to continue with the metaphor, you have to answer to a board of directors and you need to keep them happy.

So, you don't have direct control over all aspects of a project. And you are subordinate to project owners and your boss. That's why you need to negotiate and collaborate with others to get things done. For example, you may need to get sign-offs from stakeholders before making an important decision. Therefore, you'll need their support. You'll need to engage with other stakeholders to tap into their expertise.

Nevertheless, while others have authority, control, or expertise in technical matters, you are the only expert in project management. Only you dedicate the whole working day to honing your project management skills. Moreover, you will be the only one from your project team to read this book. Project owners hired you to organize their work to reach their business objectives.

That's why you need to show all project stakeholders the best approach to get what they want. Moreover, you should take complete ownership of the project management approach you selected and the team you hired. You should show that you are the most interested in reaching the project's objectives. Of course, you can't enforce it. You do it all through leadership, mentoring, and by your example. With every bit of success, you'll prove that you know how to finish the project successfully.

ROLE #2: PROJECT INTEGRATOR

Processes and tools in project management are separated and isolated. Each requires different information in different formats. As a project manager, you need to tailor these bits and pieces into a cohesive whole.

Take, as an example, a person who has zero knowledge of technical aspects of a project and project management. He simply shares his insights as best as he can. So, first, you need to convert his free-form speech into project management terms like "requirements," "the scope of work," "estimates," etc. Then, you need to capture these terms in your project management software as tasks and include them in the project plan. All these activities are project integration. This happens all the time, on all levels of the project work.

FOUR LEVELS OF INTEGRATION

Integration on the **objective** level means that you need to identify the project's objective and ensure that all stakeholders agree. Next, all your efforts and resources should aim to achieve that goal.

Integration on the **stakeholders** level means that all stakeholders have the same information about every aspect of the project. Don't assume that stakeholders communicate with each other or proactively search for the project information: you need to keep them informed and aligned.

Integration on the **processes and tools** level means that you need to make these work together. For example, you need to convert verbal and narrative information from people into tasks in your software. Or ensure that results of the risk identification meeting are captured as an action plan and risk reserves in the project's budget.

Integration on the **environment** level means that your project management approach should work hand in hand with your organization's environment.

Let me give you an example of how these different levels work. Imagine that clients ask you to make a change to a requirement. As a result, you need to tweak the behavior of an application. Moreover, the clients ask you to try to fit into the current deadline.

First of all, you need to be bold enough to question the necessity of this change. Does it help to reach the project's objective? Or is it just a whim or gold plating? It's integration on the objective level.

Next, on the environmental level, you may have various policies for such requests. For example, you may need to inform your line manager and ensure that allocated resources and people will still be available to your project. Maybe there are plans already for the engineer who can implement that request.

After that, if the change aligns with the goal, you need to communicate it to other stakeholders. On the one hand, you want to collect inputs, insights, and feedback. On the other hand, you need to keep all stakeholders informed. They may have expectations regarding your changes.

The next step is to integrate on the level of processes, tools, and your project plan. Again, it may look like it's a small requirement and just a bit of work. But you need to review the impact on all the aspects of the project: quality, risks, costs, duration, sign-offs, etc.

If you update the plan, you may need to share the updated deadlines, budget, and schedule with stakeholders.

But it's not only about changes to the project. Integration happens during planning, executing, and reporting on the project's progress in almost the same way. All processes, tools, and documentation require integration with one another.

Here's the truth:

No one wants to do all of this work. Integration feels like an administrative burden. But, without it, a project quickly becomes a mess. So, you, as a great project manager, have to assume this role and keep the project in line and in one piece.

ROLE #3: FACILITATOR

Put a software engineer, a graphic designer, and a quality assurance (QA) engineer in one room. Then, ask them to produce a cost-efficient solution for the project. Then, leave.

I'm 95% certain that this team will not come up with any reasonable outcome. They will provide you with the best solution they are capable of. However, it will be out of context and in a vacuum.

But, give them a little direction, keep them to the topic, and align them with the project goals and constraints. Then, suddenly, you have a treasure trove of valuable ideas and constructive solutions!

That's why you need to facilitate all project activities. And, in general, you need to initiate and foster professional interactions on a project.

A great project manager is miles ahead in terms of soft skills. None of the team members or stakeholders would ever know as much about leadership, management, and communications as you do. And, in the real world, lots of people you work with have below-average soft skills. That's totally fine, but it means you need to help them interact with each other.

I want to stress this as well: your product owners are in charge of the project. They might be successful businesspeople or have an executive role in a company. But it doesn't mean they automatically become great leaders like Elon Musk or Steve Jobs. So, you also need to help project owners to interact with one another and with the project team.

There's another side of the coin here. You are an expert in project management. You know how to organize the work, how to use processes and tools. However, in most cases, you don't do project management on your own. You implement your approach via the hands of the project team and stakeholders.

So, you don't want to force people to follow your project plan or to use the tools and techniques you selected. Instead, you want to sell them the benefits of doing so. Then, educate and empower the team members to use all those tools and techniques. They become the owners of the processes, documents, and tools, while you facilitate their work.

It's a small but powerful mental shift – make the team members the consumers (not the workforce) of your project management approach.

ROLE #4: PROACTIVE COMMUNICATOR

My favorite quote by (most probably) William H. Whyte, which I always keep in mind, goes as follows: "The biggest problem in communication is the illusion that it has taken place." You can track back 99% of all problems on a project to a lack of communication. I've noticed that problems boil down to these three groups:

- Stakeholders don't always communicate with each other – even people inside your organization.
- None of the stakeholders knows everything about the project. Vital pieces of information are always scattered among different people.
- People don't ask a question if they feel someone will deem it silly. Even mature businesspeople and executives can't overcome this problem.

You can overcome all three problems by becoming a proactive communicator.

First of all, you need to ensure that all stakeholders get all the information they need when they need it. Let's say you make a decision with one stakeholder without informing others. Later, other stakeholders find out. However, they may have a different opinion, leading to a conflict. So, it's better to be open at the start so you can resolve any potential disagreements as early as possible.

Second, you need to collect and digest information from all SMEs. Then, you need to share your knowledge with other stakeholders to develop a shared vision of the product, project, and all the challenges you have.

Third, you should not be afraid to bring up problems for discussion. It's uncomfortable, but you should never take it personally: it's part of your job.

Last but not least, you need to connect the technical and business worlds. First, you need to interpret the project owners' requirements, fears, and concerns. Then, formulate and communicate them to the project team in terms of requirements.

Likewise, you need to translate the technical solutions into business terminology. This means transforming technical challenges into business pros and cons. You need to explain complex topics in simple terms so that your project owners can make a decision.

You need to initiate communications to provide as much transparency as possible. Always ask about technical aspects that you don't understand. I can guarantee that 80% of people in the room don't understand them either. But they don't want to show it, and they don't want to look silly. You should be okay about asking "silly" questions. You should do the work for people who feel insecure.

Here are some examples of how to do it:

"Could you please explain it in simple terms so that I can discuss it with the project owners?"

Or:

"Could you please explain what the business impact is here? What are the pros and cons of each approach for our product?"

Also, keep in mind that stakeholders don't have much expertise in project management. So don't expect that they will ask how your project management approach works. It's a silly question. Instead, you need to continually "refresh" their knowledge.

ROLE #5: PROACTIVE PROBLEM SOLVER

The biggest issue with any problem is that no one wants to take responsibility for it. A problem means uncomfortable conversations, extra work, and conflicts. So, no one wants to take the initiative and issues pile up.

What's even worse is when problems that do not fall under anyone's responsibilities appear on a project every day. Some will fall between two different responsibility areas; some will be entirely new. But, in most cases, people think that someone else should handle it. Because of that, they don't bring the problem up. And you find about it only when it hits the project hard.

You'll undoubtedly resolve problems related to project management, your team, and everything within your responsibilities. However, it's not enough. You need to motivate your team and stakeholders to resolve the problems on their plate. At the very least, you need to encourage them to discuss the problem with the right people. They need to start the conversation. At the same time, you need to keep a running list of all the project problems you are aware of.

Usually, it's easier to resolve any issues in the early stages. To a certain extent, you'll have time to develop a proactive solution before it impacts the project. That's why you need to continuously ask whether anyone has any problems. People should feel safe to bring up any or all their concerns.

Moreover, people will make mistakes from time to time. You can't avoid it. But they need to feel they can tell you about the problem as early as possible without fear of reprisals. Of course, you should always take the blame for the mistakes of your team. Later, you can decide what to do with the troublemaker. But you should never allow anyone else to blame your team members publicly.

Last but not least, you should educate your team on problem-solving techniques. You won't have time to solve all the problems. And a forgotten or unresolved problem is like a ticking time bomb. So, your team should know how to deal with personal and technical problems efficiently in the long run.

CHAPTER 6
RESPONSIBILITIES OF A PROJECT MANAGER

Now let's talk about responsibilities. A responsibility is something that it is your duty to deal with. It's part of your job description.

And here's the truth: There's no standardized list of project manager responsibilities. Instead, every company describes the primary responsibilities based on their needs, culture, and understanding of project management.

So, I read through hundreds of job descriptions for project manager roles. Based on that, I created an ultimate list of responsibilities. I want you to read through it line by line. Here we go. A project manager:

1. has ultimate responsibility for the project's success;
2. is the main communication point with project owners;
3. promotes a productive and collaborative environment;
4. controls and enhances the positive effects of cultural differences
5. ensures professional interaction between the team and the stakeholders;
6. ensures collaboration within the team;
7. resolves personal conflicts;
8. enforces personal responsibility;
9. protects the team from internal politics

10. assists during the pre-sale process;
11. helps to produce the project charter;
12. identifies all key stakeholders;
13. develops a strategy to work with all stakeholders;
14. selects appropriate processes for the project;
15. sets up a collaboration with global and virtual teams;
16. explains the project life cycle and processes to stakeholders;
17. coordinates work between the project and key stakeholders;
18. integrates all pieces of a project into a whole;
19. works with stakeholders to identify constraints and assumptions;
20. is responsible for producing the project management plan;
21. leads and facilitates the planning process;
22. ensures collaboration of the team and stakeholders during planning;
23. identifies dependencies of project activities;
24. enforces risk management processes;
25. analyzes required time and cost reserves;
26. determines the required level of quality for the projects;
27. selects and controls processes that can deliver the required quality;
28. is responsible for developing a realistic schedule;
29. participates in procurement processes;
30. creates a change management plan;
31. actively avoids changes to the project baselines;
32. controls implementation of approved changes;
33. assists the team during project execution;
34. works with stakeholders to meet their expectations
35. ensures that the customer accepts deliverables;
36. works with the team to keep as close as possible to the plan;
37. moves the project towards its goal daily;
38. uses metrics to control project progress;
39. communicates project progress to key stakeholders;
40. keeps the team focused on risk management throughout the project;
41. spends time to improve processes;

42. works to improve project and product quality;
43. motivates the project team;
44. ensures that people leave the project motivated;
45. encourages team-building activities;
46. articulates their vision of a successful project and product
47. develops team members for the benefit of both the project and the organization;
48. organizes performance reviews;
49. solves problems;
50. controls the project in all aspects (scope, time, costs, risks, quality, etc.);
51. analyzes variances with the project management plan;
52. determines whether a change request is needed to get back on track;
53. performs project closure;
54. ensures that all contract obligations are closed;
55. logs lessons learned; and
56. updates the organization's knowledge base.

That's a huge list of responsibilities but, most probably, it doesn't cover all the aspects of our profession. So why did I want you to read it through carefully?

First of all, to show you what is NOT on that huge list. I remember when I was fresh and new to project management: I always felt the need to fill the gaps within the team.

Someone is slowing down – I'm here to help and push forward. I'm part designer, part QA guy, part business analyst, part administrator – a jack of all trades.

But I want you to know that creating project deliverables or doing the project work is not your responsibility.

The project manager's primary responsibility is to organize and motivate people to do the work in a controlled way that will help achieve the project's goal.

That is your area of expertise. You should spend time and effort helping others to do their work and finish assigned tasks on time. You should spend time thinking about how to improve the project's chances of success and how to achieve the project's goal.

Second, I want you to combine everything we have discussed so far. You should understand that your responsibilities will vary based on the size and complexity of the project, the project management culture of your environment, and your experience.

Third, notice that you can fulfill most responsibilities by following those five roles of a project manager. Again, it's easier to follow behavior patterns than to worry that you missed something from that huge list above.

IN-DEPTH ANALYSIS OF PROJECT MANAGER RESPONSIBILITIES

Now let's dive a bit deeper. Let's discuss why companies put specific responsibilities in the job description. Why do they want you to perform certain activities?

First of all, you won't see a job description with an exhaustive list of everything you should do. On the other hand, on all job descriptions, you'll find that you are responsible for overall project success or even the whole business with a client.

So, you are responsible for everything on a project. That's why I recommend viewing it as a behavior model and mindset.

Now, let's talk about several critical responsibilities that actually make you a project manager.

#1: YOU'RE RESPONSIBLE FOR DEFINING PROJECT GOALS

Why is this your responsibility, not the project owners'? Why does the employer want you to identify the project's goal? You know the saying:

"If one does not know to which port one is sailing, no wind is favorable."
  – Lucius Annaeus Seneca

If your goal is clearly defined, you know exactly what you need to do to make your client happy. Otherwise, you may create a great product or service but that tiny something will be missing. Believe me, project owners will remember and fixate only on this negative aspect. So, you want to control their expectations on what you'll deliver.

On the other hand, here's another mindset of a great project manager: You can spend allocated resources only to reach the client's business goals. Any other activities that different stakeholders try to impose on you are secondary.

Overall, knowing the project goal helps you fixate on delivering precisely what project owners want. That will make them happy clients who will hire you again.

#2: YOU'RE RESPONSIBLE FOR PROJECT PLANNING

In general, you are responsible for increasing the project's chances of success. One of the best ways to do that is by simulating project execution. Planning is exactly that. You try to think through the project from start to end.

If you use project management software, it's just like any simulation game:

- You create a Gantt chart that shows you the flow of tasks, how they depend on each other, and different events on the calendar.
- You calculate the budget and cash flow to ensure that you have enough money to support all the required activities during the whole project.
- You try to imagine all possible things that could go wrong in the process. Moreover, you prepare countermeasures in advance.

Do this for all aspects of a project, including communications, motivation, stakeholder engagement, people development, etc. This way, you'll prove that you can achieve the project goals within given constraints.

Different companies will require different levels of planning. Some may not require any planning at all. But I believe that you must plan a project. And you must put in the right amount of effort. The size and complexity of your project will dictate how serious your planning efforts should be.

Sometimes your organization or clients see planning as a waste of time. But you should try to convince them, at the very least, to allow for some basic planning. It's the most significant benefit of project management.

Why do YOU need a solid project plan?

It's all about motivation. In general, people are reluctant to strive for the finish line if they can't see it. They disengage if they don't believe that the task is feasible.

That's why you break down a project into smaller, more manageable pieces. Then, you break it down further to individual tasks for each person. Now, everyone has a step-by-step (or task-by-task) plan on how to handle the huge endeavor: It's not that scary now.

Likewise, stakeholders need to feel that you are capable of leading the project to success. Remember that all of them have their own objectives. That's why they'll want to associate their work with a successful project: This will buy their support during execution.

#3: YOU'RE RESPONSIBLE FOR EXECUTING YOUR PLAN

You are responsible for following your own plan. Moreover, you are responsible for making others follow your plan. For sure, you do it through leadership and motivation, not authority or title. But it's more complicated than it seems.

When a project is underway, there are hundreds of events and factors that could potentially derail the plan. As a result, inexperienced project managers either abandon the plan or start tinkering with it way too often. On the other hand, experienced project managers try to do everything possible to bring things back to the initial plan. Changing it is a last resort, when things have veered too far off course.

If you don't keep to your initial project plan, you neglect all the benefits of project management. You fail to manage daily activities with a proper long-term perspective. Sooner or later, you end up in the proverbial firefighting mode.

#4: YOU'RE RESPONSIBLE FOR CONTROLLING THE PROJECT

The main technical reason you need a project plan is to compare your current progress with your initial plan. A project plan clearly states what work the project team will perform on a given date and how much it should cost.

Without a plan, you can only state the amount of budget and time you have spent so far on different activities. But it doesn't answer the main questions: Does that constitute good progress? Are we on track towards our goal? Are we even pursuing the goal we planned?

That's exactly why I believe your progress reports should be pretty simple. They should state whether the project is on track as per the project management plan.

Also, if you don't compare your initial plan with your actual progress, you'll never know how good your project management skills are.

#5: YOU'RE RESPONSIBLE FOR CONTINUOUS DEVELOPMENT

One more time – you are responsible for improving the chances of success for your project. Developing your own skills is a critical contribution. As you are reading this book, you have the correct mindset already.

It relates to all projects around you:

- Your current project.
- Your next project.
- The projects that your colleagues are leading right now.

That is why, during each project, you need to learn valuable lessons. So, whether you have such processes in the organization or not, you should undertake this learning for your own development.

Why?

You never know what project will be next. Your current project is a training ground for your next bigger and more complex project.

On the other hand, isn't it great when there is always someone who can share a tip or two on running a project? Why shouldn't this person be you? Become a go-to person and make your contribution to the project management profession.

RESPONSIBILITIES EXERCISE

Your ability to fulfill a responsibility shows your competency. So, to develop professional skills, first assess your ability to perform responsibilities from the list above. Then, you can grade them by levels: none, beginner, intermediate, expert. Or you can simply mark "Yes" or "No."

Your next goal is to develop skills and knowledge for all responsibilities, at least on the beginner level. Then you can dig deeper into each responsibility, one by one.

However, the list is not an exhaustive one. For example, in your environment, you may need pre-sales or special quality management skills. In any case, though, you should follow the same learning pattern.

This book will help you cover most of the hard skills of project management that you need.

PART TWO
PROJECT LIFE CYCLE

CHAPTER 7
WHAT IS A PROJECT LIFE CYCLE AND WHY DO YOU NEED IT?

The concept of a project life cycle is critical because it helps you structure the work and make it more manageable. That's why I'm going to explain everything you need to know about it.

A life cycle consists of phases. A project phase is a collection of logically related project activities that culminate in the completion of one or more deliverables. In other words, a phase combines work that is similar in nature and requires a specific set of expertise and processes. For example, an architecture design phase requires the expertise of engineers and architects. However, during a construction phase, you need to manage the work of builders and suppliers.

The project life cycle is the combination of all the phases needed from the start to the finish of a project.

Here are some examples of phases: Initiation, concept development, planning, requirements definition, user interface (UI) design, development, integration, testing, deployment, hypercare, maintenance, hand-off, closure, and support.

Phases in the life cycle can follow a strict sequence, overlap, or run in parallel. So, your project may be a tangle of overlapping phases. Moreover, on a smaller project, you won't clearly separate phases from one another. Note that a project doesn't have to include all the phases.

Instead, as a project manager, you need to decide which phases to include.

But here's the secret! You'll rarely invent a project life cycle from scratch.

If you take a particular industry niche, you'll discover that there are just a few proven and established life cycles there. Therefore, an organization in that niche most likely uses one or two project life cycles for all of its projects. So, again, you see the influence of our environment. The organization will dictate the most suitable project life cycle based on its previous experience.

On the other hand, let's assume you are the only project manager and the organization wants you to complete a project that it's never done before. You wouldn't start inventing a project life cycle on your own. Most probably, you'd google it, or you'd find another project manager who had carried out similar projects.

Now, I have to address a popular myth: Project management is universal for all industries. Admittedly, it's mostly true: You can use the approach from this book in any industry with minor adjustments. However, the more projects you complete in a particular industry, the more efficient you become in that industry. So, project managers often specialize in one niche.

Switching from construction to software development is painful, even if you have 10 years of experience. On the other hand, changing a niche within one industry is entirely possible although you still have a learning curve.

All of this leads us to an important conclusion: You'll have long periods in your career working on projects using the same project life cycle. Quite possibly, you'll work in one industry your whole life. It simply means you must invest time into learning the project life cycles of your industry.

So, here's an important thing I want you to remember:

All projects in your niche are unique, but all will follow a typical project life cycle.

I think this is the primary benefit of project management: Typical life cycles make projects predictable.

BENEFITS OF KNOWING PROJECT LIFE CYCLES

A project life cycle describes all the types of work needed to finish the project. So, if you understand the life cycle, you know how to create products, services, and results in the niche where you work. As a result, when you have experience in this life cycle, you know how to do the work more efficiently.

But, from a project management perspective, there are further benefits to be had. Here are five main reasons to divide a project into phases (sub-projects).

#1: TO MAKE THE PROJECT MANAGEABLE

Some projects are complex, long, and require a lot of work. In such cases, planning alone may take several weeks or months. Moreover, each phase may be the size of a small project.

In such cases, the project manager divides a project into phases that have tangible deliverables. The total sum of all deliverables equals completion of the project. This way you manage a series of smaller projects rather than one huge one.

#2: TO SEPARATE WORK OF A DIFFERENT NATURE

A project may need to produce a set of different deliverables that require diverse expertise, various stakeholders, and processes. But, even if it's a small project, you will still want to separate different types of activities. For example, you may want to separate the following:

- Requirements collection (brainstorming, workshops, interviews with stakeholders, writing requirements documentation).
- Design phase (collaboration with creative experts on wireframes, designs, mock-ups).
- Planning phase (applying project management skills; working with the team to identify scope, risks, and provide estimates).

- Actual development (daily activities of construction or engineering).
- Testing (assurance of quality, benchmarking, performance measurements, etc.).

Each of these phases requires work of a different nature. As a result, you probably won't be able to manage them all using the same set of processes, tools, and techniques. Likewise, your leadership style can be different depending on the people you work with in these phases.

#3: TO MAKE THE PROJECT MORE PREDICTABLE

Different phases of the project life cycle require different levels of effort and costs. For example, more money is usually spent in the execution phases. However, some projects might need expensive materials bought in advance or an aggressive hiring process. Such projects will have peaks of costs and efforts in certain phases.

So, you need to ensure that you have the right resources and people at the right time. Moreover, you need to have enough budget to cover the costs. Knowing the project life cycle will help you plan for this.

#4. TO CREATE PROJECT CHECKPOINTS

A deliverable is handed off at the end of each phase. This is a good time to reassess the project's chances of success and to decide whether to continue or not.

Let's say that, after the feasibility analysis phase, you produce a report that makes it clear that you can't finish the project in full scope.

Project owners may deem it unacceptable. As a result, they'll terminate the project and relocate the remaining resources to a more worthwhile one. Please note that this actually demonstrates excellent project management, not a project's failure.

#5: TO REDUCE THE COST OF A CHANGE

Naturally, risks and uncertainty are higher at the beginning and decrease as you get closer to a project's end. On the other hand, it is less expensive to change something at the beginning than at the end, when it may not even be possible. A minor change in the requirements may impact the whole product or service you have already created.

That's why comprehensive project planning early on is necessary to reduce uncertainty. Clarifying the project scope at the start, in the right way, helps avoid fundamental changes further down the road.

I strongly recommend making the impact of changes during a project's lifetime as clear as possible to your stakeholders from the start. Never assume that they understand this by default. So, avoid changes near the project's end: They are costly, and you would have depleted most of your budget by that time.

Let's summarize all this. First, a great project manager has a clear picture of the project life cycle. Second, you need to continuously improve your knowledge of your industry and the niche you work in.

All in all, it boils down to an understanding of:

- what work needs to be done;
- the expertise you need to complete the work;
- the sequence of the work; and
- best practices for managing different types of work.

Here's the good thing about it: You need to focus on only one or two life cycles at a time during your career.

Next, we'll discuss the specifics of the life cycles of large, small, and agile projects. Then, we'll dive deeper into phases and how to describe them.

CHAPTER 8
THE LIFE CYCLE OF A LARGE PROJECT

Large projects provide the best examples of life cycles. They can include phases that are bigger than the projects you currently manage. Likewise, these phases produce distinct deliverables. So, they are easier to imagine.

But, before we move on, I want to address something that might cause confusion. There are no standard names for phases. Each organization develops a project life cycle that suits its needs. Therefore, you can name phases as you wish.

Also, don't mix project phases with process groups.

PROCESS GROUPS VS. PROJECT PHASES

The PMI, in its *PMBOK Guide*, introduced the term "project management process groups," of which there are five[1]:

- Initiating.
- Planning.
- Executing.
- Monitoring and controlling.
- Closing.

This is confusing, because they are the same names as those of the project phases. However, the idea is simple.

Each phase includes the whole project management process with all five process groups. However, for each phase, you can have a separate project management process. So, you can select different set of processes in each process group for each phase.

For example, you may have a planning phase. This includes initiating, planning, executing, monitoring and controlling, and closing process groups. So, yes, you will be planning the creation of a project plan. For instance, you need to know how long this will take. So, on a large project, you'll use simple planning process and estimation techniques to assess the duration of the planning phase.

Put simply, it means that you can and should treat each phase as a sub-project that you initiate, plan, execute, and so on. You set goals, identify the scope of the work, and produce tangible results at the end of each phase. But you must scale your project management efforts based on the needs of each phase.

EXAMPLES OF LARGE PROJECTS

Figure 8.1 shows how the life cycle of a large project may look:

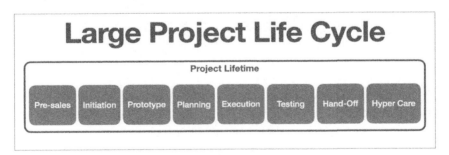

Figure 8.1: *Example of a large project's life cycle*

This is a sequential life cycle, meaning that all phases follow one another in a strict order. You might have "gates" between the phases where you re-evaluate the feasibility of the project.

It's a plan-driven life cycle because we have already planned out the phases. Someone may call it a "waterfall" approach. But that is not correct. The waterfall is a specific project management approach, not a generic life cycle.

However, in the real world, you would rarely see sequential life cycles. In most cases, some phases will overlap and you'll do the work in parallel. See figure 8.2.

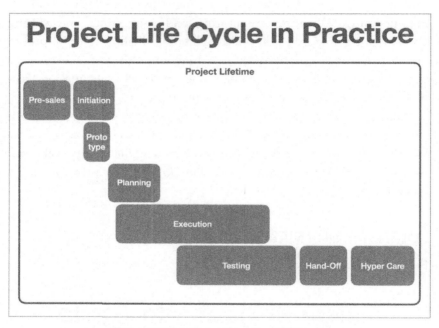

Figure 8.2: *Example of a real-world project life cycle*

Also, I need to address a common misconception. People think that you can't go backward in a plan-driven life cycle like this: that once the phase is done, it's done, and you should carry on regardless.

This is not true. It's not even true in the initial waterfall approach. If, in the execution phase, you need to make a change in the requirements, you do it. You go back to the deliverables from the planning phase and adjust them. Likewise, you may need to adjust other phases as well.

Keep in mind that, usually, you don't do the complete overhaul in the middle of a project. This is about making a small change here and there. The main challenge is to incorporate the impact of the change in all aspects of the project.

If you discover something critical on a large project, you may need to adjust the whole project management plan. But, in this case, you escalate it to a higher level. Then, together with the project owners, you decide whether to cancel the project or adjust the plan and the project's constraints.

CHAPTER 9
SMALL PROJECT LIFE CYCLE

Small projects are harder to dissect because phases overlap and coincide with the project management process. As a result, it can feel like a real mess of activities.

Quite often, it feels like you don't have phases: It's as if you have only one distinctive phase – implementation. The whole project fits in there.

However, I recommend that you assume that all phases are present. Also, each phase has its exit criteria –something you need to create or achieve to move forward. Most of the phases will take a few hours of work, but they'll stretch across a few weeks. Some of the phases will stack on top of each other and you'll grind through them bit by bit. And there'll be phases where you do not participate at all. But, still, they are there.

This approach is essential for your transition towards managing larger and more complex projects. At the very least, there's always a generic life cycle for small projects encompassing the main idea. This consists of four phases:

1. **Starting the project**. In this phase, you research, investigate, and define the goals of the project end result. The examples

from larger projects are the research, requirement collection, and feasibility analysis phases.

2. **Organizing and preparing**. In essence, this is specifying requirements, creating product design, and planning. Examples are the product design, product architecture, and planning phases.

3. **Carrying out the project work**. This is where you actually execute the work to produce the desired result. Examples are the implementation, construction, development, and testing phases.

4. **Closing the project**. In this phase, you need to hand out the final project result, service, or product. Examples are the release (to the market), transfer (e.g., to maintenance and operations), and close-out phases.

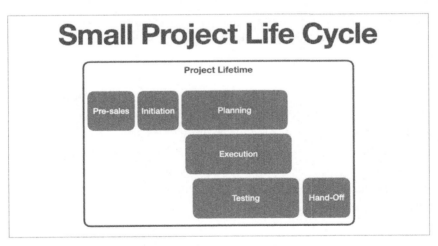

Figure 9.1: Example of a small project's life cycle

Phases and project management process groups overlap here.

CHAPTER 10
AGILE PROJECT MANAGEMENT

You must have heard about the agile frameworks we use in project management: Scrum or Kanban. If not, I recommend that you google "Scrum Guides." This will give you a quick overview of the Scrum framework.

In theory, you can use the Scrum to run a project from start to finish. You develop pieces of the project in iterations, called "sprints." Usually, these are two or three weeks long.

The biggest benefit of agile frameworks is that they allow you to change work priorities each iteration. You can also rapidly change requirements if needed. Likewise, you don't spend effort planning out the whole project at the start.

Again, in theory, it sounds incredible! But, in practice, there are pros and cons to all agile frameworks. Moreover, they have specific use cases where they excel or fail.

In the real world, you can't run a project with an agile framework from start to finish (see figure 10.1).

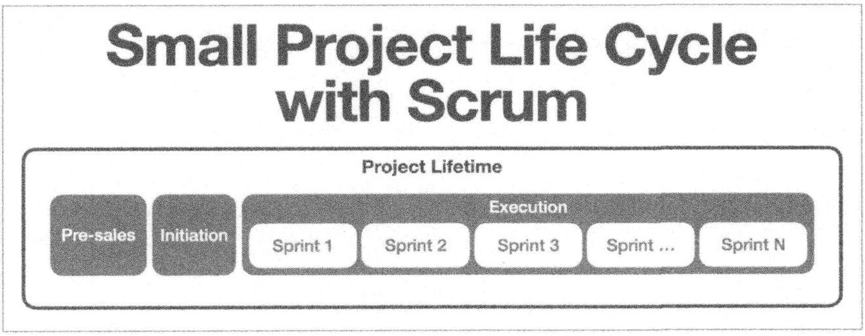

Small Project Life Cycle with Scrum

Project Lifetime

Pre-sales | Initiation | **Execution** | Sprint 1 | Sprint 2 | Sprint 3 | Sprint ... | Sprint N

Figure 10.1: Example of a project executed with the Scrum framework

There's still a place for plan-driven phases, even in agile projects. For example, you'll never run the pre-sales and initiation phases with Scrum or Kanban. That work is sequential by nature. But you'll switch to an agile framework once you get into the execution phase.

Agile project management is an approach that combines plan-driven and agile phases in one project life cycle.

So, it's just a project life cycle. And, like with any other life cycle, there is no standardized approach: It's different in different companies.

For example, the initiation and planning phases are very much plan-driven. Then, you execute the main implementation phases with Scrum. In the end, you may switch to Kanban to test and fix critical defects.

Once the team finishes the initial implementation, you may return to the plan-driven approach to deploy and finalize the project.

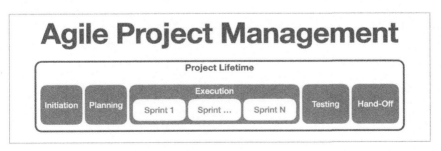

Agile Project Management

Project Lifetime

Initiation | Planning | **Execution** | Sprint 1 | Sprint ... | Sprint N | Testing | Hand-Off

Figure 10.2: Agile project management concept

WHY MIX AGILE WITH PROJECT MANAGEMENT?

Let's be clear. Scrum or Kanban on their own are not agile project management approaches: They are separate and self-sufficient frameworks.

In practice, most companies and clients are not ready to be fully agile. Scrum or Kanban won't satisfy a big organization's management and administrative needs. Therefore, most adopt a hybrid life cycle suited to their environment.

Agile project management is typically used in software development and telecommunications. Nowadays, it's a prerequisite for any project manager working in those industries.

However, I believe that all project managers in all sectors should learn agile frameworks. They offer a great set of additional tools and techniques that you should have at your disposal. For example, these frameworks can help you on projects with lots of uncertainties.

Keep in mind that these are just frameworks – don't be sucked in by all the hype and marketing buzz around the Agile Manifesto, Scrum, and Kanban.

CHAPTER 11
DESCRIPTIONS OF COMMON PHASES

Here's an exercise to help you get to grips with life cycles. As you already know, life cycles are different in each industry. Moreover, each company may get creative in its niche. Just for comparison, take a look at the life cycles below:

SOFTWARE DEVELOPMENT LIFE CYCLE

- Pre-sales phase.
- Initiation phase.
- Concept development phase.
- Proof of concept phase.
- Planning phase.
- Requirements definition phase.
- UI design phase.
- Development phase.
- Integration phase.
- Testing phase.
- Deployment phase.
- Hypercare Phase.
- Hand-off and closure phase.

GENERIC CONSTRUCTION PROJECT LIFE CYCLE

- Concept phase.
- Planning phase.
- Design and development phase.
- Implementation phase.
- Close-out phase.

FACILITY CONSTRUCTION PROJECT LIFE CYCLE

- Market assessment phase.
- Conceptual planning phase.
- Feasibility analysis phase.
- Design and engineering phase.
- Procurement phase.

You do need some knowledge and experience to describe a project life cycle and its phases. So, if you are a new project manager, you need to do your research (both online and by reading books) to learn more about life cycles in your industry. You need to be able to describe a life cycle to someone with zero knowledge in this area. But, again, don't focus too much on the names of the phases. You need to imagine the work and its nature.

So, as an example, I'll provide a detailed description of the project phases for software development, which is my area of expertise. A bonus for you if you work in IT! But this will still be relevant whatever your industry, so do read the descriptions anyway.

PRE-SALES PHASE

When a business needs a software application or a website, it hires another company specializing in this field. So, they start to look for a suitable vendor. In a large company, the process isn't that far from the client–vendor relationship. It's just an internal process of selecting which project to invest money in.

So, as a vendor, we want to get the contract to do the project for the client during this phase. Or, in the case of an internal project, to get a commitment to start it from the department or portfolio manager.

A project manager helps assess the feasibility and provides high-level estimates for the costs and duration of the project. In addition, you may need to participate in negotiations with clients, help the sales team, and communicate with SMEs to onboard new clients.

At the end of this phase, you usually either sign a contract with the client or provide a project proposal with high-level estimates.

PROJECT INITIATION PHASE

After the contract is signed, the initiation phase begins. Here you need to define the goal of a project: What would make it a success? To do this, you need to create a project charter. At the very least, you need to collect the information it should contain.

Keep in mind that a contract usually doesn't include lots of details about the project. Instead, it describes the commitments and interactions between organizations. That's why, in some cases, clients won't commit to the project unless you create a project charter that outlines its high-level scope, constraints, and boundaries.

The second important step is to identify key stakeholders. Why? You'll need a lot of input on many aspects of the project:

- User interface.
- User experience.
- Technical limitations.
- Hardware specifics.
- Development environment.
- Software architecture.

Don't expect to get all the technical details from your clients. You'll need to include internal stakeholders with the required expertise, including people outside of your team, right at the start of the project.

CONCEPT DEVELOPMENT PHASE

There are many different ways to develop software applications. However, I prefer to follow the design-first approach.

So, how does this work?

First of all, you need to develop a conceptual design and wire-frames for future application.

The design shouldn't be fully detailed. But, it should provide a framework for activities to define future requirements. And it gives tangible results to your stakeholders. They'll be more engaged in the whole project if they can see what the future product will look like following the complex software development process.

Another aspect of the concept development phase is technical.

Sometimes the required product is unique. Or it has specific requirements that don't have analogs. And no available solution will provide the desired outcome.

So, you need to develop a brand-new technological concept. You'll need the top experts in your field to generate ideas and solutions.

Therefore, most of the time, it's a gateway phase. If you create an acceptable solution, you'll continue with the project. However, if the solution requires resources and time beyond acceptable constraints, you may need to cancel the project.

PLANNING PHASE

In large IT projects, you'll need to create a complete project management plan. We'll talk about this later. However, in the beginning, you'll work on smaller projects. So planning will be simpler. And here's the reality: Many software development vendors create a custom project management approach. It forms naturally as the company grows. So, you'll need to follow either a customized approach or a variation of Scrum or Kanban.

In this case, project planning boils down to:

- identifying the project scope;
- estimates of time and costs; and

- setting milestones.

Sometimes you'll need to identify required resources and expertise. However, all other aspects of project management will be predefined by the culture of the organization.

Therefore, at the end of this phase, you'll either have a project management plan or you'll verbally commit to delivering a specific scope of work by the exact deadline.

REQUIREMENTS DEFINITION PHASE

After you plan how to manage the project, you need to find out what you need to develop.

In this phase, you can use all the following available options to define requirements:

- Brainstorming.
- Interviews.
- Focus groups.
- Questionaries and surveys.
- Document analysis.
- Mind mapping.
- Wireframes.
- User stories.

There's no specific approach to collecting requirements. But, in the end, your software engineers need to understand them.

Sometimes, simple tweaks in requirements can have a significant impact on the development. It's important to look for any opportunities to simplify the future product.

At this stage, you may want to carry out a high-level feasibility analysis. Hence, why you often see the requirements traceability matrix (RTM) on software development projects, even in an agile environment.

DESIGN PHASE

Again, there are at least two aspects here:

1. Technical architecture.
2. User interface (UI)/User experience (UX) design.

During this phase, you need to analyze the collected requirements and then develop a software architecture that'll support them. Also, you need a UI that'll make the application or service user-friendly.

The results of this phase are:

- mock-ups;
- wireframes;
- workflow diagrams;
- architecture description documentation; and
- list of technologies, frameworks, and libraries.

Once you have it all collected, you can start writing code to implement the requirements.

DEVELOPMENT PHASE

In this phase, you get into the day-to-day execution of the project plan. Finally, software developers will set up working environments and start writing code.

You'll do the actual work here following one of the selected frameworks. For better quality and engaged stakeholders, I recommend an iterative and incremental approach. You can use Scrum or Kanban in this phase. What does that mean?

You'll develop a working piece of the application to show to stakeholders. They will provide feedback. Finally, you'll integrate changes to the project. Repeat this cycle.

However, there's a catch:

Such an approach doesn't exempt you from delivering the project on time and within budget. You'll still need to stick to any deadlines and constraints you are given by the client.

TECHNICAL INTEGRATION PHASE

Nowadays, you'll rarely see an application that doesn't integrate with other services or applications.

In enterprise environments, you'll often see that employees' data and credentials are stored in a separate service with which you'll need to integrate.

The storage space is often outsourced to a third-party provider like Amazon and Dropbox. So, you need to integrate with that as well.

Quite often, integration is a part of development. However, if a lot of effort is involved, it might be better to get it done in a separate phase.

TESTING PHASE

This phase is also referred to as "acceptance testing" or "final testing."

You need to understand that you should be testing your application continuously from the beginning. Moreover, you need to avoid defects during development. Ideally, your application should be stable and without severe defects all the time.

Here you need to certify that the final version of the application you're testing is of the required quality. It doesn't mean that the application has no defects. They may be present, but they don't prevent people from using the application. You need to provide a list of all known defects in the application as part of the quality certificate.

DEPLOYMENT PHASE

Software doesn't work without hardware, be that a server, PC or Mac, or a mobile device. The deployment of a big and complex application to hardware can be a project in itself.

You need to set up servers, upload your application, and connect it with other services and servers.

With regards to mobile devices and desktops, you need to create an application file. You may also need to submit this file to the market (App Store, Google Play, etc.) with other required information.

Having your application or service available to end users marks the end of this phase.

BUSINESS INTEGRATION PHASE

Then, you need to integrate your piece of software with the company's business processes or the market where you will sell the app. This phase usually requires a lot of collaboration with different stakeholders. It can be time-consuming.

So, you better plan this one ahead of time. Pay close attention to any possible risks and resistance from people.

MAINTENANCE PHASE

Someone has to support and maintain the application throughout its whole lifetime. So, the life cycle of the product goes beyond that of the project.

However, quite often, there's a relatively short period for maintenance – the hypercare phase. This is part of the project, and the whole team works with the application after it's gone to the market. They address any critical defects reported by users.

After a few months, when the application has been used and tested by thousands of users, you can hand off the product to a separate support team. After that, the project team moves on.

HAND-OFF, CLOSURE, AND SUPPORT PHASES

Hand-off can also require a lot of effort.

You need to collate all the knowledge that has been gathered about the application and its specifics. This then needs to be transferred to the support team. Also, you may need to create documentation, specific capabilities to administrate the service, and so on.

If that is the case, you need to identify such requirements early on.

Think about the hand-off process at the beginning of the project. It will help you create an accurate plan.

TAKEAWAYS AND LIFE CYCLE EXERCISE

Notice the conversational tone of these descriptions. That's intentional. You have to explain this all the time to different stakeholders who don't know project management. So your language should be simple and it should describe the work behind each phase.

Now, I want you to do an exercise. Take a sheet of paper and a pen. First, list all the phases that you know of in your industry. Don't worry about what you call them. Invent a name for a phase if you need to. Think about all possible phases in your industry. It helps to think in terms of a large project.

The second step is to put the phases in a sequence. Leave a space between each one. Now, describe in a few words all the work that happens in the phase and the major deliverables, as if you were talking to a friend.

Last but not least, draw a simple chart depicting your previous project. Show which phases overlap, which are dependent, and approximately when they start and end.

PART THREE
PROJECT STAKEHOLDERS

CHAPTER 12
IMPACT OF STAKEHOLDERS

At first glance, it may seem like just a few people care about your project. For example, some project owners have decided to pay for the creation of a product or service. They want to get a return on their investment. Likewise, your team was assigned to the project. So, they have to work to get a salary, performance reviews, etc. Your boss will naturally also be interested in your project's success as it reflects on them.

However, it would be a dangerous mistake to assume that's everyone. In the real world, even on a small project, you'll have dozens of additional stakeholders. Moreover, they won't be as supportive as the project owners and your team.

To be a great project manager, you need to learn how to identify all stakeholders. Then, you need to manage them as a part of your project. You'll learn everything you need to know about this in this chapter.

BOUNDARIES OF STAKEHOLDER MANAGEMENT

"A stakeholder is an individual, group, or organization that may affect, be affected by, or perceive itself to be affected by a decision, activity, or outcome of a project", according to the definition from the PMI's *PMBOK Guide*[1].

But you may wonder why we are discussing stakeholder management first. Think about it for a moment. In the real world, you are likely to work in a company for a few years in a row. Therefore, even before a project starts, there are already lots of stakeholders.

So, stakeholder management is an ongoing process that is not limited to the boundaries of your current project.

You don't wait until a new project starts to build relationships with these people. Likewise, your relationships do not start from a blank page. Instead, you continuously manage internal stakeholders.

For sure, you can't know everyone in your organization. But you must know key experts who might potentially be useful. For example:

- SMEs who have the knowledge required for the project.
- Managers who control your work and provide sign-offs on critical processes and documents.
- Department managers who support every company project, like human resources (HR), IT, and recruitment.

Now, let me explain why stakeholders are essential.

A STAKEHOLDER MEANS REQUIREMENTS

You need to understand that stakeholders are the source of requirements. Sometimes these requirements feel like demands or even threats. So, they will come your way whether you ask for them or not. In any case, if you know these requirements in advance, you can incorporate them into your project management plan.

And these aren't limited to simply the product or service requirements, but also the following:

- Project management approach.
- Policies you must follow.
- Tools you need to use.
- People you can hire.
- Additional responsibilities you must take.
- Communication with the client.

The worst impact on your project comes from stakeholders who you did not identify and who demand new requirements in the middle of the project. This disrupts all the planning and work you have done so far.

For example, you started development for a new hardware product. Further down the line, you discovered that you must comply with specific safety regulations. Now, this means you have to change some components of your product and perform an external audit. What's worse, I can bet someone in your company could have known about it.

That's why the next biggest mistake you can make is to create a silo from your project team and project owners. Your organization has expertise that you can tap into. These experts can provide "desirable" requirements. A great project manager takes advantage of experience and knowledge outside as well as inside their team.

But it comes with a price. Working in a silo is much, much easier. However, sooner or later, you'll get a project where success is impossible without help from the outside. Therefore, you need to learn how to involve critical stakeholders in your project.

THE BEST WAY TO MANAGE PROJECT STAKEHOLDERS

I think we can all agree that, in life, there are always difficult personalities, demanding clients, ignorant bosses, arrogant experts, introverts, extroverts, and even plain jerks. Even if someone is great at their job, they may have a different vision of the project and project management. They may have personal problems, or simply be overwhelmed. Rarely, but still possible, you might even encounter people who are aggressively against you or your project.

This is why stakeholder management is the most challenging part of project management: Stakeholders are human beings. And there's no hiding from difficult stakeholders: You need to manage everyone.

As a project manager, you need to meet your objectives. You want to do everything to the best of your knowledge and skills to finish the project successfully. Your motivation is clear. However, not all stakeholders have the same vested interest.

When I was a novice, I thought all the stakeholders except the project owners were supportive, and willing or obliged to work with me to meet the project's needs. We work in the same company, after all, and a successful finish of a project is surely a common goal? Though this was pretty naive, it worked to some extent because there are still many good people in the world.

With experience came a different understanding. You can easily manage stakeholders if you tie their personal goals with their work on your project. For example, you help your team members to build their careers or get salary raises. Or you give them freedom and responsibility . As a result, they are motivated to work on the project because they see how their efforts will benefit them directly.

Likewise, you may help a department manager to highlight her contribution to an important project. So, you'll play along. In return, she'll help you push through some crucial decisions for your project with the executive board.

Helping stakeholders to achieve their goals benefits the project most of the time. Yes, there will be people who will take advantage of you. But, if your project benefits from this too, then it's a win-win.

That's why ad hoc stakeholder management doesn't work. Your engagement needs to be consistent and predictable, not episodic. You need to approach stakeholders strategically and with a healthy dose of cynicism. You need to have a plan to encourage (through leadership and motivation) a stakeholder to behave in the manner you need. Ideally, you also want to help them achieve their own personal goals.

Likewise, stakeholder management is not a one-off process at the start of the project; you need to carry it through until the end. And don't forget, stakeholders and their objectives may change.

CHAPTER 13
HOW TO IDENTIFY STAKEHOLDERS

Put simply, a stakeholder is someone who:

- can impact the project by providing requirements;
- can impede the project by some action or inaction;
- is affected by the project's progress or its result; and
- thinks that the project may impact them.

That's why the identification of stakeholders boils down to searching for people who fall under one of these categories. We need to know these people early on to include their requirements in the project plan. Likewise, we may need to exclude requirements that don't support the project goal. However, you can't do this at your own discretion: Project owners or other stakeholders need to agree.

It's critical to dedicate time to identify all stakeholders. That's why you need to take a broad look at your project, the environment you work in, and the environment of your project owners. Below are the possible groups and types of stakeholders you need to explore.

PROJECT OWNERS

This is a collective term for all stakeholders with direct control over a project. They include:

- sponsors;
- customers / clients;
- product managers;
- product owners; and
- project managers on the client's side.

It might be one person who acts as both a sponsor and product owner (or client). Alternatively, you may have a separate stakeholder covering each role.

When project owners come from a different organization, they share an environment with internal stakeholders. You may never contact those people directly. However, your project owners do interact with them behind the scenes.

At the very least, you should ask if they have any mandatory processes that may impact your project work with the other organization.

You need to work hand-in-hand with project owners. In most cases, they provide mandatory requirements unless you can offer a better alternative. As much as possible, you want to keep them informed and engaged throughout the whole project.

ORGANIZATIONAL STRUCTURE

Your boss and other higher-tier managers are also project stakeholders. But they have a different stake in the game. Project owners want to get results and reach project objectives. On the other hand, your boss wants stability and happy clients. Additionally, he may want you to develop stronger business relationships with the project owners. This will bring more projects and more business to the company. However, your boss may have temporary requirements for all aspects of the project based on the overall need of the organization.

But don't limit this group to your direct manager only. Explore other stakeholders who have equivalent authority.

So, in most cases, you need to keep internal executives informed about the project's progress and potential challenges. They will not be interested in all the details if you prove that you control the project.

PROCESSES AND APPROVALS

You need to adapt to the environment of an organization. It has policies and processes you have to comply with, which are controlled by people who don't provide any direct benefits to your project. However, you can't ignore them: Otherwise, they'll block your progress.

So, review mandatory processes and policies needing a formal sign-off. Sometimes, a stakeholder is a whole department or division in your company. That's fine. But do go one step further and identify the exact person assigned to work with your project. Likewise, think about departments that will help you with the project – for example, HR, recruitment, procurement, and legal (or specific people). They have a preferred way of operating as well.

In most cases, you need to inform such stakeholders about your project. Then, clarify how you plan to meet their requirements. Finally, get their sign-off. Even if they are absolutely not interested in your project, you need to keep them informed and follow the established process. Keep in mind that they have their own roles and responsibilities. Helping them to achieve their objectives usually benefits a project (though mainly in indirect ways).

RARE CRITICAL EXPERT KNOWLEDGE

Your project may require unique expert knowledge. Usually, this is costly and scarce. Therefore, it's critical to engage SMEs and use their time efficiently.

The biggest challenge here is to find something that will motivate such stakeholders to participate in your project.

END USERS

Your project might produce a flawless product but, if people do not want to use it, is it a success? I believe not.

Unless you are a Steve-Jobs-type of influencer, you need to know what your users expect from your project. Otherwise, you might be creating something that no one needs. This is particularly vital in the corporate environment when creating an in-house product.

To avoid this issue, get feedback on the future product or service from its target end users. As a bonus, they may even provide you with insights on the pain points that your product should address.

CRITICAL PROJECT TEAM MEMBERS

Most likely, you have a person on the team with expertise that no one else has. They are team leaders, your best specialists, or the soul of the team. They are your most valuable allies in the trenches. Keeping them motivated and engaged is crucial.

Let's say collecting functional requirements is not your strong suit. Ideally, you should have a business analyst in your team. That makes this person a critical stakeholder with rare expertise. They will have the ultimate knowledge of the project's requirements.

Just to be clear. Usually, we don't treat each team member as a stakeholder. This is because, individually, they don't have a major impact on a project's success. Only critical people should be treated as stakeholders. Then, you'll apply other tools and techniques to the rest of the team.

RESISTANCE

We do not live in a utopia. Your project may impact and even harm people. You need to expect resistance from their side. The success of your project may mean failure for some stakeholders.

For example, you successfully integrate a software application into a business process. It does a lot of things automatically. Now, a hundred employees have nothing to do. They might be fired in the long run.

Or think about executives in your company. They always fight for a bigger budget to run their initiatives. What's good for one of them may be bad for another.

You need to identify such people as early as possible. Then, you need to find a win-win solution that will reduce resistance.

STAKEHOLDERS UNAWARE OF YOUR PROJECT

It usually happens this way:

Your project is well underway. At some point, a person (with some degree of authority) finds out about your project and suddenly realizes that he has additional requirements or liabilities.

And he starts to panic and tries to catch up with your project's progress. This usually creates a mess. That is why it is in your best interests to ensure that every person influenced by your project is aware of it.

This person is part of a special group that can only be discovered through a proper stakeholder identification process. Someone may know that you need to inform a stakeholder in advance.

Likewise, you need to communicate proactively with all stakeholders. Don't assume they are aware of your project specifics.

SUPPORTERS

A supporter might be a project manager who had a similar project. It may be a mentor who can help you with project management and leadership.

Also, think about supporters of your team – experts in another team who can be consulted and help with tricky problems. You may want to reach out and ask for assistance in advance.

Quite often, people inside your organization can help you. So you need to find them. It all boils down to building friendly relationships with people around you.

THIRD-PARTY DEPENDENCY

This can be a third party, a vendor, or another project in your organization. Also, there are always internal or external stakeholders we depend on – for example, when the project team doesn't have expertise in the client's domain. So, again, keep in mind that stakeholders may be an organization, a group of people, or a community.

SOURCES OF REQUIREMENTS

By nature, all stakeholders have requirements. Therefore, one of the definitions of a project's success is meeting all the key stakeholders' requirements.

Remember that there will be a wide range of requirements, not only ones that are functional for the product or service you are creating. For example, there are quality, legal, compliance, organizational, project management, and many other requirements that you need to identify.

Again, think about the organizations you need to interact with. They have specific requirements for collaboration. Knowledge of industry specifics and business acumen plays a critical role here.

SIMPLE PROCESS OF IDENTIFYING STAKEHOLDERS

We have broadened our understanding of stakeholders by identifying the major types and groups, showing the variety and number of possible stakeholders.

This, in turn, should encourage you to log quite a lot of people and organizations you need to manage. But how do you actually do it in practice?

Discovering project stakeholders is all about communication. You need to ask the right questions strategically. That's why the main techniques that you use are:

- meetings;
- interviews;
- brainstorming; and

- emails/chats.

Start on the inside and work towards the outside. Here's what I mean.

First, you talk with your team members. Then, you speak with any person who helped you with pre-sales and onboarding of the new client. After that, you reach out to your leadership and internal stakeholders. And, only then, you research the client's side.

Yes, it is that simple! Just go and talk to your key stakeholders – be open and explain what you are doing. But don't say that you are "looking for project stakeholders." That's insider's language. Instead, say that you are looking for people who can help with the project.

Questions to ask:

- Who can help with our project?
- Who might be interested in our project?
- Who must be involved? Are there any mandatory processes?
- Who may be against our project?
- What drawbacks might the project have for others?

It may be a good idea to have a checklist for such interviews. And try not to make these interviews interrogations. Instead, they should be semi-casual conversations. Otherwise, people start to stress and over-think the answers.

Next, you need to repeat the process with the project owners' side if they are not inside your organization.

Now that you know how to identify stakeholders, you need to log all the collected information into a stakeholder register.

CHAPTER 14
STAKEHOLDER REGISTER AND HOW TO FILL IT IN

A stakeholder register is a document containing all information relevant to the identification and analysis of project stakeholders. It will help you prioritize stakeholders and develop engagement plans.

Inexperienced project managers don't see the benefits of a stakeholder register. So, they don't create one. But a great project manager knows that stakeholder engagement is vital research. First, you collect information. Then, you make an assumption and test your hypotheses by experimenting. After that, you repeat the process systematically until you find the correct approach to a person. A stakeholder register helps you organize all these efforts.

I want to warn you right away. You should keep the stakeholder register to yourself. Don't share it with anyone. Why? It contains sensitive information about people. Most importantly, it includes your opinions of people. And you should not adjust your opinion of someone out of fear that they may learn about it.

If you need to share the stakeholder register, you must create a copy that doesn't contain information about the impact, influence, power, and expectations of the stakeholders. Also, be mindful about sharing emails and phone numbers that are not publicly accessible.

CONTENTS OF A STAKEHOLDER REGISTER

A stakeholder register is usually a spreadsheet in Excel or Google. Here's what you need to capture for each stakeholder:

#1: **Full name**. The only trick here is to put in a phonetic transcript of fancy names. And, for sure, you want to remember all the names and spell them correctly.

#2: **Department**. Next to their name, add the department where the stakeholder works. This is the start of the analysis of relationships between stakeholders.

#3: **Location**. This is necessary only if your stakeholders are located in different cities or countries. You might also want to add any time differences next to the location.

#4: **Role on the project**. This is essential! The responsibilities of each stakeholder should be clear.

It is even more critical to ensure that all the stakeholders know the roles and responsibilities of each other.

#5: **A preferred method of communication**. If you are going to win over a stakeholder, you need to respect their preferred means of communication. This saves them time and increases your chances of getting positive feedback.

#6, 7, 8: **Impact, involvement, power**. You'll use these attributes in stakeholder analysis. I will explain this later.

#9: **Expectations**. Be realistic. For example, what does a particular stakeholder want to achieve by interacting with your project? We will discuss this point separately as well.

#10: **Engagement strategy**. After an analysis, you will need to develop an action plan to engage with the stakeholder.

As a starting point, feel free to use my stakeholder register template from the supporting materials:

https://itpmschool.com/materials

BENEFITS OF WRITING IT DOWN

There are several benefits of keeping a written record:

- Knowing where you began will help you progress toward your desired engagement level.
- You will not be able to keep everything in your head.
- You will need all the information about stakeholders later during planning.
- It will increase your chances of identifying and analyzing all the key stakeholders correctly.
- It will help you to approach the task strategically.
- You will be able to make educated decisions based on collected facts, not guesses.
- You will be able to identify where your analysis went wrong.

I think I can continue this list with a dozen more points. But you've got the idea: It is crucial to write it down!

HOW TO FILL IN A STAKEHOLDER REGISTER

Name, department, location, and role – it's easy to get this information from the email signature of a person or their contact card. Or simply ask during a call.

You can identify their preferred way of communicating by observing their habits or asking directly. In most cases, the default is email.

Impact, involvement, power, expectations, and engagement strategy all need to be researched and identified.

Power is their level of authority. It's the ability of a person to impose their will inside an organization. Power comes from their title, expert knowledge, reputation, etc.

Interest is their level of concern in a project and its outcome. It's the degree to which the person wins or loses based on the project outcome.

Involvement is the degree to which they will actively participate in project activities and their overall desire to help.

Impact is their ability to make changes to a project's planning or execution. In contrast to power, impact shows an ability to help the project to move forward.

Here comes the critical part!

There's no formula or tool to help you precisely identify these characteristics in a stakeholder. It's always your best guess, a subjective feeling. It depends on your past experience with a person, good or bad. That's why you must be pragmatic, unbiased, and have a positive attitude.

Empathy is also essential because you need to understand people's fundamental motivations and genuine attitudes. Even if you had a bad experience with them previously, you need to try to minimize any negative effects a stakeholder might have on a new project.

I can almost hear you say, "What should I do if I don't know a person? How do you fill in these columns?" You need to ask around. You need to communicate with other stakeholders or interview the person directly to learn more about them.

Obviously, you can't ask, "What is your level of power and authority?" Instead, ask about their role on the project or responsibilities in the company, or establish their credentials from their title. It will be your best guess.

So, to know about people, you need to talk to people. Do not make the common mistake of trying to identify and analyze all the stakeholders on your own. Different people can give you different perspectives.

Moreover, you have a chance to get valuable insights about the experience of working with a particular person: Their habits, perks, and quirks. Do not overthink it. You really just need to meet with people.

So, what should you actually write in the power, involvement, and impact fields? I recommend that you adopt a free-form approach as you get to know a stakeholder. Don't get too prescriptive. For example:

John is a project owner. He has ultimate **power** and **interest** in the project.

John is very busy, so his **involvement** is relatively low. But he delegates a lot to the team.

John has industry knowledge but zero experience in software development, so his **impact** is medium.

Kate is a senior engineer. She has limited **power** over the project. She has low **interest** because she doesn't like the product we are developing.

Kate is full time on the project, and she can do complex tasks, so her **involvement** is high.

Kate's **impact** is high. Lots of critical tasks are her responsibility.

In practice, you should measure power, impact, and interest in regard to your project only. I think they should be a function of involvement to some degree.

For example, the president of the company, CEO, or CTO may have ultimate power and authority over most aspects of the project. As a result, they can force you to make any changes they consider to be necessary. Also, they are very interested in the project's success and very concerned about its outcome.

However, they are never going to interact with you every day. In general, they are not involved to such an extent in any project. These stakeholders don't have time for that. So, their involvement with your project is low. All they need is to know is that the project is under control.

Therefore, focusing your attention on executives will not be the best use of your time. If everything goes smoothly, you will not hear from them a lot. So, you simply need to keep them informed.

THE TOP 10 STAKEHOLDERS

This approach takes time, but it's worth it. It gives you a wider picture of all key stakeholders. And I would rather work closely with the top 10 stakeholders than spread my attention too thinly across all of them. Remember that 20% of stakeholders will generate 80% of success for your project.

For the same reason, I don't recommend you rely too much on different power/impact grids or a salience model, even if the internet suggests that these tools are gold standard. In theory, it's an excellent way to categorize stakeholders – however, these tools create broad groups of stakeholders. Therefore, you'll need several strategies within each group. It might be a good approach for a huge project. However, on small and medium projects, it's better to take a more personal approach. Work with 10 stakeholders individually. Learn their preferences and needs. Communicate with these people often.

Next, we need to fill in the expectations and engagement plan columns. But they need a separate explanation. Continue reading!

CHAPTER 15
HOW TO PLAN STAKEHOLDER ENGAGEMENT

Let's summarize what we have learned so far. Stakeholders are valuable and useful for a project. They are many and varied. But you have only eight hours per day to manage your project. And I hope you don't go way over working hours.

That's why you need to prioritize the most critical stakeholders – those who can bring the most value or cause the most problems. It's the Pareto principle in action: 20% of stakeholders will produce 80% of the benefit/problems. Therefore, you need to select about 10 stakeholders to scrutinize.

But there's a catch.

Stakeholders and their characteristics change during different project phases. Therefore, you need to revisit the stakeholder register regularly. Your top 10 stakeholders may shift a bit during the project's lifetime.

Next, you need to identify the expectations of these selected stakeholders.

REQUIREMENTS AND EXPECTATIONS

Requirements are what a stakeholder wants from you during the project.

Expectations are what a stakeholder wishes to achieve or attain as a result of your project.

Requirements and expectations combined are like a submerged iceberg. Requirements are above the water. Expectations are below and they are more significant than just your project.

The problem is that stakeholders have requirements that they deem (to the best of their knowledge) necessary to fulfill their expectations. Read that again, because it's important to understand.

Let's give an example. On the one hand, a requirement from a quality manager is, "The project has to follow all the quality processes and policies by the letter."

On the other hand, his expectations for this requirement might be as follows:

- Pursuing the processes and policies will help the project to meet its goals.
- If they follow the processes and policies, my involvement will be minimal.
- The project is risky. I don't want to be personally involved. Let them follow standard processes and policies.
- If the project follows the processes and policies and it is successful, I can get a promotion.
- The project must be of good quality. Otherwise, I might be fired.

As you can see, there are many possible expectations and things could get even more complicated. For example, this quality manager may believe that "following the processes to the letter" will produce the expected result, and he'll get more free time to work on other projects. But that's just his assumption. It may not be true because this project is unique and requires a different approach.

So, how do you identify real expectations? I don't want to sound like a broken record but it's all about communication. It should be relatively easy with your project team and project owners. In most cases, you can simply ask. Again, one-on-one meetings are the best option.

It's a bit harder with internal and external stakeholders with lots of power. In most cases, they can't openly state their expectations because of internal politics. So you can't ask them directly, but you can get information from indirect sources. For example, you may ask their direct subordinates. Sometimes, it's evident from what they state as their goals or how they behave.

This sounds like listening to rumors and gossip. As much as I don't like it, to some degree this is true. So, be careful, because such information is not entirely reliable.

Career goals, personal hobbies and interests, and relationships will influence expectations a lot. So, ask about them.

But why do you need to know the expectations? You need to control them:

- You need to manage stakeholders' requirements.
- You need to check whether their requirements can produce the expected outcome.
- You must ensure that these requirements are aligned with project objectives.

If there are discrepancies, you need to adjust expectations and requirements accordingly.

Sometimes expectations are way beyond the boundaries and constraints of a project. Sometimes requirements won't produce the desired product or service. In either case, you need to open a dialog and adjust those expectations. The sooner you do it, the easier a stakeholder accepts the new reality.

Mediocre project managers believe that this is not their responsibility. Project owners set the goals. Therefore, they should provide the requirements to meet those goals. So, they plan and implement requirements without question. On the other hand, a great project manager always helps connect expectations with goals and requirements. They ensure that all stakeholders have realistic expectations.

WHAT DOES "STAKEHOLDER ENGAGEMENT" MEAN?

In simple terms, if a stakeholder is engaged, then they wish to help the cause of the project. Therefore, they spend time participating and prioritizing your tasks and queries.

Engagement is not as simple as being "engaged" or "disengaged." All stakeholders are engaged to some extent. They may wish to participate but only if they have spare time. So, they don't expect the project to be their number one priority.

Managing engagement boils down to incentivizing people to put your project above all their other tasks and commitments. The best way to achieve this is to fulfill their expectations.

HOW TO PLAN STAKEHOLDER ENGAGEMENT

You need to create a profile for each of your top 10 stakeholders. I recommend linking each document to your stakeholder register for quick access. Here's what you should include:

#1: **Name of the stakeholder.**

#2: **Expectations as you see them**. For example, "Jane is a new executive. She engages with lots of projects in order to push her initiative of the new reporting system. She works hard to show the impact she makes. If it works well, her project may get extensive funding."

#3: **Desired engagement level with the project**. A simple description works best – for example, "Keep Jane informed on all project challenges and risks with a weekly report. Minimize her direct interactions with the team."

#4: **Engagement plan**. Here you need to list any action you'll take to get a stakeholder to the desired level of engagement. It can be a one-time conversation, daily meetings, or weekly reports. For example, "Talk to Jane about how she distracts the team from its main aim. Suggest a workflow to prioritize her tasks. Ideally, she shouldn't distract the team from planned work with unexpected errands."

You might need something more specific, like a promise you need to fulfill or conditions you need to provide. For example, a promotion if the project is successful, freedom to make decisions, etc.

#5: **Engagement log**. Stakeholder engagement is not black and white. People are more complex. So, you need to track patterns of behavior. Here you write down how the person behaved during your last meetings, conversations, emails, etc. With each entry, you can analyze whether a stakeholder is interested in the project, bored with meetings, or overwhelmed by other tasks.

ENGAGEMENT MANAGEMENT IS ITERATIVE

Now, here's how it works. First, you make an assumption about stakeholder's' expectations. Then, you identify the engagement needed and an action plan for how to achieve it.

Next, you follow the plan and log the engagement from the stakeholders. After each significant interaction with one of them, make a simple note. Describe how they behaved. Did they follow your expected engagement plan?

At some point, you may learn that your actions aren't working. Then, you may need to adjust your assumption about their expectations or even the action plan itself.

CHAPTER 16
STAKEHOLDER MANAGEMENT STORY

At the start of my career, I managed a small software development project. I had eight people on the team. There were not many stakeholders. Most of them were internal, plus the project owners. But the project was high profile for our organization.

We were well into the execution phase, with everything heading smoothly towards the major milestone. Everyone was happy with the team's performance.

Then, out of the blue, John B., the director of development, emailed a set of small requirements for the project management approach and software development process. John was only an adviser, so he was a low-interest and low-power stakeholder. His requirements sounded fine in theory but, in practice, they were cumbersome. As a result, they had not been needed for years.

A day later, Larry C., another low-interest, low-power stakeholder, emailed with yet another batch of small process and policy requirements that built on the ones we had received from John B.

Now, I had a bunch of small and relatively unimportant requirements for project management, processes, and policies. From my perspective, introducing all these changes at once would create a lot of disruption in our development process. But John and Larry contended that they were of paramount importance. So, I tried to prioritize their requirements. As a compromise, I suggested that we implement them one by one during the next few months. But, unfortunately, this just escalated the problem.

"You must do it all to the fullest extent as soon as possible!" they announced in the email that included the CEO and all other stakeholders.

By this point, things had got a bit strange. Even on their worst day, these guys were open for a discussion. So, I decided to find the root cause of the problem. A glance at the stakeholder register showed that neither Larry nor John had enough authority on their own. So, they teamed up. But why?

Here's what bothered me. These guys requested lots of changes to the management of the project. It wasn't their area of responsibility: they controlled the technical aspects of the process. Then it suddenly became clear: They were questioning the duties of my direct manager. I'd found myself in my first internal political battle! It wasn't about me, so it didn't matter what I did or how I reacted.

So, I had a quick and informal chat with my manager. Here's what I learned.

First, Larry had had a rough meeting with the CEO a few weeks ago. He was told that there were too many technical problems and the email threads on them were too long.

Second, Larry's line of defense was that "project managers don't want to collaborate."

Things started to become clear. By highlighting and dramatizing each and every issue related to their requests, Larry and John were trying to prove they were doing their best, but they weren't getting any support. Well, at least that's the best guess I had.

So, while their new requirements for the project were aimed at improving the quality of the technical solutions, their expectations were different: They wanted to restore the CEO's trust in them and boost their authority.

As a project manager, I had to protect the team and the project objectives from this quarrel. So, once you understand your opponent's plan, you can quickly turn it against them. A quick email to the CEO from my manager did the trick. We just asked, "What is going on? And why don't Larry and John want to collaborate on reasonable timelines for their requests? Is it a planned initiative?"

There was some communication that I'm not aware of. But, the next day, the drama cooled down. We discussed what changes were needed and by when.

In the long run, Larry and John got a small win here. They installed several new processes that increased their control over the project. That's how internal politics work – a prod here and a push there to balance the scales of power in your favor.*

Of course, there might have been different resolutions to this conflict. You have to act on your assumptions because you rarely have the full picture. Nevertheless, you should always put the needs of a project ahead of any internal politics.

What are the lessons learned here? The following are a must:

- A stakeholder register.
- Stakeholder analysis.
- Overall awareness of the balance of power.

*Based on a real experience. All names have been changed.

CHAPTER 17
THREATS TO STAKEHOLDER ENGAGEMENT

Peter is a valuable project stakeholder. He has unique knowledge in big data analysis. The demand for his skills within the company is enormous. We need him more than he needs our project. So, no matter what you do, Peter puts your request at the bottom of his priority list.

Kate is a key team member. We assign lots of critical tasks to her. However, recently Kate has been more interested in the phone calls she gets. It looks like she's in the middle of a romance. Good for Kate, but now she has disengaged from the project.

Dory is a project owner. She wants to get results as soon as possible. So, she puts quite a lot of pressure on the team. But she doesn't want to hear about any challenges. She is not engaged either.

Are any of these scenarios familiar? Every project manager faces the problem of unengaged stakeholders. It may seem like there is nothing you can do about it. But that's not true!

Let me share some practical methods that will help you get round the problem and boost stakeholder engagement.

WHAT KILLS ENGAGEMENT?

Let's be clear on a few things first.

You should never act as if a stakeholder does not want to collaborate. That's not true until you prove otherwise.

I give a person at least three attempts to find common ground and willingness for collaboration. Only after that do I consider switching to more assertive tactics.

Therefore, always start any interaction from a position of mutual benefit. Even if a person acts somewhat aggressively, indifferently, or in any inappropriate manner, it doesn't mean that they are your enemy. Usually, it means that something stands in the way of a productive working relationship with you. And here are four potential reasons.

1. LACK OF INTEREST

A stakeholder simply has nothing to gain from your project. They must participate in it due to job responsibilities or someone's orders – for example, they're an SME who doesn't have any incentive to dive deep into your problems.

This is the most common reason for disengaged stakeholders. However, they don't start with a lack of interest: They lose interest because of other factors.

You will know these people: Their attitude can be summarized as follows:

- Get me a solution, and I will reject it. Then, repeat until the time runs out or I see a safe resolution to approve.
- Tell me what exactly needs to be done. Even better, please write it down. Then, I'll put my approval on it.

What can you do about it? In most cases, nothing, because they have a valid excuse – they need more details from you.

You may find something that will be interesting for such a stakeholder. Usually, it's something that challenges their professional ego. Or something that has novelty in it.

For example, once, I delegated the responsibility of creating a prototype to a technical expert who had never managed a team. It was difficult for him due to his lack of leadership experience. But he saw it as a fresh challenge and, as a result, it worked out perfectly well.

However, you need to keep an eye on these stakeholders. Lack of interest constantly diminishes all other perceived benefits.

2. OVERWHELM

People will disengage from your project if they are overwhelmed with other tasks and activities. In this case, they ignore your requests. They just don't have time for you.

It's more complicated when a person has to answer your requests due to a policy or your title, but she still doesn't have spare time. She has dozens of such requests per day.

In such a case, a stakeholder may turn your request around and, most likely, you will get back a bunch of follow-up questions. A more authoritative stakeholder may move the discussion into strategy or philosophical debate by saying something like, "We need to address the root cause ..." Or "Why did it happen in the first place?"

Their goal here is simple. They want to buy some time while you write the reply.

What can you do? Try playing on their terms:

1. Ask for the most suitable day and time they can spare to work on your project.
2. Plan it in advance and be efficient.
3. Come prepared with the critical topics only.
4. Have a focused working session, dealing with one problem at a time.

3. TEMPORARY LACK OF KNOWLEDGE

People don't like their incompetence or lack of knowledge to be high-lighted. So, they get creative to avoid such situations.

In many cases, people hide behind "following the processes and policies." They act as hard-core, old-school office workers. Tunnel vision blinds them to new technology or solutions. That's why such stakeholders insist on a proven solution only, even if it doesn't serve the project goal. It's easier to cover your back in case of failure.

What can you do? You should work in their comfort zone.

Give the stakeholder all the information and context they need, even if he is an SME. The same applies to your boss and other managers. Please don't assume that they have all the specifics of your project at the top of their mind.

Act as if they know nothing about the project – explain the details. Repeat them even if you talked about them yesterday. But never act as if you know more than they do in their area of expertise: It is not true. Most likely, that person just didn't have enough capacity to learn the specifics of your request. So, it's a temporary lack of knowledge.

This stakeholder doesn't need to feel like he is the best in the world. You only need to make him feel like he knows a bit more than you do. Then, you need to make him feel comfortable to discover new solutions or technology. Protect his ego and help him save face. After that, he'll tune in.

If you know of such a stakeholder, never kick off a discussion in a meeting with lots of other experts. Instead, prepare for a separate, quick meeting to get him up to speed.

4. CONFLICTING REQUESTS

This usually happens due to miscommunication or the absence of communication from your side. People need to be given clear instructions on what tasks to prioritize, and ideally at least a few days ahead.

The same is true when a person has two bosses. Both may have different priorities and expectations. It may even create a conflict and the stakeholder is caught in the middle. He has to wait until the conflict is resolved, which puts him under pressure.

So, when you only have a limited amount of someone's time, you need to ensure that they don't have to guess what task is more important. Instead, you and the other manager should discuss it and give clear priorities. Moreover, it may require continuous communication so the person can manage their daily commitments.

Remember that it's not about the person's ability to prioritize and manage their time. Instead, it's about the pressure that leaders put on them.

So, these are the four main reasons why people don't want to engage with your project. I would always check them first. If you can eliminate the root cause, it will be easier to engage with your stakeholders.

Now, what can you do to create engagement?

CHAPTER 18
HOW TO BUILD ENGAGEMENT

You can't simply ask a stakeholder to be interested in your project or behave in a certain way. Building engagement is instead about motivation, manipulation, and influence, which are no bad things if done for a good reason and within ethical limits.

Building engagement is not a one-off: It needs to be done continually, step-by-step with small interactions.

Below is a list of proven tactics that I learned during a decade of working as a project manager. But, before we get into it, I want to give credit where credit is due. To clearly explain how I work with stakeholders, I got inspiration from Josh Kaufman's book *The Personal MBA*[1]. It provided the correct terminology and explanation of how people work. I strongly recommend you to read this book. It will help you improve your business acumen.

These ideas are also present in the *PMBOK Guide* to some extent. However, they are incorporated into the processes and tools, so you can't see them on the surface. But I'm going to show you under the hood so that you can fully understand why these are the best practices of project management.

KNOW YOUR STAKEHOLDERS TO PUSH IN THE RIGHT DIRECTION

So, it all starts with stakeholder analysis.

You simply must know who the stakeholders are. What do they want and why? You need to find out what they value the most. To this extent, you should have some awareness about their personal lives without prying.

Why does it matter? You can't motivate a person to do something if you don't give something back that they consider valuable. And I'm not just talking about money and titles here. Actually, people value responsibility, freedom, challenges, community, free time, or sleep even more.

So, knowing your stakeholders is the first step to an efficient engagement plan. And you must have a plan!

Have you ever noticed how professional psychologists work in movies? They always record their sessions and they keep notes during the process.

Why do they do that?

They test and verify the result. Then, test again and check whether there is a pattern, whether their patient is moving in the right direction. Finally, they look for an approach that will work for each patient.

You should work in the same way when engaging stakeholders.

Plan, do, check, correct. Plan, do, check, correct. Yes, that's Deming's Cycle in action. Google the term if you've never heard about it.

RELATIONSHIPS WITH OTHER STAKEHOLDERS

How important is it to know that your junior team member is a close friend of the CEO?

How important is it to know that several key stakeholders are pulling strings for another person who is behind the scenes?

Would you plan and act differently knowing that the sponsor follows the suggestions of his CTO without question?

Many stakeholders seem relatively unimportant if you analyze them separately and out of context. However, if you dig deeper, you will soon see that they are all interrelated and have a place within the organization's hierarchy of power.

Most of them have superiors or peers whom they want to impress or influence. These people have friends, foes, and associates. Some of them have shared goals.

Once you have a clear picture of the relationships between stakeholders, you will have a better chance to define real expectations. You will also be on a firmer footing in any related negotiations.

By understanding the influencers and their expectations, you can propose solutions that will benefit all the parties. But I must stress again: You still need to check whether these expectations are within the goals of the project.

BUILD RELATIONSHIPS TO BUILD ENGAGEMENT

The most common mistake is to build engagement with a stakeholder only when you need it. That doesn't work.

You need to always keep them interested. You want to make it appealing to work with you – in advance. So, keep the required stakeholders informed on the project's progress and ask for their opinion, ideas, and insights.

On the other hand, you don't want to overwhelm stakeholders with all the project details. You just need to keep the door open for them to contribute.

WHAT'S IN IT FOR ME?

We often assume that our colleagues owe it to us to do their best for no other reason than they work for the same company. They get a salary, don't they? Therefore, they are obliged to help us. But it doesn't work that way in the real world.

Look around your office. Most probably, you have several established experts there. They are valuable, they are proven, and there's almost nothing that can impact their career. Moreover, they are experienced enough to balance their commitments to maintain a secure position in the company.

For sure, most of the time, these experts are decent people and honest professionals. They are willing to collaborate and help you. However, don't forget that they might be overwhelmed or, for example, have family issues.

Now, there's literally nothing that could make them prioritize your work over their family problems.

That's why I recommend that you always think about what's in it for them (beyond salary and job security). How can you make working with you appealing?

Think about challenges, responsibilities, a better working environment, less stress, and fewer distractions. Sometimes they need a free day to sort things out. That's what people actually crave in the modern workspace.

ASSESS HOW KEY STAKEHOLDERS ARE LIKELY TO BEHAVE

I like to approach this by asking "what if?" I investigate the pros and cons of involving or not involving a stakeholder in some activities. Here is an example of the thought process:

> What if I send Peter the full progress report every week? What benefits will I get? So, he is a team leader. He will be better informed and aware of the situation. I hope it will make him more engaged as I share information intended for project owners. He may find some inconsistencies and point them out. But, on the other hand, it may distract him and take up too much of his time.
>
> What if I don't send him the report? Nothing will really change. I may lose some opportunities for his engagement, motivation, and process improvement.
>
> So, it seems like it's better to send the report to him.

Here is another example:

> What if I send the proposed solution directly to the customer without consulting Peter?
>
> He is the leading SME. I have feedback from his previous work. I know they had serious problems when the project manager promised something Peter

couldn't deliver. And, let's be honest, this happens way too often on all projects. Well, most probably, he will be upset.

On the other hand, I want to keep him engaged as much as possible. So, I'd better contact him in all cases. He likes that. The trade-off is that it may cause delays. So it is wise to plan communications well.

This simple behavior analysis may help you select the best strategy to work with any person. I recommend starting with this analysis and brainstorming all possible scenarios that will either build or kill engagement. Use your gut feeling if you can't operate with facts. So, yes, it is mostly using your instincts. Of course, you can interview people to collect their thoughts and experience of working with the relevant stakeholder. But, still, it will be a subjective opinion, not a fact.

GIVE AWAY OWNERSHIP TO BUILD ENGAGEMENT

Often additional responsibilities help to improve motivation and engagement. But with responsibility should come authority. People don't like to commit to a project when they don't control the assigned tasks.

Think about this example. Heather, a high-level expert, agrees to help you with a project. She is a rising star in her department. In addition, she leads some projects on her own.

On your project, you make Heather a team leader. However, you don't fully trust her and you control every decision she makes. Moreover, you ask her to follow your process and don't allow any changes.

That's not as exciting as leading your own project, is it?

Keep in mind that delegating responsibilities is more efficient than delegating tasks. Therefore, you should always assess the pros of fully delegating ownership over a part of a project: It may build tremendous engagement.

However, don't abuse this option. It should be a weighted decision and, what's more important, you should be available to provide support when needed.

ACKNOWLEDGE CONTRIBUTION TO BUILD ENGAGEMENT

It goes without saying that you acknowledge the contribution of your team. Hopefully, you thank them every day.

But what about someone outside your team who had only a small role to play? Do you remember to acknowledge their commitment? If not, that might be a reason why stakeholders do not want to engage with your projects. Remember that a simple 'thank you' also builds engagement. All it takes is one email.

Giving recommendations on LinkedIn is another form of acknowledging someone's contribution that is particularly effective if you do it without needing to be asked.

EVERYTHING IS A TRADE-OFF ON A PROJECT

Every project works under the constraints of scope, costs, and time, with each having an effect on the other. For example, if you increase the scope, it's going to cost more money, take more time, or both; if you finish ahead of time, you might reduce costs; and so on.

Every time a stakeholder wants to do something, he makes a trade-off because it means something else can't be done.

You should teach each stakeholder this concept and be ready to stand your ground if it's being challenged.

Every change request should result in one or a combination of the following:

- A change of the project scope: A part of the project should be removed or modified.
- Getting additional resources, whether that's more money, staff, or equipment.
- A change to the schedule. Milestones and deadlines should be moved to include new work.

This concept is quite transparent at the start of a project: If you want something extra, it's going to need more time and resources.

However, things get complicated when the project is already underway.

Raising awareness of these trade-offs among stakeholders helps their understanding of the processes needed and the consequences of reckless decisions.

Let's take a look at it from a stakeholder's perspective.

During the execution phase, a project owner asks to make a small change to the project's scope. It is quite expected, and you are even prepared for it, so you agree to integrate the change without a trade-off.

Then he asks for a second, third, and fourth change.

Now your schedule and your team are stretched. It will be hard but still possible to meet deadlines.

Then comes a fifth change request.

You see that there's no way to fit this into your schedule, and only now do you start to negotiate a trade-off.

It might seem like the previous four change requests didn't require trade-offs, but they did. You gave away any slack you might have had in your schedule, maybe some capital reserves, and, therefore, increased the risk level for the project. Additionally, you put your team under stress, which may influence their motivation.

But it shouldn't feel like we are bargaining all the time. That's why we need to use the next concept.

ALWAYS PROVIDE THE NEXT-BEST ALTERNATIVE

Let's assume that you did not communicate the concept of trade-offs and the actual consequences of the first four change requests from the example above. The project owners may not make it easy at this point:

> *You made four changes without a problem before*, they might think. *But now, suddenly, you can't make another "simple" change? Moreover, the project is now at heightened and significant risk. How could you let this happen?*

At this point, you and the stakeholder can't reach an agreement. Your client will search for the next-best alternative. Given that he doesn't believe (or understand) you, he tries to force you to accept the change anyway. He'll do it either directly or via your management.

While trying to please the customer and make him happy, you must include the change without a trade-off.

Usually, your boss will try to satisfy the client however they can. That is because your organization wants to preserve long and beneficial relationships, especially if it costs just a "bit" of stress for you and your team.

Such misunderstandings happen way too often. Unfortunately, some clients cynically take advantage of this situation to get as much as possible for what they paid.

But let's be optimistic and assume they are genuine.

What would be the next-best alternative?

That's right! It is a trade-off.

But you need to present it as a no-brainer. More importantly, you should be proactive. Don't allow stakeholders to come up with something unfair simply because they don't see any other options.

One of the obvious alternatives that clients don't think about is for all of their suggested changes and improvements to be carried out as a follow-up project.

If you continuously communicate about trade-offs and viable alternatives, you'll soon collect enough requirements for another project. Then, it will be easy to convince project owners to do business with you again. You delivered the first project on time and within budget. They might even put the product on the market and start getting income from it. In the process, you identified many possible improvements for their product or service that they didn't think of initially. Why would they go to someone else to make those improvements?

To make this process more efficient, you need to increase the perceived value of your suggestions.

INCREASE PERCEIVED VALUE

When you know a person, you know what they think is valuable.

Each part of a project has a different value for a stakeholder. Likewise, each functional requirement, characteristic, or trait of the end product also has its value.

Project owners can calculate the monetary value of delivering a requirement. However, in the real world, they operate with a perceived value. It is the number of resources, time, and money they are willing to give for a product or result. Quite often, perceived value and actual costs are different.

It is one of the most challenging aspects in managing stakeholders' expectations. First, you need to sync perceived value with the real value of your product or service. Second, you need to transparently explain how costs add up, and how much time and effort each piece of work requires.

Any next-best alternative or trade-off also has its perceived value. The good thing is that you can increase the attractiveness of your suggestions by:

- visualizing the plan and the end result;
- removing stakeholders' hassle in the process as much as possible;
- ensuring that everything is under control; and
- making a stakeholder feel good and look good in the eyes of others when they accept your offer.

In general, you should always focus on the most significant benefit of your suggestion that stakeholders perceive as valuable. This way, you can influence stakeholders and make their decisions more predictable.

OVERCOME ABSENCE BLINDNESS

"Absence blindness is a cognitive bias that prevents us from identifying what we can't observe," says Josh Kaufman in *The Personal MBA*. This human trait has a significant impact in many areas of project management.

Both stakeholders and project managers have a hard time identifying better approaches once they have selected one.

While everything works fine, we tend to become blind to new problems until they appear. Absence blindness is so widespread that it is present in all aspects of life, not just project management. I would say that risk management was basically invented to overcome absence blindness.

By the way, this is often why project managers are underappreciated. If a project runs smoothly, that's due to great project management. But most people tend to miss that because they haven't seen all the bad things that you've managed to avoid. As a result, it may seem like a project gets finished on time and within budget while you are sitting doing nothing.

Absence blindness makes risk management, preventing defects in quality management, and process improvements less appealing. It is hard to see that these processes and activities are beneficial because they simply lead to the absence of problems rather than producing something tangible.

Absence blindness creates another challenge: People feel uncomfortable and out of control when you do nothing as something terrible is happening.

In project management, it is often better to stick to the overall plan or the agreed risk responses to overcome problems. However, stakeholders tend to escalate problems when they do not see you "doing everything possible" to solve the problem straightaway. For that reason, it is important to keep stakeholders informed about upcoming risks and tell them that you've got everything under control.

HELP TO AVOID LOSS AVERSION

People hate losing things that they already own. Businesspeople hate to lose opportunities even more. So, quite often, this aversion to loss prevents stakeholders from making the right decisions.

You will often see this when negotiating scope reductions. Even if project success is at stake, it is hard to convince stakeholders to give up a feature or functionality. Everything is a "must-have."

Sunk costs are money, time, and effort spent that can't be recovered. It's another concept that influences stakeholders.

Customers and sponsors don't like to give up sunk costs. They try to invest even more resources in the hope of getting back their investment. It spirals down into a rabbit hole and they end up throwing good money after bad.

However, if something didn't work out as expected, you should not consider sunk costs – only the value of the final product or result matters.

You should show empathy towards project owners with loss aversion, because it will help you to convince them to make the right decision.

HELP TEAM MEMBERS OVERCOME PLANNING FALLACY

Always keep in mind that people tend to underestimate how much time and effort is needed to finish a task.

Even if you are doing everything by the book, there will be uncertainties, risks, and interdependencies that you will not be aware of. Even if you are very accurate with your estimates, there will always be some waste between activities and phases.

You can strive to predict every possible problem. However, there's never been a project that hasn't needed to be changed in some way. That's why I prefer to have a flexible plan that can withstand a reasonable number of unexpected events without being thrown off course. Don't make your plan too detailed because it will require changes on a daily basis.

It takes a lot of experience and authority to produce a plan that stakeholders will accept and that still has a good chance of being accurate. So, for now, I would recommend you allow for some slack in your projects.

Slack is just an empty period of time between two tasks. In practice, I add slack between deliverables. You always have work without a name when you try to finalize a deliverable and start a new one.

Slack seems like an indulgent luxury in our world. Nevertheless, I suggest you try to explain the concept to stakeholders. It might help you to shore up your deadlines and make planning more realistic.

In addition to that, help team members to overcome planning

fallacy by adding your gut feeling buffer. For example, increase their estimates a bit. In the long run, it will remove lots of unnecessary stress during execution.

TREATING PEOPLE AS "RESOURCES"

Key stakeholders are usually busy people. They may be responsible for hundreds or thousands of employees, other stakeholders, or users.

It's not possible to work with all these people on a personal level. So they tend to group them into "teams" or "projects."

It is not we are mean or cruel. It is just the way our brains work: It is called "cognitive scope limitation."

Stakeholders put a lot of stress on a project team by setting unrealistic demands or pushing deadlines. They try to achieve their goals.

So, they tend to forget that "teams" and "projects" include people who have lives outside of work, with their own hobbies, families, goals, needs, and problems. Stakeholders usually don't know your whole team. They remember one or two names. A human brain just doesn't have enough mental capacity.

The only way to influence stakeholders and overcome this problem is by personalizing your project. Use your team members' names, put their photos as avatars in your communication tools, acquaint them with the key stakeholders, and guard their personal time.

Overcoming cognitive scope limitation will help you create a healthy professional environment whereby people feel belonging and friendship. They'll feel valued by the project owners.

SHOW STAKEHOLDERS BEHIND THE SCENES

The idea is simple. Whenever you communicate with stakeholders, you should vividly describe the efforts it takes to do the work.

For example:

- When a team works on a challenging task, say they are working hard and doing their best.

- When the team has to work overtime, describe how committed they are.
- When you are working on creative tasks, explain how engaged the team is.
- Acknowledge a team member who did some critical work.

You don't need to be super-creative here. Simply stating these facts is enough.

Your stakeholders should always feel they are working with a committed team. It works the same way as leading by example. Your team should inspire stakeholders to behave the same way.

This will make stakeholders more reluctant to waste the team's time, delay answers, or request unneeded changes. Also, it is hard to stay passive alongside such an engaged group of people committed to the project's success. This tactic works really well in overcoming cognitive scope limitation as well.

Likewise, don't assume that all stakeholders know how a project team operates on a daily basis. Giving them a glimpse behind the scenes will help them better understand the dynamics of the work. It will help them become a part of that team.

ALWAYS ADD A CLEAR CALL TO ACTION

The last thing I wanted to tell you about is a call to action. This concept is widely used in marketing. Whatever you communicate to stakeholders, you must direct them to the action you want them to take.

They can't read your mind. So you need to tell them exactly what you want them to do at the end of every message.

It is better to have only one call to action per message. It will increase your chances of getting the response you are looking for. Even if you do not expect any actions from a stakeholder, it is a good idea to give him a way to clarify things and ask questions. Invite him to write back with any questions he might have as a call to action. It opens up a constructive dialogue, improves engagement, and helps to prioritize your request.

You might not see an immediate or profound effect from these tactics. Instead, they encourage patterns of behavior, understanding of the project management process, and collaboration with people. Therefore, you need to apply them continuously during all interactions with stakeholders you need to influence.

So, if you expected a step-by-step action plan to win over people, I have bad news for you. Unfortunately, such a tool or technique doesn't exist. Every stakeholder is different and unpredictable. So, you need to develop a personal approach for each of them. That is why stakeholder management is the most challenging part of your job. But a great project manager knows that, if you don't do this well, your project will fail.

PART FOUR
RISK MANAGEMENT

CHAPTER 19
RISK MANAGEMENT OVERVIEW

I was sitting in the office early one morning. I'd created a perfect plan to fix a problem that I believed would appear in a few days. It was my first project. And it made me a little proud that I'd discovered a potential risk!

In a few days, it happened!

With barely concealed enthusiasm, I escalated it to management. At once, I provided my plan to overcome the problem. After a few hours of intensive meetings, senior management accepted my plan.

We solved the problem quickly and efficiently. But once everyone left, my mentor came to me. "What the hell was that?" he said. "Fixing the consequences is a passive mindset. You should be proactive! If you knew the solution, you should have prevented the problem."

That's a lesson that I've remembered through my whole career. If you think about it, he was right. By discussing the problem with an expert in a quiet meeting before it arose, we could have reached the same result in a cheaper, less stressful way without troubling senior-level managers and engineers.

So, risk management is all about preventing problems or reducing their impact on a project.

But why do we talk about it before we've even discussed how to start and lead a project?

First of all, you inherit risks from the environment of your organization. Think about internal stakeholders, processes, lack of support from leadership, absence of expertise, recurring or seasonal problems. They're all present in this environment already. So, here's the good news! The more you work in one company, the more you know about its inefficiencies and weaknesses. But rest assured that the same challenges will reappear for all new projects. Unfortunately, organizations don't fix these problems quickly.

Second, you may participate in the pre-sales phase of a project. So, again, there's the potential to avoid a treasury of risks from the start by adjusting stakeholders' expectations. But you need to know how to identify and track those risks.

That's why we need to focus on risk management from the start. You need to apply the processes and tools we discuss in this chapter throughout every aspect of the project. Risk management activities must be baked into your project plan.

Repeat this mantra after me:

"I will perform risk management activities throughout the whole project lifetime and in between projects. It never stops."

SHORT GLOSSARY OF PROJECT RISK MANAGEMENT

There is no such thing as a universal risk management approach. Instead, you need to select tools, techniques, and processes for each project individually. Moreover, organizations often develop their own approaches to risk management that you need to follow.

The *PMBOK Guide* describes a simple framework for risk management[1]. It gave me inspiration, so credit where it's due to the PMI. See what I just did? I acknowledged the stakeholder's contribution.

It gives the following definition of a risk[2]:

"An uncertain event or condition, that if it occurs, has a positive or negative effect on a project's objective."

Conversely, an opportunity is an event or condition that has a positive effect. As a project manager, you need to try and leverage opportunities as much as avoiding risks.

The "impact" is the effect of risk or opportunity. This may change the feasibility, costs, durations, overall risk level, availability of resources, or personnel. In general, a risk may impact any aspect of the project.

We can assess a risk's impact qualitatively as low, medium, or high.

We can also describe the impact as a monetary value of a risk like $2,450, or as a delay of four calendar days, or both at once.

But don't limit yourself only to project costs or duration. Risks will appear in all aspects of project management and may have a complex impact. For example, a risk may impact quality, team motivation, resources, and staffing all at once.

"Probability" is the likelihood of a risk or opportunity happening.

Again, it can be qualitative (low, medium, high) or quantitative (a percentage).

A "risk response" or "risk response plan" details the action you will take to avoid or mitigate risk.

RISK MANAGEMENT FRAMEWORK

Below is a quick overview of the risk management framework. Notice that each step of the framework is a separate process, all of which will be discussed in detail in the following chapters.

Additionally, keep in mind that it's just a framework. You can add or remove tools and techniques in each process. However, in the long run, you need to tailor your risk management approach for the given project. The primary consideration is the costs of your efforts. Risk management is not free of charge. It requires the involvement of the whole team and stakeholders. So, you need to balance your efforts with the benefits of overcoming risks.

STEP #1: PLAN HOW TO MANAGE RISKS

As with everything in project management, risk management starts with planning. There are three main reasons for this:

1. Risk management requires the input of all the project documentation, processes, and workflows. You need to plan what you'll analyze and how.

2. You don't do risk management alone. You need input from stakeholders, so you need to know who they are and plan their engagement.

3. You need to collect the assets and knowledge of your organization. This helps you to avoid reinventing the wheel.

There are too many moving parts for this to be kept in your head. So, you need a simple project risk management plan. It should cover each detailed step discussed below.

You can get my risk management plan template from the additional resources to this book. Use it as a starting point.

https://itpmschool.com/materials

STEP #2: CONTINUOUSLY IDENTIFY RISKS

The next step is to identify risks with techniques outlined in the risk management plan, in conjunction with all the information you have at your disposal.

We'll talk about different risk identification techniques in detail. However, I want you to focus on one in particular that can help you kickstart the process, even if you have never done it before. It's the analysis of risk categories.

The only problem is that your company probably doesn't maintain a list of risk categories. But I've got you covered. In my experience, there are 43 risk categories. Take these as a starting point. Then, expand the list with categories from your industry. Finally, keep it updated throughout your career.

How many risks should you identify? Even on a small project, there could be up to a hundred.

So, what should you do with all of them? First of all, you need to log them all in a risk register. But don't evaluate them – just write them down for now!

STEP #3: PERFORM QUALITATIVE RISK ANALYSIS

Qualitative risk analysis is all about assessing each risk's impact and probability in simple terms like low, medium, or high.

Remember, mitigating is costly: You will never work on a project that allows you to do this for every possible risk. That's why the primary goal of the qualitative risk analysis is to shortlist the known risks: Those that have the most adverse impact on the project and are a distinct possibility.

Soon, hundreds of risks will be whittled down to maybe a dozen. The next step is to plan risk responses for each of them.

The others remain in a "watch list" section of the risk register. Why is this needed? The impact and probability of risks evolve during the project lifetime.

Here's a key piece of advice: Don't overcomplicate it!

If you can prioritize risks using simple grades of low, medium, and high, then do so. Going beyond this is only beneficial when you have hundreds of risks or require a more complex analysis.

STEP #4 (OPTIONAL): PERFORM QUANTITATIVE RISK ANALYSIS

You may analyze risks further by using percentages for probability and dollars (or whatever currency is relevant) for impact.

Using these figures, you can calculate the expected monetary value (EVM) of each risk.

But, for smaller projects, this isn't usually worth the effort required because it's unlikely to be needed.

In some cases, it may help you to analyze a costly and critical decision. If you are doing it for the first time, ask your peers and leadership for guidance.

STEP #5: PLAN HOW TO OVERCOME RISKS

So, now you have identified a dozen risks. What next?

- You can do something to avoid a risk.

- You can do something to reduce the impact and/or probability of a threat.
- You can do nothing but, when the threat materializes, you can use the risk reserves to minimize any negative impact.
- You can do nothing, and just accept the risk and its effects. Then, you may need to adjust the project plan.

The risk response plan will help you achieve one of these results. But don't limit yourself to a cookie-cutter solution. An efficient response plan comes from collaboration with stakeholders.

Sometimes you need to look beyond your Gantt chart, your budget, and your team. Sometimes informing the right people may eliminate the risk altogether.

STEP #6: IMPLEMENT RISK RESPONSES

Each risk response plan is a part of your project management plan:

- It's a budget allocated for a specific risk.
- It's a separate task someone needs to perform.
- It's a new process you developed.

More often than not, someone needs to implement the risk response plan before a risk materializes. At the very least, this person should monitor the risk and report on the effectiveness of any response. But, in most cases, that shouldn't be you because you don't have the time to track dozens of risks.

So, you need to do the following:

1. Assign an owner to each risk. This person will monitor and work specifically on their allocated risk when the time comes.
2. Communicate with stakeholders about the upcoming risks and responses you've planned.
3. Collect data about the risks: The number of risks that did or didn't occur, the efficiency of responses, and the impact on

schedule, budget, and scope of work. Also, don't forget about the client's happiness.

4. Identify any residual risk following your responses.

These activities are relevant across the board for all project management efforts. Each risk response is like a micro sub-project. But they are always a part of the wider project, not a stand-alone activity.

Here's an expert tip:

Delegate ownership for implementing risk responses as much as possible. You need to focus on the bigger picture of project progress, overall risk levels, and new sources of risks. In general, you should only tackle the risks that are in your area of expertise.

STEP #7: CONTINUOUSLY MONITOR RISKS

When controlling risk management activities, you first need to ensure that your planned risk responses are efficient and timely.

After that, you need to keep an eye on new risks as they appear. And they do surface all the time! Likewise, known risks may change their probability and impact. These new and updated risks may challenge the feasibility of your project.

Next, you need to control the overall risk level for the project. You should do this periodically. Then, based on your analysis, you may need to make changes to the project baselines or your risk management approach.

What if Risks Messed up Your Project?

Following this process doesn't safeguard you from problems:

- You may fail to identify a severe risk.
- Your risk response plan may be inefficient.
- Small risks may snowball into larger ones.
- Some risks will be out of your control.

When a risk seriously hits your project, you need to focus your efforts on getting back to your initial plan. Don't re-plan the whole project because that will create new risks.

But that's the worst-case scenario. You're unlikely to see too many risks that can instantly ruin the whole project. Even if there are, such risks are usually known, and you try to avoid them from day one by creating a prototype or performing a feasibility analysis.

In the real world, you should be worried about the compound effect of numerous small risks and risks that you failed to identify. They won't bring your project down at once, but they'll gradually cause delays. They will make your project owner unhappy to the point where they start questioning your competency. You definitely want to avoid that! That's why I'll explain how to conduct all these processes in the following chapters.

CHAPTER 20
HOW TO IDENTIFY RISKS

Hopefully, you've reviewed my risk management plan template already. So, the first thing you need to come up with is a list of tools to identify risks, called "risk identification techniques." Then, you need to understand when to use them and how to apply them to your project management documentation.

There are several established methods of analyzing project information, and discovering threats and opportunities. The most popular include brainstorming, interviews, document analysis, checklists (risk categories), root cause analysis, and assumptions analysis.

Put simply, a risk identification technique helps you to discover problems that you were unaware of.

WHEN DO YOU IDENTIFY RISKS?

In practice, you should use an integrated risk management approach. This means that you should talk through possible risks for each and every activity during the project.

For example, when you collect requirements and write specifications, you and your team should always be on the lookout for risks:

- Track all the assumptions you make.
- Check if the requirements are ambiguous i.e., do people understand the exact same requirements differently?
- Don't hide uncertainties. Instead, transform them into risks.

So, you capture all the identified risks as you go. You can then analyze them separately.

But that's not enough. You also need in-depth risk identification sessions at specific critical points in project planning where you take a broader look at the project as a whole.

For example, here are some important times at which to consider the need for dedicated risk identification sessions:

- When clients identified the project goal.
- After you've identified key stakeholders.
- When you've reviewed risk categories for the first time.
- After you've collected most of the requirements.
- After you've created a draft of the work breakdown structure (WBS).
- After you've identified the required resources.
- After you've drafted the project schedule.
- After you've drafted the project budget.

HOW TO USE RISK IDENTIFICATION TECHNIQUES

Some techniques, like brainstorming, are universal. You can apply them to anything on a project.

Other techniques, like requirements analysis, are specific to a piece of project documentation, and you do it once.

You don't always use all the techniques on everything. However, you might apply several techniques to one input. For example:

1. You can review the project schedule with the team and brainstorm possible threats.
2. After that, you'll check common risk sources in the risk categories.

3. Then, you'll take the schedule to a senior project manager and interview her to get her insights.

It all boils down to efficient use of your time and resources.

THE ONLY SIX RISK IDENTIFICATION TECHNIQUES YOU NEED

In real life, it's tough to make risk identification techniques timely and efficient. As I've said before, the key is to keep things simple. Team members and stakeholders should be able to use them without special training or experience.

Therefore, I've selected the following six techniques that you can use on any project no matter how experienced you are.

#1: ANALYZE RISK CATEGORIES TO DISCOVER TYPICAL RISKS

Most organizations carry out projects of a similar nature. Processes and policies are the same. Some stakeholders never change. So, a new project inherits all the same sources of risks from your environment.

Risk categories are just a list of these common sources of risks in your organization. In practice, that means all organizations in the same niche share the same sources of risks. So, this technique is really worth your time because you can reuse it throughout your whole career.

The list of risk categories comes from lessons learned in risk management. Ideally, project managers should share these lessons with others. However, that is rarely the case. That's why you won't find such a list in your organization. What's even worse, for the same reasons, you probably don't even have your own list of risk categories right now. But I've got you covered. I'll give you one in the next chapter.

This technique:

- helps you to identify risks that you may not be aware of;
- prevents you from forgetting about some risk sources; and
- structures your risk identification efforts.

So, the process is simple – you need to get through the list to identify risks that may apply to your current project. You can approach this in different ways.

You may review the list alone and shortlist the categories, then discussing the shortlist with your team. Or, you can brainstorm through the whole list with your team. Usually, the best time to do this is when you already know the project's scope of work.

I also recommend keeping the list close at hand as a cheat sheet or template for other risk identification sessions. It will be a good starting point for identifying new possible sources of risks.

#2: PERFORM REQUIREMENTS REVIEW

A requirements review is just one part of assessing the project documentation, but I want to focus on it separately because it's critical.

Requirements contain significant risks for a project. Therefore, you need to analyze them to find any ambiguous or unclear aspects. This will help you to assess how much work is actually required to fulfill each requirement.

Poor requirements are the number one cause of project failure. It's not just their quality and level of detail: It's also important to have enough time to analyze the project specifications. You need to have a chance to review and discuss each requirement with the team, with the big picture in mind. You need to ensure that the requirements don't conflict with one another. Not giving yourself the time to do all of this is a risk in itself!

In the real world, you clarify requirements throughout the whole project lifetime. Therefore, you need to re-evaluate the risks progressively here. So, here's what you need to do in practice:

1. Select some requirements.
2. Select a group for analysis (the whole team or just group leaders).
3. Let them read through the specifications, designs, emails.
4. Plan a meeting to analyze the requirements.

5. Let one person explain the requirements to the others.
6. Clarify requirements to the point where everyone has the same understanding.

If you have never done this before, try it at least once, even if just out of curiosity. You'll notice that different people read the same words and sentences differently.

Likewise, I'm a big fan of visualizing workflows, information flows, and user experience. If your product, service, or result has a user interface or any tangible form, take time to draw it out. You will identify a lot of new use cases, weak spots in requirements, and inconsistencies. As the old saying goes, a picture is worth a thousand words.

#3: REVIEW THE PROJECT MANAGEMENT PLAN WITH THE TEAM

This is the more general part of reviewing project documentation that can be applied to any assessment of risk.

So, what documents should you review to find risks? The answer is every one! For example, once you have a first draft of the project management plan, review it with your team.

First of all, engaging the project team in the planning activities is vital. So you need to ensure their buy-in from the start. A disengaged and unmotivated team that doesn't believe in the project plan is a huge risk by itself.

On the other hand, your team is the primary source of information and risks. When you walk the whole team through the project plan, I can promise that each person will find at least one risk related to them. It's better to find out such risks early and adjust the plan accordingly.

There are many aspects that you need to talk about with the team. At the very least, you need to discuss the following:

- Units of measurement. Did they provide estimates in effective or ideal hours, working days, etc.?
- What did they include in those estimates? Is there a buffer?
- Do they know how to report the money they spend?

- Do they know how to log their progress and when?
- Do they know your project management approach in general? What about risk management?
- Do they understand the definition of a completed task?

The list goes on and on. Never assume that team members see and understand your plan the same way as you do. Moreover, don't assume that all team members have a common understanding of all project activities.

Once I have a draft of a schedule, I show it to the team. They review dependencies, flow of tasks, any buffers that we have. They also think through their personal plans, vacations, and other errands.

For example, a team member sees the project schedule. He has several critical tasks next week. Then, suddenly, he remembers that he's planning an important trip he has not told you about yet. You can then adjust the schedule to allow for his absence.

Moreover, different parts of your project always depend on others, and you want to make sure that nothing blocks your progress. So, team members may discover hard dependencies that I've missed. Therefore, it helps me to correct the plan early on and include these possible delays.

I use the same process to verify our WBS. Draft after draft, I collect feedback from the team and correct the WBS. This often reveals insufficient details in requirements. Therefore, we need to take a step back. Occasionally, we discover a new piece of work when we look at the product as a whole.

I also recommend creating and reviewing project workflows. At the very least, you need them for:

- starting, reporting on, and finishing a task;
- identifying and controlling risks;
- reporting on project status;
- identifying and fixing defects;
- integrating a change request; and
- elaborating requirements from concept to an approved specification.

You can draw the workflows on a piece of paper or create them in a tool like diagrams.net. But I believe you do need to visualize them. If you use project management software, you need to tie it all to "statuses" and "fields." You don't need any flashy diagrams here: Just make it clear to team members.

The good thing is that you'll only need to do this once for each organization. Then, you can adjust it for new projects. But it will help you identify roadblocks, areas of diffused responsibility, inefficient communication, etc. Another source of risks is your superiors who need to approve your work. All these show up on a diagram of project workflows.

Do you really review all the documents on your projects?

No, I don't. This is because some of them are pretty similar to the ones I used on previous projects. So, I just make sure that the same plans, templates, and workflows will work for the new project.

#4: USE BRAINSTORMING AND INTERVIEWS TECHNIQUE FOR DEEPER ANALYSIS

In general, I don't like to identify risks with wild brainstorming. However, there are critical points in project planning when I use brainstorming for risk identification on a higher level. These are:

- when analyzing essential requirements;
- while reviewing the WBS;
- when reviewing the schedule and HR plan;
- while creating a quality management plan; and
- before finalizing the whole project management plan.

So, for example, once I have a draft of the WBS, I plan several brainstorming sessions. Then, I analyze major deliverables one by one with the team. My main question is, "What could go wrong when we implement this piece of the project?" And I point at one of the deliverables.

Then, I ask, "What challenges do you see in putting it all together in one piece?" So, we take a broader look at our future work once we know enough details.

I use interviews with SMEs in the same manner. Unfortunately, these experts usually don't have time to participate in all risk management activities. So, instead, I try to get feedback and validation on the most critical risks and related response plans.

#5: APPLY ROOT CAUSE ANALYSIS FOR SYSTEMATIC RISKS

In practice, I use root cause analysis for risk identification in three scenarios:

1. To analyze severe problems of past projects. It might be my previous project. It might be a similar one in the organization carried out by another project manager. It can also be relevant notes from lessons learned or a list of risk categories.
2. When I'm trying to solve a systematic problem. This usually relates to inefficient communications, poor-quality, inaccurate estimates; or ambiguity in requirements.
3. To group all identified risks by the root cause. It helps to see the primary sources of problems and identify even more risks.

So, in a real-world project, you don't carry out root cause analysis during planning. Usually, it's a post-mortem or analysis after a significant problem. So, first, you collect lessons learned. Then, you allocate time at the end of the project for a root cause analysis session. You can use the fishbone diagram, "5 Whys" technique, or a scatter plot diagram. Later, develop a systematic risk response plan for the next project.

Don't assume that the same risks will not occur in the next project. On the contrary, they undoubtedly will – especially those related to your project management approach and your organization's environment.

Always put such risks on your risk categories list.

#6: ANALYZE ASSUMPTIONS TO IDENTIFY THE MOST IMPACTFUL RISKS

By nature, assumptions involve risks. If an assumption is wrong, a project is in trouble.

So, first of all, you need to keep track of all major assumptions. I keep a separate list of project-level assumptions. In addition, I log all assumptions related to specific requirements right in the specification document. After that, you need to review and validate the assumptions regularly.

We make assumptions all the time. But most are made right at the start of a project. So, they may impact the project later down the road. Assumptions that you make due to problems in the organization are the most risky. These include the following:

- An assumption that you'll get the required resources in time. Why?! Do recruiters always hire people quickly?
- An assumption that your SME will be available to your project. But what if he's assigned full time to another critical project?
- An assumption that a third party will provide their deliverables on time. Usually, they don't, and the whole project stalls.

You need to work hard to validate an assumption and either make it a fact or transform it into a known risk.

HOW TO FIND TIME FOR THESE ACTIVITIES?

First of all, efficient delegation is the key. You don't need the whole team for risk identification.

Second, you can incorporate these techniques into other processes and meetings. There's no need for separate meetings unless you want to explore possible risks in depth.

Third, when you educate people about risk management techniques, they start using them on the fly: they include risks and assumptions in all their conversations.

On the other hand, you need to explain the benefits of risk management to the project owners. You need to strike the right balance between your efforts and the potential benefits they provide, and ensure that you ask for enough time to achieve those benefits.

CHAPTER 21
SOURCES OF RISKS

Listing risk categories is a simple yet powerful technique for identifying risks. It's even more valuable if you do not already have robust risk management processes in place.

It's pretty straightforward. Simply go through the list and see what sources of risks apply to your project. Then, you need to brainstorm specific risks in each selected category.

You can work with the whole list several times during project planning. Likewise, you can revisit parts of the list based on the current phase of the project.

How do you come up with this list? In theory, all project managers should contribute. It's a by-product of the lessons learned process that you should perform after every project. But most organizations don't have a process to collect lessons learned and maintain this list. That is why I'm going to share my list. You can use it as a starting point.

PROJECT MANAGEMENT CATEGORY

Project management itself can be a significant source of risks. I know you are a diligent project manager. However, do check whether the following apply to your project.

1. Project manager cannot dedicate enough time and effort. The root cause may vary. For example, you work on several projects at once and do not have enough time to manage each one of them properly. Or you combine two roles like project manager and business analyst. Therefore, you can't dedicate enough time to planning. You need to overcome such risks with proper delegation of responsibilities.

2. Lack of knowledge by stakeholders. When stakeholders know little about project management, they cause trouble. In most cases, they won't follow the processes you've established. Instead, they'll do everything as they see fit. Moreover, they may believe project managers don't bring any value.

First of all, do not assume that stakeholders know how to manage a project. Instead, you need to lead them whether they're your boss, project owners, or technical experts. They pay you to be the expert, don't they?

Second, you need to educate them continuously about their role and how to leverage your project management approach.

Finally, be mindful that this won't happen overnight. So, expect delays and miscommunications that lead to false expectations.

3. Imposed requirements to project management approach. Both project managers and stakeholders tend to be familiar with one particular project management approach. It's the method they use most often. However, it may not be suitable for your current project. In this case, you'll need to cover inefficiencies with risk reserves.

4. Project schedule. At the start of a project, someone sets a deadline. They do it out of the blue or based on business needs. It doesn't automatically mean that you can reach the project objective by that date. So, you need to prove whether it's feasible or not.

In general, the project schedule incorporates risks from other knowledge areas. For example, if the scope is poorly defined, then more work is needed, putting pressure on the timeline. Likewise, an unrealistically tight deadline never works because it puts pressure on every aspect of the project. Moreover, it demotivates the team.

5. Product or service quality. If your product or service is regulated through mandatory audits or has strict quality requirements, it's a source of risks.

Inefficient quality assurance and defects always result in additional work and delays. In general, you won't be able to finish a project with lots of defects. Project owners won't accept it.

So, you need to think in advance about how you will assure quality and what you would do if the team missed some defects.

STAKEHOLDERS CATEGORY

We discussed the impact of stakeholders on a project. They have a wide variety of possible effects.

6. Executive support. Sometimes you just need a formal sign-off from your boss. Sometimes you need support to make an organizational change – for example, to avoid major recurring risks related to the processes, policies, or stakeholders.

Therefore, you need a commitment from these stakeholders. Unfortunately, it's often hard to get this because they have little time or interest in your project. You may even end up with no support at all, which will lead to project delays or failure. As a result, any dependency on top-tier stakeholders is a risk.

7. Sponsor-caused risks. Business people have a different mindset. Once a project is up and running, their focus switches to the next idea.

If your project depends on the sponsor's engagement or approval, there is a risk that the schedule and the scope could change.

8. Conflicting stakeholders. Stakeholders have different expectations for your project. Whenever you get requirements from several equally authoritative stakeholders, it's a risk.

They may provide conflicting requirements. Or they may pursue different goals. Moreover, the balance of power between them may change. This means that requirements may change in the middle of a project. What's more important, this type of risks requires keeping a close eye on all the company's internal politics.

9. Unidentified stakeholders. Nothing is worse than an authoritative stakeholder appearing in the middle of a project. And, of course, he has his own vision and new requirements! But they are not aligned with the goals of the project. As a result, they are not in your project plan.

So, if you've already missed the stakeholder identification process, write this down as a significant risk.

SCOPE AND REQUIREMENTS CATEGORY

Requirements are the most significant source of risks. Period.

10. Poor rolling wave planning. You do not need to plan the whole project in detail. Sounds good, right? However, sorting out the finer points as you go, otherwise known as "rolling wave planning", can be a source of serious risks. It is based on assumptions. Some of them will be proven to be wrong. Overall rolling wave planning requires proper risk management with risk reserves of time and resources.

11. Inconsistent requirements. This is subtly different from conflicting requirements. Some stakeholders may be focused on only a part of a product or service that you need to deliver. Therefore, they will not bother considering all possible uses.

This often happens when requirements come from different departments or even different organizations. If that's the case, you need to mitigate such risks by adding more time to analyze all requirements.

12. Unclear requirements. This one's pretty straightforward. All of us started work without fully described requirements. In the end, there's a chance we won't meet stakeholders' expectations.

So, if you begin the execution phase before finalizing requirements, this is a risk that entails reserves for rework and change requests. Alternatively, you may fix the root cause of the problem by applying agile methodologies like Scrum and Kanban.

13. Feasibility of requirements. Quite often, requirements are not feasible within given constraints. Therefore, you cannot implement them fully or with the required quality.

Nevertheless, you are forced to press ahead. That's a risk – you need to communicate it continuously.

14. Poorly defined scope. Overall, it's hard to identify 100% of a project scope. That's why we use so many tools and processes. If you are not proficient with the requirements traceability matrix, WBS, or scope statement, you should log risks.

Likewise, if you don't have a professional person to collect project and product requirements, this will also lead to a poorly defined scope.

15. The absence of a WBS. The WBS is a cornerstone tool in project management which:

- links different aspects of a project with the scope of work;
- serves as a hub for all project information; and
- gives structure to a project.

If you don't use this or an equivalent tool, that's a risk.

CHANGE MANAGEMENT CATEGORY

16. Inconsistent change management. A change to the project is a risk by default. You need to go against your initial plan. Moreover, a change to the plan always impacts several or all aspects of a project. Therefore, change management has several sources of risks. They include but are not limited to:

- number of changes;
- failing to actively avoid changes;
- careless analysis of the impact of a change;
- inconsistent logging of change requests;
- inefficient control over the implementation of changes; or
- poor communication of approved and rejected changes.

If you get a lot of changes in the middle of the project, you need to double your risk identification efforts. Likewise, you should be ready for unexpected threats. Therefore, when you accept a change, consider adding risk reserves.

HUMAN RESOURCES MANAGEMENT CATEGORY

The next big risk category is related to the project team and resources.

17. Poorly managed conflicts. Conflicts within a team are inevitable. Nevertheless, I do believe they are important and valuable.

But when you leave them unresolved or resolve them in the wrong way, they can cause many problems.

If you don't already, use a conflict log. It is a must-have tool for any project.

18. Inappropriate resources. You are often obliged to work with people and resources simply because they are all that is available at the time. For example, your team might have been assigned long before you knew the scope of the project. It means that the team members may not be up to the tasks at hand.

19. Team motivation. This is the key to any project management approach or methodology. None of it works without people.

Moreover, there's no efficient and proven way to manage demotivated people. So, if your team is unhappy with the project or your management, expect all sorts of trouble.

20. Team acquisition timelines. You often have to share resources with other projects. Therefore, you need to be ready for delays or even the absence of resources you requested and secured. Also, there might be additional communication and management overheads.

Likewise, the hiring process is unpredictable. You may not get the desired experts by the time you need them.

Moreover, there's always a learning curve you must take into account.

21. Unclear roles and responsibilities. You need to establish responsibilities on different levels:

- Responsibility for project deliverables (RACI matrix).
- Responsibilities and accountability that are related to daily activities (project workflows).
- Role-related responsibilities, including leadership hierarchy (job description).

Until you establish all of these in your team, you should expect risks.

COMMUNICATIONS AND DECISION-MAKING CATEGORY

22. Inefficient communication. If the only way to reach critical stakeholders is by email, this will cause delays. Emails may go back and forth but problems stay unresolved. So, allow for time in the project schedule to get information from such stakeholders.

As I've mentioned before, always define the correct means of communication for each stakeholder. And keep to the best practices of how to write emails. We'll discuss this the Chapter #56.

23. Unreliable means of communication. Keeping specifications in emails rather than in shared documents is a bad practice. Storing important files locally on your computer is another one. Likewise, emails might not be the best way to discuss daily challenges.

A project manager should define the best method of communication for all stakeholders and activities. Otherwise, your messages may remain unseen for good.

24. Insecure communication. Often you work with sensitive information. Do you have a protocol to share and store such information? Is there a risk of leaking this information to the wrong person?

The worst thing about this risk category is that security problems arise long after the project is finished.

25. Poor decision making. Have you ever thought about the quality of your decision making?

Do you often need to make decisions under pressure and on the spot – for example, during a short call with the client? Well, if you do, it's a major source of risks. The best way to fix the root cause of the problem is by planning one step ahead.

26. Incompetence in decision making. This is common when, for example, a businessperson is making critical decisions about technology. That's why you need to know how to explain technical aspects in simple terms to stakeholders.

27. Slow feedback. Some stakeholders, usually external organizations and departments inside your company, have a predefined response time. As a result, it may take a day or a week to hear back from them. So, you need to allow for this in your schedule.

THE ENVIRONMENT OF THE ORGANIZATION CATEGORY

We usually assume that the organizational environment is suitable for project work. This is rarely true. In fact, it can be the cause of quite a lot of serious risks.

Here are just a few of them:

28. Resistance to changes. Technologies and approaches change rapidly. But companies do not. Your organization may not be flexible enough to take on a new technology stack or update its project management processes. When your project depends on embracing something new, be sure to consider resistance from within.

29. Lack of expertise. If the nature of a project is new to the organization, it will not be fully ready at once.

You'll find no lessons learned or experienced teams. The level of uncertainty will be high. Thus, there will be more risks in all aspects of the project.

30. Inefficient processes. The world is changing. Organizations need to refresh processes and policies in order to be efficient.

An example here is an organization that adopts agile methodologies. They start working with Scrum or Kanban but not all departments have updated their processes and policies. Therefore, they impede the performance of Scrum teams.

31. Security measures. Do you have tight security in the organization? If so, you will have a limited range of technologies you can use. Security introduces difficulties in transferring information. Sometimes you will need special approval. You can expect delays. In the worst cases, some solutions may be restricted.

32. Internal politics. Major stakeholders will always change the balance of power. They may be using your project as a good platform for their own ambitions and goals. What's even worse, they may not be interested in your project at all.

33. Infrastructure. Poor infrastructure of an organization, whether it's weak or overly complex, negatively impacts almost all aspects of a project.

LACK OF RISK MANAGEMENT

This may sound ridiculous but risk management is also a source of risks.

34. Secondary risks. Risk response plans address identified risks. However, quite often, they may introduce secondary risks. Unfortunately, project managers tend to forget about these.

This is why project planning is iterative. After the initial round of risk management activities, you need to repeat risk identification. You need to ensure that your actions do not create threats in other areas.

For example, we usually forget to analyze the impact of our actions on the project team.

35. Residual risks. The same goes for risks that were accepted but no action was taken. However, risks are not static. They change their probability and impact on a project with time.

Failing to monitor these risks may lead to serious problems that appear unexpectedly.

36. Unidentified risks. A lack of risk management efforts or inefficient processes is most definitely a risk. It's critical to continue risk identification throughout the whole project's lifetime.

37. Risk management in procurement. Risks in this category range from the total absence of required contractors to the poor performance of vendors and suppliers.

LACK OF AUTHORITY

38. Lack of leadership authority. This is a broad risk category. You may lack the power to make serious decisions. Your influence on stakeholders may be weak.

You may have problems managing a highly experienced team. Or your lack of authority may have a detrimental impact on negotiations.

As a junior project manager, you should be ready for these kinds of risks. However, it is usually hard to put them into your risk register, isn't it? Instead, categorize them under poor decision making and allow for delays.

TECHNICAL SOLUTIONS

39. Dependency on technical solutions. Whenever your project depends on hardware or a service, you must assume that these will perform to the required level.

But what if the hardware or service performs less efficiently? Or the workload is much higher than expected? And you learn this in the middle of the project?

You need an action plan to verify all assumptions related to the selected technology.

40. Design and architecture. An evolving product or service must have a flexible and scalable architecture. Otherwise, changes may require disproportionately more effort. This also applies to legacy systems.

41. Integration. Whether this is technical or business-related, you need to be prepared that something will simply not work.

Therefore, always brainstorm ideas of what may go wrong with your project.

EXTERNAL RISKS

42. External events. There is a multitude of these that may impact the project, like *force majeures*. They might be a regular occurrence, depending on the location and timescales of your project.

This risk category may include:

- tropical storms;
- local strikes;
- blackouts;
- transport collapses; and
- seasonal flu.

43. User acceptance. You finished the project within constraints. However, no one wants to use the product you created!

How would you respond to such a risk? As a project manager, you may need to find stakeholders among the end users. You need someone who can explain pain points from the trenches.

On the other hand, organizations creating their own services and products should incorporate product management techniques into the overall development process.

Either way, every requirement should have a justification based on end users' feedback or collected data.

ASSUMPTIONS

44. Every assumption is a source of risks. That's why you need to log and work with all assumptions that you make on the project. And you need to do it continuously. Wrong assumptions usually lead to dramatic problems.

In no way do I consider this list complete. It's a living document that we need to update regularly. So, consider it as a starting point.

CHAPTER 22
RISK REGISTER

The risk register contains information about identified risks, results of risk analysis (impact, probability, effects), and risk response plans. You should also use the risk register to monitor and control risks during the whole project life cycle.

At first glance, it's a simple document. You just need to fill in the information you collect about each risk. But don't be fooled!

You need to keep in mind that the risk register is a living thing:

- The information it contains changes rapidly.
- Risks evolve and adjust.
- A risk response plan may not be efficient enough.
- Threats and opportunities may disappear or become irrelevant.

In practice, only a handful of project managers keep the risk register in good shape during the whole project lifetime. Why? Because most overcomplicate it! Instead, you should keep it simple, adaptable, maintainable, and close at hand. So, remove unnecessary information that you don't use in your risk management approach.

WHAT SHOULD YOU PUT INTO A RISK REGISTER?

A risk register usually takes the form of a spreadsheet. If your project management software has a built-in capability to track risks, you can create one there (although it may need adapting).

Here are the primary entities (columns) that I suggest you include in the risk register.

RISK ID

This is a unique number that identifies a risk. Throughout the project's lifetime, you'll log hundreds of risks – even on a small project! Therefore, you need a simple way to identify the correct risk in the register.

Four-digit numbers should suffice in most cases. Start with 0001, then 0002, and so on. Continue in sequence, even if you remove a risk.

WORK BREAKDOWN STRUCTURE ELEMENT

I suggest you integrate the risk register with the WBS.

The WBS is the tool that helps you break down the whole project scope and identify all of it. It consists of big pieces of tangible results called 'deliverables' and smaller pieces called 'work packages'. These all have a unique identifier that clearly states their position in the hierarchy called the 'WBS index.'

For example, linking to the top-level item means threats to the project outcome. On the other hand, if you link to a deliverable or a work package, that's an isolated risk.

Therefore, in this column, you'll have a WBS index like 1.2.4 or 1.3.5.1. This shows the exact location of an element in the WBS.

Some project management software applications allow you to log risks into a WBS element. In this case, you don't need a separate spreadsheet.

If you don't know what this is, don't worry, I'll explain it in the Chapter #39.

RISK CATEGORY

Grouping risks by categories can help you to fight the root cause of a problem. So, it may show you a way to tackle several risks with one risk response plan.

You need to decide what categories to use beforehand. Below are some examples.

- The common ones: scope, schedule, cost, quality, and HR.
- Industry-specific ones (e.g., IT): requirements, design, implementation, testing, and deployment.
- PESTLE: political, economic, social, technological, legal, and environmental.

Again, it's up to you to identify the most appropriate categories. I recommend starting with simple industry-specific categories.

RISK TITLE

Describe each risk, its nature and severity, in one sentence.
Check out these examples:

- David may leave the company.
- David most probably will leave the company, which will impact the deadline.
- David leaves the company on June 16, which will impact the deadline by a month.

A title may be the only thing you need to describe a risk. It's usually sufficient on small and medium projects.

RISK DESCRIPTION (OPTIONAL)

You may need to add a fuller description than just a risk title for two main reasons:

1. You have complex risks that impact multiple areas in different ways.
2. There's a need to share the risk register with other stakeholders as is, so more context is needed.

Above all, you want to ensure that anyone who reads the risk register understands the risks within it. So, again, use layman's terms, as you would talk about it with a colleague.

EFFECTS

This is a narrative description of the potential impact on the project. You won't find this on any other template. But I strongly recommend adding this column.

Not all your stakeholders, including project owners, will be proficient with risk management terminology and concepts. Moreover, impact and probability expressed in numbers will not suffice.

For example:

You want to get approval to add $10,000 to the project budget as a risk reserve for a deliverable.

Will you get it because you've described risk #0023 as having impact 7 and probability 6? I doubt it!

Therefore, write it out as if you're describing the risk to a non-technical person with no project management experience. Two or three sentences should be enough. Later, you can reuse these descriptions in all your communication with stakeholders.

PROBABILITY

Probability value comes from quantitative risk analysis. We'll discuss this in the following chapters. It's the likelihood of risk happening. You can use a 1–10 ranking grade or just low, medium, high.

IMPACT

Impact also comes from quantitative risk analysis. It's the severity of the effect on the project. Again, you can use a 1–10 ranking grade or just low, medium, high.

RISK RANK (OPTIONAL)

Risk rank = probability x impact. I use this value for sorting risks by severity. You will get values from 1 to 100.

This is the easiest way to shortlist the most critical risks that you'll need to work on directly.

QUALITATIVE ANALYSIS VALUES (OPTIONAL)

This is optional because it's important not to overwhelm the risk register with unnecessary information. It is only necessary for a small number of top priority risks, and it might be a good idea in any case to keep the results in a separate document. But it's up to you to decide.

RISK OWNER

This is simply the name of the person responsible for monitoring, managing, and reporting on the risk.

Ideally, you should not put your name to any risks that are not related to project management. All technical risks should be delegated to SMEs.

RESPONSE PLAN

This is the action plan to avoid or mitigate the risk. Alternatively, you can state that you are going to accept the risk and do nothing. We are going to discuss risk responses in the following chapters.

PRACTICAL APPLICATION OF RISK REGISTER

RULE #1: KEEP IT CLOSE AT HAND

The rule of thumb is that you start filling the data during the risk identification process. But you already know that a great project manager is always in risk identification mode. Therefore, you should start logging risks in the project initiation or even pre-sales phase.

On the practical side, you should do the following:

- Create a bookmark in your browser to the risk register spreadsheet.
- Put the file on your desktop.
- Create a separate view in your project management software just for the risks.
- You should be able to open up the spreadsheet and capture risks quickly.

RULE #2: THE RISK REGISTER IS ALWAYS IN DRAFT

Writing down your thoughts, concerns, and high-level risks is okay. You will be able to refine them later.

As you get more information from SMEs, you need to make changes to your entries.

After that, you need to review your risk register with stakeholders. Why? First of all, you want to get their feedback. Second, they will help you overcome some risks. Consequently, each risk will go through several updates.

RULE #3: DON'T MIX IDENTIFICATION AND ANALYSIS

Write down the description of a new risk. Then, come back to analyze it later.

Don't think you need to fill all the columns at once. You can write down the risk titles at meetings or during calls. Later, you can find time to add the details. Moreover, involve team members as much as possible.

RULE #4: GIVE AS MUCH DETAIL AS POSSIBLE

Are you the only user of the risk register? If so, you don't need to add all the information I've described above. If you need to share the risk register with stakeholders, however, then more details will reduce unnecessary communication.

Bear in mind that risk management is not free of charge. It's your time and effort. But, more often than not, you need the team's input to fill in the risk register.

RULE #5: DON'T DO IT ALONE

At some point, you need to start delegating risks to your project team or stakeholders. Each risk should have an owner.

Always remember that you are an expert in project and risk management. You can't know every aspect of the project and related activities. On the other hand, you have access to experts who can perform better analysis and suggest better action plans. Use their expertise.

RULE #6: SHARE THE RISK REGISTER WITH THE TEAM

Keep your whole team engaged in all risk management activities and give them access to the document.

However, please don't assume that all team members know everything you know. You need to educate both the team and the stakeholders on your risk management approach.

You'll need to repeat the same information about risk management over and over.

RULE 7: REVIEW THE RISK REGISTER REGULARLY

Make sure you review the risk register regularly. As well as having a recurring calendar event, the following should prompt a review:

- After each change request.
- When you start and finish working on a deliverable.
- When a risk occurs.
- When a risk response plan is inefficient.
- When you've managed a risk successfully.

You got the point. Check it regularly!

RULE #8: KEEP THE RISK REGISTER UP TO DATE

Risk management is a continuous effort. It doesn't end with planning. Moreover, the impact and probability of risks change over time. They change because of other risks, change requests, external factors, etc.

So, you need to monitor risks during the whole project life cycle.

RULE #9: MAKE IT PRESENTABLE

Risk management provides more value when you can efficiently communicate future risks to stakeholders. Moreover, it helps to manage their expectations, secure their engagement, and prepare them for problems.

So, make it easy to communicate the information from the risk register.

CHAPTER 23
QUALITATIVE RISK ANALYSIS

Qualitative risk analysis is the process of grading each risk in terms of its probability and impact using a predefined ranking system.

The goal of the process is simple – you need to prioritize the most severe risks. Then, you'll develop action plans (risk response plans) for them.

Why is it necessary? On the one hand, you have a limited amount of time and resources to address risks. So, you can allocate budget and resources only to critical risks that are the most likely to impact your project. But, on the other hand, you need to demonstrate that your risk management is worth the effort by showing the benefits.

You therefore need to look at the biggest risks first. Then, for the remaining dozens or hundreds of minor risks, we'll try our luck or work them out as we go.

There are a lot of additional benefits of qualitative risk analysis:

- You can focus on risks that are crucial for the project's success.
- The team is encouraged to share their concerns and fears rather than hiding behind buffered estimates.
- The process itself creates engagement opportunities for stakeholders.

- There is greater transparency of threats and opportunities.

INTERPRETATION OF IMPACT AND PROBABILITY GRADES

From the definition above, you can see that you need a "predefined ranking system" for impact and probability. Here's the crucial part: This ranking system is subjective and depends highly on your project and your project owners. There's no universal grade for impact and probability.

I will share some examples below and you can find more on the internet. However, I strongly recommend that you use them as a starting point only. You need to take some time to develop interpretations that are aligned with your organizational environment and project owners.

Let me elaborate further.

Impact is the effect that a risk will have on the project. Probability is the likelihood of it occurring.

You can describe both of them as low, medium, or high grades. Or we can use numbers from 1 to 10. But these grades will be meaningless unless you clearly describe what each one implies in terms of project metrics.

You don't develop these interpretations yourself. You need to work with your team and stakeholders to create descriptions that everyone understands the same way. It's like a secret language – everyone knows what you mean when you say "medium risk".

Table 1 is an example of an impact interpretation map:

TABLE 1: IMPACT INTERPRETATION MAP

Impact Interpretation map

Rating		Interpretation
High	10	One or two of such risks will lead to project failure
High	9	Over budget or delay by more than 40%
High	8	Over budget or delay by 30-40%
High	7	Over budget or delay by 20-30%
Medium	6	Over budget or delay by 10-20%
Medium	5	Slight budget increase. Three to five risks will lead to 10% budget increase
Medium	4	Large reduction of risk reserves
Low	3	Medium reduction of risk reserves
Low	2	Small reduction of risk reserves
Low	1	Minimal impact

Keep in mind that we describe the impact on the overall project status. So, if you have a risk related to a separate task or deliverable, in most cases, the impact won't be 40% of overall project budget or schedule. Risks with 7–10 impact should be rare.

The probability interpretation map (Table 2) is even more simplistic:

TABLE 2: PROBABILITY INTERPRETATION MAP

Probability Interpretation map

Rating		Interpretation
High	10	It's not a risk, it's a fact.
High	9	It's about to happen.
High	8	Most likely will happen.
Medium	7	Most likely will happen.
Medium	6	A good chance that it will happen.
Medium	5	Quite possible.
Low	4	It may happen.
Low	3	Low probability.
Low	2	Most likely won't happen.
Low	1	Very unlikely.

When you have a big project and the number of risks exceeds 50, you need to switch from low–high grading to a scale of 1 to 10. It will give you more precision when prioritizing. Unless you have a small and straightforward project, start with 1 to 10 grading.

RISK APPETITES, RISK TOLERANCE, RISK THRESHOLD

Here's what I learned in practice: It's even more critical that the grades of impact should be mindful of the project owners' appetite and tolerance for risk.

The project owners and other stakeholders will have a certain attitude towards risks and their impact. This can be broken down into the following:

- Risk appetite is a general and subjective description of an acceptable risk level towards one of the project's constraints.
- Risk tolerance is a measurable and specific level of risk.

147

- Risk threshold is a particular point at which risks become unacceptable.

For example, the sponsor may state that the budget is limited but there are no strict deadlines. This means that risk appetites for costs are low, while more risks can be taken with the schedule.

On the other hand, there may be a $10,000 contingency for risks within the budget. If that is the maximum limit, then that is your risk threshold.

Ideally, you need to find out these values directly from stakeholders. Why do you need them?

If stakeholders don't have an extra budget, they won't accept additional expenses as an impact. Instead, any risks will have a bearing on the project's scope or deadline. For example, they'll ask to remove a deliverable, or do it later when they have the money.

In this case, there's little value in grading impact in terms of extra costs. Instead, it's better to consider the effect on the timeline or efforts required.

Likewise, if you don't manage the project budget directly, you don't need to include the impact on the budget. Instead, you describe the impact on required efforts from the team.

I believe it's better to have these descriptions carefully aligned with your current project owners rather than to develop a one-size-fits-all system.

QUALITATIVE RISK ANALYSIS MATRIX

There are different names for this chart: 'impact/probability matrix,' 'qualitative risk analysis matrix,' or just 'risk matrix.' But they all refer to the following – see Table 3:

TABLE 3: IMPACT-PROBABILITY MATRIX

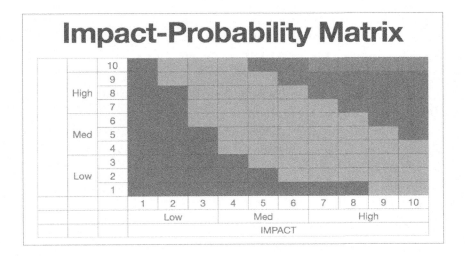

You have impact grades on one axis and probability on the other. Taking into account your interpretations, each square is given a color:

Red – risks that warrant a response.

Yellow – risks that require further analysis and investigation.

Green – risks that you can ignore (for now).

This is just a visualization of priorities. But it can help you communicate with stakeholders when setting the boundaries of their risk tolerance. Then, you can negotiate the amount of resources and time they are willing to spend on risk management.

QUALITATIVE RISK ANALYSIS PROCESS

Let's pull all this together. The process is quite simple:

1. Put all identified risks into the risk register.
2. Using impact and probability ranks, evaluate each risk.
3. Log the risks in the risk register.
4. Prioritize the list of risks.
5. Analyze the list for the required outputs.

In most cases, you will need to arrange interviews, meetings, or brainstorming sessions. Qualitative analysis can be a part of any discussion. My formula is simple:

Discussing the topic (80%), Risk identification (10%), Risk analysis (10%).

Sometimes you identify too many risks to analyze on the spot. In this case, you'll need an additional meeting.

You should educate your team in risk management. Then, you'll be able to discuss risks on the spot. Here's how it usually happens:

Dmitriy: "So, we're on the same page on how this new functionality works and looks. And we identified that we shouldn't develop the whole module from scratch as it would take us a few months. So, we can use a ready-made solution. We have one good option here. But there's a risk that not everything will work as expected out of the box."

John: "Yeah, as always, it looks like this third-party library does what we need. But I can't be sure until we integrate it and see how it works. There's a slight chance it won't work at all."

Dmitriy: "How slight is this chance?"

John: "I think very small, like one or two on our scale. But if that's the case, we may need to implement custom integration. It would take about a month."

Dmitriy: "A month is like 10%–15% of our project duration and efforts. Let's say the impact is 6 then."

John: "Sounds good to me. But I can verify it in the next few days."

Dmitriy: "Okay, that will be our action plan for now. If the risk happens, we'll discuss the possible solutions."

Lora: "I think we should also consider what we'll do if the library, you know, won't have some minor features and we have to tweak it. In all these requirements, I see a lot of fine points where it may not work as described in the specification. So I would say it's most likely the case. But we can handle it with a few extra days of work and testing."

Dmitriy: "Okay, good, let's put it down as a risk with probability around 7. And impact maybe 2?"

Lora: "I think 3 is better. It's not only development. There will be a few rounds of testing as well."

Dmitriy: "Very well, let's make it 3."

So, the analysis can occur at any moment and after every important meeting. You can work with any number of known risks. Nevertheless, there are several key moments in real-life projects where you want to analyze all known risks and fill out the risk register.

WHEN DO YOU PERFORM THE ANALYSIS?

In general, it's better to analyze risks in small batches on the go. You literally do it constantly. However, from time to time, you need to pause to review all identified risks. For example, when you finalize the first draft of the project management plan.

Likewise, you need to perform qualitative analysis during project initiation. It's a rapid phase where you have lots of urgent risks that impact the project's overall feasibility. You need to address them right at the start. So, you'll perform the analysis before you start project planning.

Moreover, during project execution, you need to analyze risks periodically. The impact and probability of known risks can change.

WHO SHOULD BE INVOLVED?

You should always participate in all risk management activities. At the very least, you need to facilitate them. Then, you need to decide who should help you:

- **Separate stakeholders**. In some cases, it is efficient to analyze specific risks one on one. Likewise, you may want to consult with senior-level colleagues regularly.
- **Expert groups**. Most of the time, you will work with a group of dedicated people who possess the necessary expertise.
- **Whole project team**. If the size of the team allows, it may be beneficial to involve everyone.

THE RESULTS OF RISK ANALYSIS

What should you get in the end? Here are the main outputs:

1. **A prioritized list of risks**. Your risk register should communicate which risks you'll explicitly address in your project plan.
2. **List of risks grouped by categories**. Grouping risks helps to identify any significant root causes of problems and to find a solution. Or address the root cause in the first place.
3. **List of risks for additional analysis and investigation**. In some cases, you will not have all the required expertise at hand. So, you won't be able to assess risks on the spot. Therefore, you will need additional consultation on the risks.
4. **List of urgent risks**. Some severe risks may require immediate action. Otherwise, they may have a damaging impact on a project that has not even started yet.
5. **Watch list**. This contains risks that you need to keep an eye on. They do not require a response straightaway. However, they might cause problems in the future.

As you can see, the qualitative risk analysis is simple. But it requires time and effort to conduct all these meetings. Moreover, you need to continuously educate your team members on how to perform risk analysis.

CHAPTER 24
WHAT TO DO WITH A RISK?

This is where your risk response strategy/plan comes in. It is an action plan outlining what you will do with a risk. The main strategies for threats are mitigate, avoid, transfer, actively accept, passively accept, or escalate.

Here's the biggest challenge with risk responses. There's no set formula. Moreover, the strategies described above are merely a theoretical attempt to categorize possible responses. In practice, each risk response is a separate and unique microproject. So, you need to invent a solution.

For sure, there are some common risks and common ways to overcome them. But critical risks that can break your project are usually unique. That's why you need to be open-minded about possible actions you can take to tackle a risk or leverage an opportunity. The following two chapters are full of real-world examples showing the wide variety of options you should consider.

RISK RESPONSE OPTIONS FOR THREATS

Let's recollect the workflow:

1. You need to identify risks and log them in the risk register.

2. You need to conduct a qualitative risk analysis.
3. For the most severe threats, you'll decide on the best response.
4. The main types of risk response strategies are avoid, mitigate (impact and / or probability), transfer, actively or passively accept, or escalate.

1. TRY TO AVOID A RISK

Avoiding a risk means you need to do something to eliminate the root cause of the threat.

#1.1 EXAMPLE OF RISK AVOIDANCE IN SCOPE MANAGEMENT

Clients and other stakeholders provide requirements for the project. Usually, they think that these requirements will help to achieve the project's business objectives.

Quite often, these requirements will pile up, leaving you with insufficient time and money to fulfill the ever-burgeoning project scope.

When this happens, it's apparent that you need to remove some requirements or move deadlines. But, more often, you'll find yourself in a situation where you are expected to make do within the existing constraints.

That's when you need to log a risk that you don't have any free reserves of time or budget (otherwise known as 'a buffer'). If something goes wrong, you may fail to deliver the whole project on time.

So, at this point, you can develop a risk response that removes a piece of the project scope. This will happen only if, for example, you are 10 days or more behind schedule.

This will help you control expectations. You warn stakeholders that this risk might happen before the project has even begun. If they accept the action plan, it will be easier to descope the requirement if something goes wrong. That's why you should always identify the most critical deliverables and implement them first of all.

#1.2 HOW TO AVOID RISKS WITH LEADERSHIP AND STAKEHOLDER MANAGEMENT

As a project manager and leader, you need to ensure that your team members are happy, motivated, and engaged in the project.

For sure, you can't always get people who match perfectly with one another. Moreover, constructive differences within a team are a good thing. However, sometimes conflicts can escalate beyond professional behavior. People may feel dissatisfied with the organization in general. This is when the situation can become destructive and demotivating for other team members.

As much as possible, you need to try to mitigate the impact of conflicting team members. But, sometimes, nothing helps and you go beyond the point of no return in your relationships. In this case, you want to avoid risks of further demotivating the whole team by dismissing someone.

Likewise, you may have an authoritative stakeholder who conflicts with team members or with you. In this case, you'll need to take measures to isolate that person as much as possible. This is when you need to become embroiled in internal politics and find leverage through your leadership or policies.

#1.3 HOW TO AVOID RISKS THAT IMPACT THE WHOLE PROJECT

Before I became a project manager, I was a sailor. I once worked on a big container vessel. We were unloading in Amsterdam when it started raining. In a few minutes, we heard over the radio that someone had fallen around 40 feet from the fourth-tier container onto the deck.

Port authorities stopped the unloading. We called a helicopter to get the stevedore to a hospital. In the end, unfortunately, he died.

I very much hope that nothing as awful as this happens on your project. You must do whatever it takes to avoid such risks. The delays and extra costs are nothing compared to the possible impact of a threat.

That's why many industries forbid any work in bad weather to avoid the risk that someone gets hurt.

2. MITIGATE IMPACT/PROBABILITY OF RISKS

This is about how to lessen the impact of a threat or reduce the likelihood of it occurring.

#2.1 MITIGATION OF UNCERTAINTY

In the IT industry, we often create solutions using brand-new technologies or working in a way that no one has tried before. Therefore, there's a lot of uncertainty.

Is it even feasible to achieve a project's objectives?

You don't want to start full-blown development to discover that the cornerstone technology can't provide the required functionality. To mitigate such risks, we begin with a prototype, a proof of concept (POC), or a feasibility analysis phase.

These are essentially mini-projects aimed at:

- creating a minimal viable product;
- testing the compatibility of different solutions; and
- checking the capabilities of new technologies.

This way, we try to guarantee the feasibility of at least 80% of the requirements.

It's a quick and dirty implementation. But it's just a fraction of the budget and resources of the whole project. And sometimes, several POCs may be needed before finding the most efficient approach. But still, it's worth the investment.

This way we can also get early feedback from clients and adjust the requirements to the capabilities of the technologies we want to use.

Always keep in mind that risk management is not free of charge. You need money and time to address such risks. So they should be a part of your project plan.

#2.2 RISK MITIGATION IN PROCUREMENT

Whenever you have a third party involved in a project, it's a risk.

There are many reasons why:

- They have a different project management approach.
- They have different quality standards.
- Their team is not in sync with your team.
- There's a hard dependency on their deliverables.
- There are difficulties in communication.

And that's just the tip of the iceberg.

You need to mitigate ALL possible risks from their side. But, usually, you don't have direct control over them.

That's why you need a mitigation response strategy that provides you with more information from the third party. You can request or even state it in the contract that:

- they need to provide a weekly progress report;
- managers should participate in daily or weekly sync-up meetings; and
- you can visit them at any time to audit the work.

This way, you can get early warnings about any problems they might have.

#2.3 MITIGATE RISKS VIA EDUCATION

You can't identify every possible risk. But you should try to mitigate the possibility of an unexpected, severe risk in the middle of the project.

The most efficient way to achieve this is by educating your project team and stakeholders in proper risk management activities.

Also, you need to create an environment where people are not afraid to report new risks as soon as possible, even if they committed to finishing the work on time.

It's much easier to avoid or mitigate a risk when you know about it in advance. You can't avoid it if it's already happened.

3. TRANSFER RISK TO ANOTHER PARTY

This basically means making someone else responsible for a risk.

#3.1 OUTSOURCING PART OF THE PROJECT SCOPE

Imagine you work for a furniture company. Your leadership decides that an e-commerce website and mobile applications are needed to boost sales. You are assigned to the project. Now you are an IT project manager! Right away, there are huge risks:

- You don't have the expertise and engineers to start the project.
- There are no infrastructure and practices to run a software development project.
- Your recruiters don't have expertise in hiring developers, quality assurance engineers, etc.

This is why companies transfer such risks to vendors with expertise, infrastructure, and HR. Of course, it doesn't eliminate all related risks and often introduces new ones: Procurement, third parties, etc. But, most probably, you have the same kinds of risks in the furniture industry. You know how to deal with them.

Notice how we've changed totally unknown risks to risks that you know how to manage.

#3.2 INSURE AGAINST COST RISKS

Sometimes projects depend on a piece of costly machinery. Or you rent some equipment. Or you need to purchase and store lots of materials.

The risk is that you can't afford these things if something goes unexpectedly wrong.

Like in everyday life, buying insurance for a relatively small sum can mitigate this risk. Of course, if a disaster happens, there will be a delay. However, the insurance payment will allow your project to recover and carry on.

#3.3 USE FREELANCERS TO FILL KNOWLEDGE GAPS

Sometimes your organization will not have the knowledge or expertise needed for a particular project.

For example, you need to hire a graphic designer. However, in-house recruiters have no experience or understanding of this role. Therefore, it might be better to find an agency or a freelance recruiter who can find a suitable expert. In the same way, you can hire an experienced interviewer for a few hours.

Likewise, you may need to avoid risks related to the procurement, accounting, or legal aspects. If you don't need full-time involvement, you can transfer these risks to part-time specialists. So, hiring freelancers on an hourly or per-task basis is an option here.

4. ACTIVELY ACCEPTING RISKS

This means developing a (contingency) plan and having reserves available to deal with a risk. However, you will act only if and when the risk happens.

Note the difference: You don't actively fight against a potential risk. Instead, you react to it if it happens and try to reduce the negative impact. But, still, you prepare in advance.

In the real world, this is the most common type of response plan.

But here's the catch: You can use the allocated reserves of time or money ONLY if the dedicated risk happens. If not, you need to release the reserves and switch to the next set of tasks.

Why?

Parkinson's law states that work will always expand to fill the available time and resources. Moreover, you want to control the accuracy of your risk analysis. It may provide you with insights into the risks that are yet to come.

#4.1 ACCEPTING RISK WITH A RESERVE OF TIME

If you lead a long project, there'll inevitably be a time during winter or a cold and rainy snap when people catch colds. If you see that some critical due dates fall into such seasons, you need to plan accordingly.

The simplest way is to allocate a week or two of time reserve to your schedule – just put a buffer on the milestone.

Also, think about the next-best alternative here. You may propose to project owners substituting a person on sick leave with someone else, if they can get up to speed quickly. Nevertheless, there may be additional costs. So, you'll also need to budget for those in your risk reserves.

#4.2 ACTIVELY ACCEPTING RISK WITH RESERVES OF BUDGET

Sometimes requirements are not clear and no amount of business analysis helps. So, if you have such ambiguity but deadlines are set in stone, that's a risk.

In this case, you want to get feedback from clients on what you've created as soon as possible. This is likely to mean changes in the requirements and some rework.

You may actively accept such a risk and reserve an additional budget for paid overtime for the team to make the required changes during weekends.

5. PASSIVELY ACCEPTING RISK

This basically means doing nothing. If a risk happens, you will need to decide if there is a workaround. Or you simply soak up the impact.

#5.1 PASSIVELY ACCEPTING A RISK AND FINDING A WORKAROUND

Let's revisit the previous example of a company getting insurance cover for its expensive machinery. In the case of passive acceptance, we won't do that.

We may decide that, if the machinery breaks, we will try to carry on without it. Yes, it may take more time and some manual labor. But that may be an acceptable workaround.

Likewise, we may decide to find funds to make repairs. Again, it's additional costs and will delay the work, but it might be okay.

6. ESCALATING RISKS AS AN OPTION

This means engaging with a stakeholder who can eliminate or mitigate risk.

There will always be some risks that you can't handle yourself. However, there may be someone who can. So, you just need to grab their attention.

EXAMPLES OF POSITIVE RISK RESPONSE STRATEGIES (OPPORTUNITIES)

Now, let's quickly review the response plans for opportunities.

Exploit – Do some extra work or change the project plan to realize an opportunity:

- Assign work with lots of risks to the most experienced team members.
- Suggest a more efficient approach.
- Suggest a solution to get a new contract from the client.
- Finish the current project earlier in order to move on to another project.

Enhance – Do something to increase the chances or impact of an opportunity:

- Buy the equipment beforehand when the price is lower.
- Negotiate the transfer of exceptional experts to your team as early as possible.
- Incentivize the team to finish ahead of schedule in order to start a new project sooner.

Share – Team up with another organization to help both parties realize potential benefits and opportunities.

- Create a partnership with a third party to achieve your goals.

You can actively and passively accept opportunities as well as threats.

ALL YOU NEED TO KNOW ABOUT RISK RESPONSES ON A PROJECT

Let me answer a few common questions that I'm always asked.

Should You Create Risk Response Plans for All Known Risks?
Should we really do something about each risk? No, you cannot eliminate all the risks. It is impractical and barely even possible.

You need to operate within your constraints of budget, time, and scope. You may have a specific budget for risk management.

What Is a Risk Response in Your Project Management Plan?
You need to understand this:

Your risk management efforts are a part of your project. They are not stand-alone.

Risk response plans may require:

- Updating project scope: Adding or removing deliverables, work packages, tasks.
- Updating project budget: Adding reserves, allocating money for additional work, resources, expertise.
- Updating schedule: Starting work on specific dates, adding reserves of time to critical tasks.
- Introducing new processes and workflows.
- Hiring a particular expert, consultants.
- Outsourcing part of the project scope to a third party.

- Changing the project life cycle by introducing additional phases.
- Changing the project management approach.

Here's the catch:

You plan risk responses later during project planning. So, you need to update the required areas of the project management plan with the planned responses.

It should be clearly depicted in your plan.

What Is a Risk Owner's Role in the Risk Response Plan?

Remember this:

You don't control all risk response plans personally. Instead, you must assign an owner to each risk and log their name and contact details in the risk register. This person is responsible for monitoring the risk.

Sometimes the risk may start impacting your project sooner than you anticipated. Or you may simply have underestimated the risk. So, it is the owner's job to keep the assigned risk at the top of their mind.

When the time comes, the owner implements or controls the implementation of a risk response plan. To some degree, you do as well – but on a higher level.

The risk owner also controls and reports to you on the efficiency of the strategy. If something goes wrong, they should escalate these problems to you.

It's totally fine if one person owns several risks – so long as all those risks don't happen at the same time. Otherwise, the person will be overwhelmed. And don't become that person yourself.

How to Implement a Risk Response Strategy?

First of all, you need to identify the top risks that warrant a response.

Next, you need to work with your team and stakeholders to develop possible responses for each risk.

It means that each risk will require some extra work, some action or decision, or reserves of time and money.

It will help you to know risk tolerance and thresholds in order to develop the most appropriate responses.

Then, you need to communicate these options to project owners and some key stakeholders. You may need to get their approval. At the very least, you must inform them.

Once everyone agrees to the suggested risk response plans, make them a part of your project management plan.

So, you need to review the plan and identify secondary and residual risks. You may need to repeat the whole risk management process several times until you get a good plan. Then, you execute the response plan as you would any other task on the project.

EVERY RISK RESPONSE HAS CONSEQUENCES

Here is another important concept of risk management: Every action has consequences. Therefore, by eliminating one risk, quite often, you can introduce new ones.

There are two types of risks you need to be aware of:

1. **Secondary risks** – any new risks created by the implementation of a risk response plan.
2. **Residual risks** – these remain after the implementation of all risk response plans. Usually, they have less significant impact on the project.

You should appropriately document and communicate these to stakeholders.

CHAPTER 25
RISK MANAGEMENT EXAMPLES

In this chapter, I shall outline a mixture of unique and common risks to demonstrate the various possible actions you can take to overcome them.

FIXED DEADLINE

You will face a lot of such cases. It happened on all the projects I led.

Clients come with a particular scope in mind. They think that all their requirements are "must-haves."

Moreover, they have a fixed deadline to release a product or service. And the budget is fixed as well!

The first impulse is to request as many people and resources as possible, do as much of the scope as possible, then pray that project owners will be happy with the outcome and your efforts.

Pardon the pun, but that's a risky approach.

RISK RESPONSE

In many cases, adding more people doesn't increase productivity proportionately. Moreover, putting people under too much stress over a long period of time is a recipe for disaster. They disengage the moment they feel it is impossible to achieve the project's goal. So there is no benefit from working hard for the next few months and failing in any case.

There is a better response plan, one involving an integrated approach to mitigating threats. Usually, your team and some internal SMEs have crucial expertise – more than project owners have.

Use their knowledge and authority to break down the scope into three groups:

- Must have.
- Should have.
- Nice to have.

Don't agree to put everything into the first category. It is never the case. Instead, identify the scope of work that is crucial for the (first) delivery. Additionally, promise to deliver as many of the "should-haves" as you can.

Notice the difference:

You don't suggest de-scoping the project, removing features or capabilities. Instead, you promise to deliver what's critical for project success. Plus, you add everything that fits into the deadline.

It's entirely possible that you will be able to deliver everything in the end. However, if not, you have an acceptable contingency plan.

HUGE UNCERTAINTY IN PROJECT SCOPE

We had a significant and complex enterprise-level piece of software. Without going into too many details, we had to add new functionality without changing existing behavior.

In this case, the risk impacted the feasibility of the project. From the beginning, it was clear that it was a big piece of work. But, as usual, there was a question. Should we do it ourselves or buy it? Even if we bought it, there might be efforts to integrate and customize the solution.

So, we may go from inserting an existing solution and it works as-is. Or it doesn't work at all. In the latter case, we'll need to do a lot of work to customize it, which might not be possible. So, in the long run, it may result in an even more costly decision.

What can you do to mitigate such a risk?

RISK RESPONSE PLAN

The team decided to make a proof of concept. So, we introduced an additional phase to the project.

First, engineers found available solutions that we could use with our product. Then, we negotiated a free trial with vendors of those solutions. It allowed us to do a quick and dirty integration. As a result, we were able to identify the costs and additional work to customize this solution.

The idea here is simple:

We didn't start a project with significant uncertainty in scope and budget. Instead, we did just a bit of research beforehand and eliminated the guesswork.

This was done even before we started planning. So, we began the project with risk management.

This is not something you do on a daily basis. However, it demonstrates how you can go that extra mile. Do keep in mind that your response should reflect the impact of the risk. In this case, performing this proof of concept cost several thousand dollars. However, it eliminated a risk that could have cost hundreds of thousands of dollars. So, it was worth it.

INEFFICIENT QUALITY

This example shows that you can change processes to overcome risks.

We worked on a product that converted images and text into speech on a mobile device. It helped people with speech disabilities.

My team had all the expertise to do the work but were relatively inexperienced. Also, due to the complexity of the product, there were lots of defects.

With changes in different areas, the defects mounted up and caused severe delays. We tried simply adding risk reserves. However, this was based entirely on guesswork.

Moreover, there was a complication. The time it took to find, fix, and deliver a corrected version of the application grew with its complexity.

I had to find a profound solution.

RISK RESPONSE

The initial workflow was as follows:

Analyze requirements, implement the requirements, test your work, create and hand-off deliverable the QA engineer.

Then, the QA engineer tests the deliverable, logs defects, and returns the deliverable back to the developer for rework. Even on a small project, this defect feedback loop can take a day or two.

So, I introduced a "quality checkpoint" – at the moment when the developer had tested his work and just before handing off the deliverable to the QA engineer.

It required the QA engineer to quickly review the work before it became a deliverable. Usually, this takes 5 to 15 minutes. In comparison, the entire round of testing may take several hours to several days.

It was a quick win. The number of defects decreased by almost half. Moreover, the severity of those defects was lower as well.

Admittedly, it was not a perfect solution:

- It took additional effort.
- It introduced distractions for the QA team.
- It reduced the ownership for the quality by developers.

Yet, despite these side effects (residual risks), the approach worked well.

RISK OF LOSING AN IMPORTANT TEAM MEMBER

You have planned your project and the plan looks realistic. Clients love it!

Now take a look at your schedule. Do you have only one person who can do some specific tasks?

Look into your RACI matrix. Is the same person responsible for most of the deliverables?

Look into their assignments. Is this the person who has unique knowledge and experience?

What will happen if this person leaves in the middle of the project? Unfortunately, this scenario is all too common. Every project has indispensable people.

RISK RESPONSES

A whole set of preventive actions is required to mitigate the probability of such a risk.

First, talk one-on-one with this person regularly. Try to identify concerns she has related to the working environment – her happiness, satisfaction with the impact she makes, etc. (this is to mitigate the probability of the risk).

However, the main question stays the same:

What am I going to do if this person leaves? You may have a suitable candidate ready to take the role. It might not be a perfect solution. But the impact will be lower (mitigate risk impact).

You may try to find someone outside of the company urgently (actively accept the risk).

You may be transparent with clients and agree to take on the impact. Make changes to the plan. Soak up the effect until you hire a substitution (passively accept the risk).

In practice, I use all of these options. You need to choose the most cost-efficient one for your project.

INCORRECT REQUIREMENTS

This example is about assumptions and incorrect requirements. It happened when I worked on a product for people with speech disabilities. We were to develop new functionality.

In this particular project, we made a critical assumption: That we clearly understood the needs of our end users.

The challenge was that our end users had special needs and severe problems with fine motor movements. So we developed a solution that helped such people interact with phones and tablets.

There were several possible approaches for implementation but we didn't want to make a bet on just one of them.

That would mean spending lots of time developing and getting this feature to the market. It would take even more time to collect actual feedback from end users.

In the end, there was a significant risk (about 30% probability) that our assumption was wrong. So, what did we do?

RISK RESPONSE PLAN

We decided to create a prototype. It took us less than a week. During this week, clients were able to organize a workshop with users. They demonstrated a prototype and let the users try it out.

In general, it validated our approach. However, there was a catch (isn't there always?!): We discovered that everyone used the device in the same way but they all had different reaction speeds.

So, as well as verifying our assumption and avoiding the risk – as a bonus – we identified an improvement for this feature before the product reached the market.

VENDOR FAILS TO FULFILL COMMITMENTS

There is an empiric rule here: All interactions with third parties take three times longer than you expect.

The worst case is when several vendors work for one client and on one product. If you depend on any deliverables from others, your schedule is at risk. Delays happen all the time.

They finish their work late. Then, it appears that the deliverable is not functioning at all. Someone goes on vacation and can't fix it. Then, you find a defect during integration. They must fix it, and all your planning efforts are wasted. You have to do it all again.

And that's not even taking into account other potential issues like communications overhead, unclear responsibilities towards other vendors and your project, etc. Never assume that things will go according to plan, even if you have successfully worked with the same vendor before. Review the lessons learned, but treat them with caution.

RISK RESPONSE

In many cases, you don't have much leverage over third parties. So, the best approach here is to allocate risk reserves of time to mitigate possible delays and rework. Adjust your schedule accordingly.

However, if you have authority, you can try to force the update of a typical contract. At the very least, you can add a clause for them to provide weekly reports and attend some meetings.

Recently, I witnessed a case where a company enforced a change in the overall project management approach. Each and every vendor had to comply with this approach to fit into the delivery strategy of the whole enterprise.

Updating contracts on the go is hard. However, you can provide your ideas to the procurement department for all future contracts with vendors.

You can suggest the same to your client. They can adjust the work of other third parties you need to interact with.

SICK LEAVE

This is so typical that it should be handled by default on any project.

This example also shows the need for common sense in the process. Risk management is not always about expert knowledge or project management tricks.

We had a critical project at hand to get our product compliant with the recent General Data Protection Regulation (GDPR). It had a strict deadline. Otherwise, the product would be removed from the market-place. Therefore, we had to triage the scope and still be ready to release everything we could possibly finish in time.

And it was early fall. The weather was changing dramatically, which, usually, resulted in increased numbers of people taking sick leave.

That is something I had to take into account. How does a project manager usually think?

If a person catches the flu, he is out for about a week. Moreover, if they are a critical person, the project will be delayed for a week. If more than one critical person is out, then the delay gets worse.

Usually, stakeholders do not accept time reserves for sick leave, especially that large. I can understand why, but that's what makes people come to the office when they are ill. Therefore, I don't support such an approach.

So, what did I do instead?

RESPONSE PLAN

First of all, I took steps to try and avoid as much as possible the situation happening in the first place. I reminded staff to wrap up warm, take care, sleep well, and think about their health.

They must share responsibility. It is a crucial project for the company. They committed to doing it. Therefore, they should do what they can to try and prevent themselves falling ill.

Second, I banned from the office anyone who caught a cold or felt sick.

Third, I put in place working-from-home arrangements from the start. This happened before the pandemic. So, it wasn't as easy as it would be today.

But, of course, that was all common sense.

Now, to the project management aspects. How much time reserve did I need? If you cannot measure it, you cannot manage it.

So, I got sick leave statistics for the past two years from HR. These are usually readily available.

It appeared that the numbers were lower than I expected. On average, there were 10–15 days of sick leave absence during fall.

Therefore, there was no need to plan for an epidemic. I know it may differ for your project and organization. However, the main point here is to use objective data, not subjective perceptions.

So, what's left? We need to mitigate the risk of one critical person falling ill.

Avoid tasks that can only be done by one person in the team. This can be addressed during planning.

If I have "indispensable" people to do the work, I take more time for preparation. I try to ensure that someone else can handle the task, even if they can't do so as effectively.

Therefore, we document and communicate the selected approach and technologies. In the long run, the goal is to find an efficient substitution.

Sometimes I have to look for the substitution outside the project team. The key is doing so beforehand. That person is not sitting idle. Their manager should plan to share them if possible.

On average, for three months of work, I reserve only about a week for sick leave for a team of 10. Of course, a bigger team may require more substantial reserves. But, on the other hand, they have greater capacity to cover up losses.

RISK OF UNCLEAR REQUIREMENTS

A few years ago, I worked on a complex enterprise product. From the start, one crucial requirement lacked clarity. We had to add a few settings to adjust how the application behaves. But, it was just a vision, nothing concrete. So, project owners didn't see the impact those settings had on all the existing functionality.

However, it made it into the scope statement. Product owners promised to deliver detailed specifications soon. Of course, it was logged immediately in the risk register, initially as a high-level risk.

Such risks often have different impacts. Product owners can delay the promised specification. Or it can be of poor quality. Poorly defined requirements always imply poor product quality.

We scheduled the delivery of this requirement close to the project's end – we wanted to give time to the customer. There was a date by which we were to receive the specification. Beyond it, we'd have to clarify requirements on our own. As a result, we set deadlines, and planned time and cost reserves. Nevertheless, we monitored this risk closely all the time.

Much of the functionality of our service relied on this feature. There were hundreds of use cases. Closer to the deadline, it was clear that we would never get the full spec.

So, we decided to be proactive and not to wait for the deadline. We created a change request that explained that we needed to act straightaway. Moreover, we'd do it ourselves out of the cost reserves.

RESPONSE PLAN

We analyzed the complexity of the requirement. It seemed like it didn't require technical skills. It was more about fundamental business analysis. We evaluated that a junior-level QA engineer should handle it. Then, we acquired one for a week.

I asked him to get familiar with our product and focus on one specific functionality. His primary task was to draft out all use cases for our new feature.

He did the job within the week. However, there was still time before the implementation.

So, the main team reviewed the draft and elaborated the specification. Then, in the long run, they defined an algorithm that covered all the cases.

We implemented the feature flawlessly without any severe defects. I doubt we could have done it any better under other circumstances. Moreover, I believe we even saved a lot of resources in the long run. But, there is no way I can prove that!

Risk management is all about the prevention of problems in the first place. The difficulty is proving your success. It is so hard to demonstrate that you saved money, time, and effort.

RISK OF INTERNAL STAKEHOLDERS

Usually, your employer expects you to build business relationships with your clients. Developing new business opportunities means increasing the project scope or starting a new project for the same client. But it also means increasing the risk for the ongoing project.

Likewise, you may have a dedicated stakeholder in the company responsible for developing business with your client – maybe a business development manager or something similar. Of course, both of you have one goal in mind – to make the client happy. But your criteria for success are different.

This happened to me. There was an internal stakeholder responsible for business development. He was not part of the team and, therefore, he had a loose understanding of what was on the team's plate at the time. However, he had enough authority to recommend improvements and new requirements to the product we developed.

Sometimes, he promised something that we couldn't deliver. Sometimes, he underestimated the work at hand. As a result, he put commitments we had at the time at risk.

RISK RESPONSE

There's no easy way to mitigate such a risk. You see, in the eyes of the company, this stakeholder did some good things, like great features that clients liked, additional scope, and more people in the team. All of that meant more income for the company from our project.

On the other hand, he jeopardized our commitments. One failed project could eliminate all the benefits mentioned above. Moreover, the responsibility for all new initiatives was also on me: It was my headache to work out how to deliver all the promises he made.

The only way to mitigate such risks is through internal politics. You need to ensure clear responsibilities between you and such stakeholders. You need to have clear boundaries between their promises and your commitment to delivering them within the constraints of the existing project. At the very least, you shouldn't allow any promises on your behalf.

So, it was a constant struggle. Depending on the current state of affairs, the business development manager or I had more power. Ideally, we should have worked hand in hand. But our priorities and goals were so different.

This case demonstrates that your colleagues can create risks for your project even if they have good intentions. Besides, you may have to deal with such risks for years while working in the same organization. Again, that's the influence of your environment.

CHAPTER 26
RISK MANAGEMENT RESOURCES

I realize that I've just given you quite a lot of information about risk management to remember. Moreover, it will be challenging to implement it all from a blank page. That's why I've prepared a whole list of resources that can help you:

1. A one-page cheat sheet on risk management.
2. A risk management plan template.
3. A risk register template
4. A risk categories list that you can copy for your reference.
5. A video explaining how to implement this approach in an agile environment.

Get supporting materials here:
https://itpmschool.com/materials

PART FIVE
HOW TO START A PROJECT

CHAPTER 27
BUSINESS GOALS AND PROJECT BOUNDARIES

Why do people start and fund a project? They want to achieve a specific business objective. It's always about making or saving money, even if it's a charity, social, or non-profit project. If you accept this, project management becomes a bit easier.

For example, a company wants to create a website for selling its products. It wants to make money.

An organization starts a project to build a new office. In the long run, it will save money on renting similar space.

A bank needs to make a change to its online banking system to stay compliant with legal regulations. This means it wants to remain competitive in a changing market and to keep the income stream.

However, for some reason, clients and sponsors don't like to share their underlying business need to start a project. Or they've never even thought about it.

When you work with a big, established organization, it will always have a business justification to start a project. If it invests a certain amount of money and resources, it expects to get a return on that investment.

Smaller clients have a vague definition of the business need. Don't expect that they did any calculations. They want a product, service, or result from you. They'll figure out how to make or save money with it later.

So, why do these business objectives matter to you as a project manager? Let me show it to you through an example.

SIMILAR PRODUCTS, DIFFERENT OBJECTIVES

Imagine you have two clients. Both want you to develop a new social network. So, they need an estimate of the project from you.

They provide you with some high-level requirements on how the website should look like, its capabilities, and so on. But neither of the clients disclose their underlying business objective.

You do the estimates and plan the project. Later, you discover the business objectives of these clients.

The first client needs a social network for in-house use. There will be a thousand users maximum. They want their employees to interact with each other and share personal photos. However, they don't want the distraction that LinkedIn provides and they are concerned about privacy.

The second client needs a social network that will compete with LinkedIn. They want a market share. They have a business plan on how to achieve it but the product you need to create is more complex than the first one.

Imagine you didn't know the business need from the start. Would you create a website capable of handling millions of users by default?

I think you'll agree that – to make your clients happy – you need to create a product or service that will satisfy their business needs.

However, usually, project owners have only a vague understanding of what this is. They have a business idea but that is not enough for project management purposes. You need to make them think about it and formulate it in a measurable way. This will help you justify the requirements and estimates you'll provide for the project. So, don't assume that project owners understand the complexity of the project simply because they initiated it. You need to prove it.

That's why it's critical to tie business objectives with project goals. This brings me on to another essential aspect of project management.

PROJECT SUCCESS IS A RANGE OF OUTCOMES

Project goals are like a shooting target. In the center, we have the bulls-eye. At the start of the project, that's our focus: To get the highest score. However, a project can be successful even if you hit one or two circles beyond the bullseye.

So, in real life, the project goal is never a single point. Instead, it's a range of possible outcomes that will satisfy the clients, sponsors, and stakeholders.

Take a look at our social network example above. You can create a huge variety of features and capabilities, a combination of which produces something that is capable of achieving the ultimate business goal.

That's why it's critical that we also set boundaries for the project. How do we do that?

First of all, we need to clearly specify the tangible results needed for the project to qualify as a success.

For example, do we just need to create the product or service? Or are supplementary educational materials needed as well, like a user manual, instructional videos, etc.? Or do you need to support the product when it goes to market?

These can be a part of the overall project or a separate set of projects. In any case, you need a mutual understanding of the desired end result.

Next, it's equally important to know what is not a part of the project.

Let's go back to the LinkedIn competitor in the social network example. Who would collect requirements for features of this product? It's a considerable amount of work. You need to conduct thorough research to understand what requirements will help you make a superior product. So, is this a part of the project? Or does the client already have these requirements? If it's not a part of the project, you need to make this clear.

Who will create designs and user experience diagrams for the product? Is this a part of this project? Your clients probably don't have the necessary expertise, in which case it will be a part of the project.

Notice that each part requires different expertise. In addition to actual software development, you may need graphic designers, technical writers, video editors, etc. You may not have this expertise available in your company. So, to avoid serious problems, you need to state explicitly what is excluded from the project scope.

Conversely, you will have certain expertise at your disposal within the company. This will define the boundaries of which technologies, tools, materials, and vendors you work with.

Sometimes, your management will want you to go beyond these boundaries, which will mean a bigger allocated budget or higher profit from the project. Just keep in mind that, without proper planning and realistic assessment of your expertise, serious risks will be introduced.

THE IRON TRIANGLE

Every project has three main restraints:

- A deadline for when the project is due.
- A budget that can be spent on the project.
- The scope of work (what needs to be produced within the limits of allocated time and budget).

This is known as the "iron triangle."

The idea is to achieve the best possible result within these constraints. Or to prove that it's impossible to achieve the goal within these constraints. Pause here and let this idea settle in.

Believe me, it's always better to manage a project with explicit constraints set by project owners. You can manage their expectations with hard facts from your project plan. They are more willing to negotiate changes to the project scope, deadlines, or budget if you can prove that their initial assumptions are incorrect.

When you have an unlimited budget, or you define the scope of the project on your own, stakeholders put a lot of trust in you. By giving you *carte blanche*, they have elevated expectations that you'll achieve their business objectives. In this case, they disengage from daily participation in the project's life. And you don't want that.

To summarize, don't assume that project owners have justified the business case for the project. In most cases, it's not true.

Take the lead in specifying the project's objectives. Try to tie them to the business needs of the client. But ensure that they are feasible within the constraints that they've set. In the long run, it will be easier to prove that you have achieved those goals.

If you don't have a clearly defined goal, only a bullseye might satisfy your clients – but don't rely on it. Success is a subjective feeling. That's why we need to create a project charter before we start any work.

CHAPTER 28
PROJECT CHARTER

A project charter (aka project definition document, project initiation form) is a document that contains high-level information about the project, its goals, and its boundaries.

In theory, project owners create a project charter to authorize the existence of a project and provide formal approval to use resources for its activities. In the real world, YOU will do it. Most likely, you'll be the only person interested in this process.

Unless it's specifically requested, there's no need to create a project charter as a formal document. It's more important to collect the information it should contain. You can do this in meetings, calls, or emails. Then, summarize the collected data, and get feedback and confirmation. Finally, keep this information in a shared resource that you can quickly refer to.

So, how big should a project charter be? Many project managers think they are too bureaucratic, long, and complicated, and simply not worth the effort. That's not true. Remember that a project charter is simply an agreement on the vision of the project.

It should be short, no more than five pages long. A person should be able to read it in just a few minutes. Otherwise, no one will.

Keep it as simple as possible. A branded, rich text document works the best. Any bells and whistles will only distract stakeholders from the primary goal of this exercise – to create a shared vision of the project. Now, let's review what information you should include.

WHAT'S INCLUDED IN A PROJECT CHARTER?

Below is a full list of standard clauses within a project charter. But there are no hard rules as to what to include or what to remove. Use common sense. The document should provide a common under-standing of the project.

However, keep in mind that this vision is not only between you and the project owners: All key stakeholders need to share it. They may benefit from the additional information that seems obvious to you. So, put yourself in their shoes.

There's a project charter template in the supporting materials at:

https://itpmschool.com/materials

PROJECT TITLE (KEEP IT SHORT)

First of all, you need an official name for the project to differentiate it from other projects in your organization.

Keep it short and catchy: Something people will remember and associate with your project.

PROJECT BACKGROUND

What's this project all about? Ask project owners the following questions:

- Why did you start this project?
- What is the business need?
- Who are the end users?
- What are the pain points?
- What problem do we solve?

The background of the project will profoundly impact the decision-making process. Keep in mind that project results, services, or products create value for people first of all. Therefore, the project's background will help you make decisions and solutions that benefit the end users.

In the long run, it's all about getting people to use your product or service. In most cases, this means that your client's business will grow. They will hopefully then reinvest the money into more projects with you.

Remember that other stakeholders and project team members need to access this information. So, use everyday language that all stakeholders understand! Avoid insiders' language and jargon as much as possible.

BUSINESS CASE

What is the justification for the project? Is it a financial, legal, or market matter? What was the reason behind it?

A business case may be a separate document that justifies undertaking a project. It should be summarized in the project charter, with a link to the full document.

The business case stated in the project charter is vital! During the execution phase, you should check any change to the project against the business case. If the change does not align with it, you should automatically reject it.

PROJECT OBJECTIVES

You can implement project requirements in many different ways. Thus, you can get different end results. However, project owners start a project to achieve a particular business goal. Therefore, while your final product, service, or result may be functional and wonderful, it might not accomplish the project's objectives.

Quite often, fulfilling the business need takes some time after you finish the project. This could be several months after going to market. Therefore, you need to identify measurable objectives for the project (not the product!). Meeting these project objectives will mean you finish the project successfully. Additionally, it implies that you will reach the business need in the long run, potentially.

If you have not done this before, start with the SMART technique for setting your goals – making sure they are Specific, Measurable, Achievable, Relevant, and Timebound.

KNOWN REQUIREMENTS

Here you need to include high-level requirements as they are known at the time. However, remember that you can refer to other documents here – there's no need to put the full specification in the project charter. Instead, write a short description and link to the entire document if it feels right.

DESCRIPTION OF PRODUCTS/SERVICE/RESULT AND DELIVERABLES

Here you need to write a short description of the end result, service, or product you are aiming for. Then, you need to list all the deliverables you'll create in the process. This may include the WBS, risk register, budget, etc. Likewise, it can be intermediate results for product development. We'll discuss possible deliverables in the following chapters.

ASSIGNED PROJECT MANAGER

This is the only document that formally states that you are the one who makes decisions on the project. The project manager role brings a lot of responsibility. So, at the very least, ensure that your authority is recognized.

PROJECT MANAGER'S AUTHORITY

Nevertheless, your authority has limits. Here you need to clarify whether you can determine, manage, and make changes to the budget, scope, schedule, or hire people on your own.

PREASSIGNED RESOURCES

At the start of a project, it's unlikely that you'll have a team in place. But someone with technical expertise should help you to decide what needs to be done. So you will have some preassigned people beforehand. Add their names and expected availability. These people should understand their involvement.

STAKEHOLDERS

List the key stakeholders who can influence your project or will be affected by it. This will be subject to an in-depth analysis later but – for now – it is identifying the champions of the product or service you create.

If you list a person here, you need to ensure that they are aware of the project. Moreover, they need to confirm that they will participate in the project.

ASSUMPTIONS

For planning purposes, these are factors considered to be true, real, or certain without proof or demonstration. For example, at the start of the project, we assume that we have all the required expertise in the organization. Therefore, we won't need to hire anyone. We'll have to plan the whole project based on this assumption.

CONSTRAINTS

These are applicable restrictions or limitations, either internal or external, that will affect the performance of the project – for example, the overall budget or deadline.

PROJECT APPROVAL REQUIREMENTS

This section should state what items of the project should be approved and by whom. In most cases, you'll need to get approvals at critical points in the project life cycle – e.g., for the:

- WBS;
- project schedule;
- project budget;
- risk management activities; and
- list of required resources.

Usually, these requirements come from the policies of your organization or the project owner's requests.

PROJECT RISKS

This section usually contains only high-level risks: The most critical risks that may impact the project's feasibility. Later, we'll elaborate on them during our discussion on risk management processes.

Likewise, there might be urgent risks that you need to address as soon as possible.

SIGNATURES OF PROJECT SPONSORS

Every project sponsor should sign the project charter.

CHECKLIST TO DEVELOP A USEFUL PROJECT CHARTER

Step #1: Check who is responsible for creating the project charter. Is it mandatory?

Step #2: Find a starting point:

- Check whether there is a template in your organization.
- Ask your manager and/or peers.
- If there's no template, create one.

Step #3: Talk to the sponsor, client, customer, and key stakeholders.

Collect information about the business case, background, high-level requirements, constraints, assumptions, risks.

Ask the right questions about the project's goals.

Step #4: Try to understand the project objective and how it is aligned with the business case. In most cases, you will need to formulate it for your stakeholders.

Step #5: Try to identify real expectations of the project, including those of internal stakeholders.

Step #6: Make the first draft. Keep it short and clean.

Step #7: Consult with SMEs, review historical data, look for similar projects. Focus on identifying major deliverables and risks.

Step #8: Update the draft, if needed, with risks and assumptions from other projects.

Step #9: Meet with preassigned team members and get their input. Focus on elements of the project scope that you might have missed.

Step #10: Update the draft if needed.

Step #11: Plan a meeting with key stakeholders and walk them through the charter.

Step #12: Update the draft and finalize the project charter.

Step #13: Get sign-off.

This whole process takes one or two days, depending on the availability of your stakeholders. It is possible to nail it in one meeting and a follow-up email. So, don't think it's a huge effort. If you participated in the pre-sales phase, you would already have all the required information.

Of course, the process may differ from project to project. Some steps might not be formal or mandatory. In any case, I recommend that you include the project owners in this process as early as possible. Also, communicate with colleagues with greater expertise and authority first.

BENEFITS OF CREATING A PROJECT CHARTER

"Do we need a project charter if no one requests it? Seems like a waste of time!" I get this question way too often. And it always comes from project managers who lurch from one crisis to the next. If you don't create a project charter, you're shooting yourself in the foot – and then allowing stakeholders to repeatedly stamp on the wound.

Your organization or your project owners may not require a project charter. But that doesn't mean that you should deprive yourself of the critical advantages that it provides.

Again, you don't need a formal document. All it takes is to ask the right questions and listen to what the project owners have to say. Then, collect that information and get agreement on the main points.

It's a critical step in any project management approach. Let me elaborate on the benefits.

ALIGNED UNDERSTANDING OF THE PROJECT

Most expert opinion suggests that a project manager should create a project charter – unless one is issued by a sponsor. In the real world, you invite all key stakeholders to a meeting in order to achieve a mutual understanding of the project's goals, expectations of deliverables, and the main risks, assumptions, and constraints.

You literally need to speak through every point in the charter. This will provoke questions, clarifications, concerns, anger, and resistance. It's your job to get project owners to clarify all these views, resolve any conflicts, and agree upon a shared vision for the project. This vision will be stated in the project charter and signed by the project owners.

Later, if a stakeholder demands to change or add a requirement, you can always refer back to the project charter.

CAPTURING THE OBJECTIVES OF THE PROJECT

How can you tell whether a project is successful? Hitting your target on time and within budget is not enough!

A project should achieve its business goal. This should be concrete and measurable. Otherwise, how will you know if a 4% or 10% performance improvement is good enough?

Unless you have a specific goal, you cannot prove that you have successfully finished the project.

MUTUAL UNDERSTANDING OF THE PROJECT BOUNDARIES

Moreover, any solutions need to be proportionate to the project's goal. The law of diminishing returns applies here – that is, adding more resources will not necessarily lead to a proportional increase in results after a certain point.

In pursuit of the best possible outcome, you may throw a lot of money and resources at a problem. However, you should be sure that the results are worth the investment for the client. So, unless you have clearly defined goals against which you can measure your efforts, you can't tell how successful your project currently is and when you need to stop.

By giving a project clear justification, requirements, and goals, a project charter sets boundaries. As a result, it ensures that each dollar is well spent.

SETTING A FOUNDATION FOR CHANGE MANAGEMENT

Changes are inevitable and a project charter will help you to control them. How? Every time someone asks for a change, you should ask them, "How does this change help us achieve the project objectives?"

If it's needed, then by all means add it to the project plan. On the other hand, if it's not aligned with the project objectives, let's put it on the backburner.

You will check and ensure that every change request is aligned with your current project's objectives. And if you get too many change requests from project owners, but these changes do not align with project objectives, it's time to verify those objectives. Maybe it's time to cancel the project and start a new one?

THE ASSIGNED PROJECT MANAGER AND HIS LEVEL OF AUTHORITY

I firmly believe that there should be only one person responsible for the entire project. Also, they should be the only person who can make hard decisions. That's why their name should be on the project charter.

On the other hand, there should be an upper limit of their authority to mitigate critical risks. Beyond that limit, a project manager should get a sanity check and approvals from the sponsor.

CHAPTER 29
REAL-LIFE CASE STUDY OF A PROJECT CHARTER

PROJECT TITLE

Image library service site update (codename: project "redesign")

DESCRIPTION

We did the last update three years ago. As a result, it is outdated in terms of appearance, performance, and user experience.

We conducted an investigation to help develop performance requirements and a new vision of the UI.

The purpose of this project is to develop and implement a brand-new site.

BUSINESS CASE

All our competitors have up-to-date, responsive, and fast websites. Customer satisfaction with our service has dropped significantly.

This project is called to update the image library services site.

The new site should have good search and filtering capabilities.

The UI should be clutter-free and focused on finding and previewing images in the library.

The site should be fast, responsive, mobile-friendly, and support key accessibility features.

We expect to regain our position as the number one image content provider within a year of the new site coming online.

KNOWN STAKEHOLDER REQUIREMENTS

There are requirements for the new site's performance and a general description of the vision for its design, as per attachments to this document.

In no way should the new website reduce existing functionality for users.

Any updates or improvements to the database should not be performed unless needed.

The marketing team needs a fixed date for the release of the new site. They'll conduct a promotion campaign based on that date.

The new site deployment is not a part of this project. Instead, due to its complexity, this will be done as a separate project.

PRODUCT DESCRIPTION/DELIVERABLES

1. Full design of the new site as storyboards.
2. WBS.
3. HR plan.
4. List of project-related risks.
5. List of milestones.

The main deliverable is the new version of the website that has been tested in development environments and is ready for deployment.

PROJECT MANAGER AND AUTHORITY LEVEL

Nizhebetskyi Dmytro is assigned as the project manager. He has the authority to select the required team and determine the final budget.

RESOURCES PREASSIGNED

Patricia Smith from the design team is already assigned to the project on a full-time basis. The project manager will identify and request any other internal resources.

STAKEHOLDERS

Andrew Peterson manages the design department.
Ray Jackson represents the customer support team.
Lora James represents marketing.
They are all available to support the project as needed.

ASSUMPTIONS

- No new hardware is required.
- No changes to the database are required.
- Internal resources are capable of finishing the project.

CONSTRAINTS

- The new site should be ready for deployment no later than October 20, 2022.
- The WBS should be provided by July 10.
- The list of risks should be provided by July 25.
- The final design should be ready and approved no later than August 20.

MEASURABLE PROJECT OBJECTIVES

The objective of this project is to develop a site with the speed performance level stated in the requirements.
Attrition should be reduced to 3%.
Budget limits and deadlines are the next priorities.
Release date: Due no later than October 20, 2022.

Summary budget: $120,000.

PROJECT APPROVAL REQUIREMENTS

The head of the design department should approve the final UI designs.

Sponsors should approve the WBS.

The Project Management Office (PMO) manager should review and approve the list of risks.

HIGH-LEVEL PROJECT RISKS

We have little experience in improving and measuring customer satisfaction. Therefore, it is possible that the new site will not meet end users' expectations. Consequently, we may not reach our goals.

Due to customer attrition, project delays may cause severe customer losses.

Project sponsors authorizing this project:

_____ John Late, Vice President

In the long run, a project charter will help you to deliver the result that sponsors paid for. It will protect you from unnecessary changes. Why? Each piece of work should clearly align with the project objectives.

However, keep in mind that no single document can guarantee project success. Building mutually beneficial relationships and mutual understanding of the project is the key. Hiding behind the charter is also a bad strategy. Instead, you need to show empathy and guide your project owners towards the right decisions.

PART SIX
PROJECT PLANNING PROCESS

CHAPTER 30
PLANNING PROCESS APPROACH

Project planning is a challenging and complex activity. You need to apply knowledge and skills from all domains of project management, leadership, and negotiation. And you operate with an enormous amount of information and some level of uncertainty. Moreover, you are in a race against the clock because project owners want to start implementation ASAP. As a result, you'll need to balance the expectations of many stakeholders simultaneously. That's why planning is both the science and art of project management.

Planning is one of the most exciting activities for me. Though, in the beginning, it was the most confusing one. The information I found in books and online didn't provide a clear picture. At each moment of the planning process, it seemed you need information that you don't have yet. And most of the processes are interrelated. So, you don't know where to start from.

I tried dozens of different approaches before coming up with my own step-by-step workflow in which I always use outputs from the previous steps in the following step. And you don't need to jump from one area to another.

Nevertheless, planning is an iterative process. This means that, when you get through each step, you collect more details about the project. This new information may prompt you to reconsider the results of the previous steps.

For example, you may analyze the feasibility of requirements as you collect them. As a result, you may learn that you won't be able to achieve some project objectives. Consequently, you may need to revisit the project charter.

Another example is when you create the first draft of the project schedule or budget. Here, you may notice that you got beyond the project's constraints. So, at this point, you go back to negotiate what parts of the project scope you can remove. And you update the plan accordingly.

You will also need to review the whole plan and ensure that it's still valid after including all the risk responses identified during risk management.

Thus, you repeat the process several times. But you don't do it from scratch. Instead, you go back to quickly validate and adjust information in each step. So, in general, each iteration will take less time. And, in most cases, it will be minor adjustments, not a total overhaul.

But before we dive into the planning process, we need to ensure that our expectations and mindset are correct.

HOW LONG DOES IT TAKE TO PLAN A PROJECT?

There are many steps in the planning process. Some of them take a few hours of work; some of them need days or even weeks. So, let me give you some perspective.

On a small project, you'll need one to five days to develop a plan. Most likely, you'll spend most of the time on requirements.

In agile environments, there is no project planning phase. But you may need to come up with a product roadmap or release timelines. Usually, you can come up with a high-level plan in a day or two.

A medium-sized project may require a week or two to finalize the project plan. You'll work with more stakeholders, variables, and risks. Therefore, there will be more negotiations and discussions when selecting the best approach. Hence, you'll have to work through several versions until you develop a realistic plan.

A large project may need a month or two to get an approved project plan. Most likely, the plan should comply with lots of regulations. It should be a formal written document.

So, consider the size and complexity of your project. Based on that, you need to ensure that key stakeholders have realistic expectations of the efforts required to develop a reliable project plan.

WHAT IS DONE DURING PLANNING?

You'll spend around 80% of the time on communication. You'll have meetings with project owners, key stakeholders, the project team, SMEs, etc. You'll talk with people one on one. You'll write emails. You'll conduct brainstorming sessions.

Then, you'll spend 20% of your time creating and reviewing project documentation. Again, most of this time will be spent specifying requirements and identifying the scope. On the other hand, estimates, schedule, budget, and risks take a relatively small amount of time. Moreover, you don't do this on your own.

WHO DOES THE PLANNING?

There are different activities in the planning process.

For example, when you collect requirements, there's a lot of work with stakeholders. So, you and a business analyst do the heavy lifting. After that, you analyze their input with the project team.

Conversely, the project team should do the bulk of the work to identify project scope, estimate duration and costs for tasks, and plan quality assurance. But, still, a project manager should facilitate all their activities. Risk management is for everyone. So, include the team, stakeholders, and yourself.

The communication plan and stakeholder management are mostly a project manager's responsibility.

In any case, it's always good practice to get insights on all these activities from your team.

HOW OFTEN SHOULD YOU MEET WITH THE PROJECT OWNERS?

As often as possible! Ideally, you need a daily meeting for an hour. Of course, you may not use every minute but the time should be available if required.

Remember to factor in the time it takes to process the project owners' input into requirements, specifications, and estimates. This could take your team several days. In such a case, you can reduce the number of meetings. But I prefer daily sessions because there are always a lot of clarifications and follow-up questions.

In the daily meetings, keep the conversation to the following:

- They provide input on new requirements.
- You ask questions on requirements from previous days.
- You discuss risks and assumptions related to the requirements.
- You discuss estimates for each deliverable (later).
- You discuss the project schedule as a sanity and feasibility check (later).
- You discuss project risks (later).
- You explain the project management approach you will follow (one time).

You and your team work on several requirements during project planning. You, as the project manager, update the project plan with the information you obtain daily.

WHAT ARE THE KEY CHALLENGES IN PROJECT PLANNING?

The primary challenge is that you never have enough time – stakeholders want the project team to deliver value from day one. You are constantly switching between managing and hiring the project team, getting new requirements, and updating the project plan.

WHERE DO I GET A PROJECT MANAGEMENT PLAN TEMPLATE?

You'll never find a template that will work in your organization for your project. So, don't waste your time searching. I'll elaborate on the project management plan in the next chapter. Keep on reading.

CHAPTER 31
STEP-BY-STEP PROJECT PLANNING PROCESS

It's essential that you determine whether each step (process) is necessary for your project. You may not need all the steps I have on my list. But don't skip a step because it looks complicated or you've never done it before. Every step is critical.

You need to make an educated decision for each step. First, you need to understand it. Then, you may decide to skip it. But that's unlikely. Instead, you may need to scale it down or simplify it.

STEP #1: DETERMINE HOW YOU WILL PLAN THE PROJECT

Before you start planning your project, you need to have an approved project charter. Or, at the very least, the information that I recommend you discuss with project owners. In essence, you will elaborate and specify everything you capture in the charter. And, likewise, everything you do on a project should align with one of the sections of the charter. It's the guideline for all your future planning efforts.

At this point, you need to take a holistic look at your project, your experience, and project owners, and make several decisions.

Firstly, analyze the nature of the project: The main requirements, assumptions, and constraints. Then, you need to define the most effective project life cycle and project management methodology. As I said before, there won't be too many options here. But, still, you may need to make a choice.

Let's say your organization works in a plan-driven environment. Trying to start a Scrum-based project will be a bad idea. Instead, you need to define the most suitable processes and policies for your environment.

Secondly, I recommend that you review the steps below and just think through how to implement them. Don't get stuck here. Think about it for an hour and move on.

STEP #2: DETERMINE EXISTING TEMPLATES, POLICIES, AND PROCESSES

I've said it before, but it's worth repeating: You don't do projects in a vacuum. There's always an environment with policies, processes, templates, and people you need to work with.

Each organization has a preferred project management approach. At the very least, there are several mandatory processes and procedures. Organizations use them to monitor and control critical operations on all projects.

Likewise, there's senior management with responsibilities related to your project. And you will have to work with them to move your project forward. Ideally, you have already identified your internal stakeholders. If not, this is the right moment to start noting who they are if you are new to the company.

You need to know the requirements and rules of your organization. So you need to collect the templates, tools, and techniques that it already uses. The better you understand how your environment works, the smoother your project will run. You need to analyze all the processes for the whole project life cycle. Always think about how you'll close and hand off the project.

STEP #3: OUTLINE THE PROJECT MANAGEMENT PLAN CONTENTS

At the end of project planning, you need to come up with a project management plan. A project management plan is scalable: From a short note in Google Docs to an 80-page formal Word document. A project plan usually consists of several subsidiary plans that describe different aspects of the project.

If an organization requires a formal project management plan, there should be a template and guidelines on filling it out. At the very least, other projects will have created such a plan before. So, you should ask them to share a draft. For this reason, I'm not providing you with a template: Most probably, it won't work in your organization.

However, if you are unlucky enough that there are no templates, you should use the scope and risk management templates I provide as a starting point and add other subsidiary plans in the same style.

At this step, you need to draft the key points of each subsidiary plan (scope, risk, cost, quality management plans, etc.). Use the predefined processes and tools that your organization requires. You'll add more details as you go.

However, you should be totally clear on how you'll collect requirements and identify the project scope because that's the next step in the process.

It's perfectly fine to not have a formal project plan at all. On a smaller project, you can keep it in your head.

STEP #4: DETERMINE DETAILED REQUIREMENTS

At this point in the process, you need to define the detailed requirements for your project. This may take quite a lot of time and effort.

You need to take high-level requirements and objectives from the project charter. Then, you need to clarify all functional and non-functional aspects that you need to deliver. This may include sketches, designs, requirement specifications, performance, safety, or reliability characteristics. You need every possible trait and feature that the final service or product should have.

Again, you may need to identify more stakeholders to help you here. Functional requirements mostly come from product owners. Non-functional requirements come from internal and external stakeholders, and controlling bodies.

You, as the project manager, should not collect requirements. A project manager facilitates the process. It's good practice to have a dedicated specialist for this – a business analyst or a business solution analyst – because they are trained and skilled at systematically defining requirements. Their primary responsibility is to build a bridge between business needs and a technical project team. Yes, they do speak in a different language, even though it sounds like English!

I worked with many great business analysts. They have a specific mindset and skill set that a project manager doesn't have. That's why a project manager will never be as good at working with requirements as a dedicated business analyst.

On the flip side, you may not have a business analyst on the team. This means that you and project owners have to write the requirements documentation. In this case, you should ensure that your team understands the business requirements of the project.

STEP #5: DETERMINE QUALITY STANDARDS, PROCESSES, AND METRICS

Keep in mind that each industry and niche has its own unique quality standards. There are best practices but no one solution will fit all projects.

So, quality should be an integral part of a project. And quality has its costs. It directly impacts the project schedule, scope, and required resources.

But building quality products is cheaper than dealing with defects and related problems. So, you need to ensure that compliance with quality standards is part of your project scope.

If you are new to the industry, the best way to learn about best practices in quality management is to ask other project managers in your organization. Or you may have a person or a whole department dedicated to quality compliance.

STEP #6: CREATE THE PROJECT SCOPE STATEMENT

This is a critical milestone and checkpoint for you. You need this step because you don't control the business aspects behind the project. Let's say someone decided that, to fulfill their business needs, they needed a project to create a software application. And you defined the project scope for that. But it was their assumption. So, you need to share responsibility for this assumption with the project owners.

You did your best. You took the objectives of the project, worked with stakeholders, collected and described project requirements. Based on those requirements, you should have an understanding of the main deliverables. Then, on a high level, you need to explain what work you need to perform (project scope) to create those deliverables.

You need to make sure that project owners and other key stakeholders understand and approve the project scope. Moreover, you need to have a mutual agreement that this project scope and these deliverables will achieve the project objectives. Why is this so important? Because you'll create a project plan to implement the exact scope of work that they approve.

That's why you need to create a project scope statement. This describes what you will deliver and how. It includes the following:

- Project and product scope.
- Description of deliverables.
- Acceptance criteria.
- Exclusions (what is not a part of the project).
- Assumptions and constraints.

It is also a good idea to specify places where the scope might be misunderstood and, therefore, may change. We'll discuss the project scope statement further in the next part.

STEP #7: DETERMINE THE PROJECT MANAGEMENT TEAM

If your employer or project owners ever ask you to plan a project on your own, run! Leave, and don't look back.

As a project manager, you should never plan alone. So far, you have worked with people preassigned to your project. Maybe you reached out to other experts in your organization. Now you need expert knowledge to proceed. You can't and should not try to proceed alone here.

So, it is time to define the resources and expertise that you need.

Then, you'll use them to understand the amount of work, complexity, required technologies, solutions, risks, etc.

Ideally, you need senior-level experts from within your company. They'll be the backbone of the team. They'll help you to hire or acquire all other team members. You should try to secure these experts in advance for the duration of the project.

Alternatively, you might plan the project with one group of people but then need to hire a new team to execute it.

STEP #8: CREATE A WORK BREAKDOWN STRUCTURE

A WBS is mandatory on any project. It is a hierarchical list and/or a diagram that shows the entire project scope. It helps you to visualize the extent of the project.

On the highest level, the WBS details a product or an expected result. Below that, there are major deliverables broken down into work packages.

Work packages are smaller deliverables. Moreover, the sum of all work packages gives you a deliverable.

Then, you take each work package and break it down further into actual tasks.

You need all of these to perform the bottom-up estimate and to create a project schedule.

Here's a tip if you lead on a big project: Use the rolling wave technique.

This is a progressive elaboration technique in which you plan for imminent deliverables from the WBS in more detail. Of course, elements that are further in the future remain on a high level. But you plan for them in terms of project scope, budget, schedule, risks, etc. Then, later, you elaborate on the details for those WBS elements.

You can also apply this technique when defining requirements. First, you may capture requirements on a level sufficient for a high-level estimation of scope, duration, and costs. Then, during the project execution, write out detailed specifications and do the planning.

STEP #9: ASSESS WHAT YOU NEED TO BUY OR OUTSOURCE

Now that you have a clear picture of what you need to deliver, it is time to identify the resources and materials that you need to buy.

Some parts of the project may be so complicated that you do not have the required expertise in the organization. So, you need to assess whether outsourcing these elements will be beneficial.

Note that you may need to go back to this step several times during project planning. At any point, you might learn about something that will have an impact on the project. Each time, you'll need to decide whether it can be handled within the existing team or not.

This is the starting point for procurement management. You need to raise this with the company. If it doesn't have a dedicated procurement team, ask your direct managers. If they don't know what to do, it's a significant risk. I'll explain what to do in this case later in the Chapter #49 on procurement management.

STEP #10: BREAK DOWN WORK PACKAGES AND DELIVERABLES INTO TASKS

Ideally, everything should be carried out within your project management software. It may not be possible to capture requirements or create a WBS all in one tool. Nevertheless, at this step, all information should be logged into some dedicated project management software. Excel won't cut it: You'll waste your time. If you don't have project management software in the organization, buy it yourself. It's not that expensive.

As we've discussed, you need to identify the tasks for each work package. It's good practice to create tasks that one person can perform from start to end. It makes it easier to control the work.

A task description can contain quite a lot of information. As far as it is practical, include duration, cost estimate, required resources and materials, dependencies, and risks.

STEP #11: IDENTIFY DEPENDENCIES BETWEEN TASKS

One way or another, all activities are related. There are many types of dependencies: The main ones are external and internal, hard and soft logic.

While some tasks may not be strictly dependent on each other, you still need to assign discretionary dependencies to structure the project workflow.

I'm sure you've heard about network diagrams. They illustrate the sequence of all tasks and their dependencies, and are a must-have on complex projects; less so for smaller projects.

Your project management software should create a network diagram for you. If not, don't waste your time doing it manually. A Gantt chart will be enough for the project schedule.

STEP #12: ESTIMATE REQUIRED RESOURCES, EXPERTS, AND MATERIALS

Once we know the scope of our project, we can identify what resources we need in terms of people, materials, and tools.

For each task, decide:

- What kind of expertise do you need?
- How much experience should an expert have?
- What hard and soft skills do you need?

Next, group similar tasks together and create a "role" to perform these tasks. Then, assess how many people will be needed to carry out this work. Additionally, consider whether you need a team leader.

You will end up with a list of roles or positions on your project. For example, ten carpenters, three bricklayers, and one designer or three senior back-end software engineers.

In the long run, you'll need to create a job opening. Always use the titles that you see on the hiring market. Then, adjust the job description as required.

If your team is preassigned, make a plan based on the people you already have. Try to use their expertise as best as you can. However, you need to consider whether or not you have all the required knowledge.

In the same way, you take each task and assess the required materials, tools, and equipment.

STEP #13: CREATE A HUMAN RESOURCES PLAN

Here, you need to list all your staffing requirements and when you'll need them by.

Some of these people may already be at your organization. For example, there might be a "bench" for people who are not involved in any project. Some projects may release people soon. Or you simply negotiate the transfer of a person to your project. In any case, you need to work with your direct management to secure these resources. Write down the dates when people will join the project.

Then, you'll need to hire the rest of the team. You need to work with recruiters in your company to develop a job description for each role on the project. Recruiters will post the job opening through all available hiring channels. But you need to state when you'll need someone to start. Recruiters should confirm that they will be able to hire someone within a given time frame. Otherwise, it's a risk.

Just a side note: I never call real people a "resource" day to day. I would use a name or a title. But, when speaking about an open position on your project, it's okay to call it a resource.

STEP #14: CREATE A MATERIALS AND TOOLS ACQUISITION PLAN

Just as with human resources, you need to identify the exact date when you need to get materials, tools, and equipment.

Give your list of tasks (and the required materials and tools for each of them) to the procurement team so that they can plan accordingly. In the long run, you need to get a commitment from them to fulfill your project's needs. Their plan will feed into your project schedule and budget.

STEP #15: ESTIMATE DURATION OF TASKS

First, you need to consider the nature of the work in your industry, and how much time and effort is required for those tasks. We'll talk about this in greater depth in the following chapters. For now, let's just say that we have a task and we know who should perform that task.

Ideally, that person should estimate the time and effort needed to complete the task. If they don't have enough experience, a senior-level team member may be able to help.

But it's entirely possible that you don't have that person yet. Instead, you only have an open position. In this case, you need to estimate the work required for a person of "average performance" in this kind of role. Senior experts will always complete a task faster than a junior. Pitch your estimate somewhere in between. In any case, don't forget to include a learning curve for this person in those estimates.

Later, you'll fill that position with a real person. You'll need to ensure that their performance meets your expectations. So, it pays to be cautious with your estimates in such cases.

STEP #16: ESTIMATE COSTS OF EACH TASK

If project owners pay for the whole team throughout the project's duration, you don't need to estimate the per hour cost of a task. Just include a lump sum of the team's rates into the budget. You may need to adjust it based on when people actually join and leave the team.

If you bill the project owners on an hourly basis or a contractor does the bulk of the work, you need to estimate the cost of each task. In most cases, it is the duration multiplied by the hourly rate of those who did the work.

In addition to that, you need to estimate the costs of materials, equipment, and other required services. In some cases, it's critical to identify the dependencies and duration of tasks before you estimate the costs. For example, prices of materials and equipment may fluctuate. Likewise, it might be harder and more costly to hire people in specific periods of the year.

These are general considerations. In practice, cost management depends heavily on the industry, niche, and specific company you work in. If you are new to this environment, you need to learn the details of cost management from your peers, accountants, or leadership.

STEP #17: DEVELOP A PROJECT SCHEDULE

If you follow the process within your project management software, you will eventually come to the Gantt chart. Each task has a lengthy bar that represents the duration. Next, you connect these bars with arrows that show dependencies.

Easier and less risky projects have one long sequence of tasks. But, most probably, this won't meet the project's deadline. So, tasks will need to overlap and work in parallel. Therefore, you'll have parallel sequences of tasks.

This is an iterative process. You will play around until you come up with a realistic schedule.

Keep in mind that you have already identified and allocated resources to each task. After you make a change, you need to ensure that you don't overload a person with 16 hours' work from different sequences of tasks on any given day.

When you have the first draft of the project schedule, do a sanity check. Does it fit into the project's constraints? If not, there's little value in continuing planning without getting approval for a new deadline, change in scope, or additional budget.

After several iterations, you'll develop a schedule that fits into all the constraints. But you're not finished yet. You still need to perform risk management and include the results in your plan.

Moreover, keep in mind that the Gantt chart is not the project schedule. In essence, the project schedule is the planned start and end date for each task. Only these two dates matter.

STEP #18: DETERMINE THE CRITICAL PATH

The longest path within your network diagram (read Gantt chart) is your critical path. It's the shortest project duration. Any delay on the critical path has a knock-on effect for the whole project, so it provides a valuable insight into the risky areas of your project. You need to have tight control of tasks on a critical path.

It is also a good idea to determine a near-critical path: One that is close in duration to the original and that has a chance of becoming it during execution. Moreover, if all your sequences of tasks are on a near-critical path, you have a very optimized and very risky schedule. Be ready for serious communication overhead.

STEP #19: DEVELOP THE PROJECT BUDGET

By now, you should have a clear picture of the work that the project team needs to do. You know when they'll do it. You have estimates of activities, required materials, and resources. You should also understand what work you will outsource.

The next step is to think about other related expenses, like costs of hiring people, traveling, training, team building, etc. To make your life easier later on, link to the associated deliverables as much as possible. Don't let the expenses float around. It will be hard to prove that you needed them to achieve the project objectives.

On a larger project, you have big budgets. In most cases, you'll get the money in installments. Therefore, you also need to develop a payment plan that ensures that those installments will cover ongoing project costs. Sometimes the situation is reversed and installments are on fixed dates. Then, you need to adjust your project plan to align with those dates. In the long run, you should never run out of cash.

Again, note that we haven't performed risk management yet. Thus, this is not a cost baseline yet. You still need to define risk response plans and calculate risks contingency reserves. But you need to have this first draft of the project budget because it's a source of risks in itself.

STEP #20: CREATE THE PROCESS IMPROVEMENT PLAN

A project manager should always try to improve the management and product development processes. Any improvements should be measurable and must be aligned with some goals. So, it's good practice to plan such activities.

I recommend that you select one or two areas that you want to improve per project. Then, think through a possible solution you can try.

Don't skip this step. Otherwise, you'll be stuck in that comfort zone of "it's always worked this way" or "if it ain't broke, don't fix it." It's a sure way to impede your professional development and career growth. Moreover, successful and measurable improvements of processes look really great on your CV.

STEP #21: DETERMINE ROLES AND RESPONSIBILITIES

Most responsibilities are outlined in job descriptions. But, there are always some tasks that fall between the responsibilities of two or more people. These will tend to rear their head after you've done most of the planning.

In general, you want to make clear the attitude you expect towards the work and project. These are your professional ground rules for carrying out everyday responsibilities. You want to stress things like proactivity, collaboration between team members and stakeholders, engagement in all aspects of the project, etc.

On another level, you want to assign responsibility for different deliverables. A RACI matrix is an excellent way to do that. People responsible for a deliverable will report to you on the overall progress. They'll oversee the work of other team members. Usually, your goal is to assign capable team and group leaders.

STEP #22: PLAN PROJECT COMMUNICATIONS

In the real world, you don't need a plan that explains how to communicate with the project team. Instead, it comes naturally based on the preferences of project owners and key stakeholders.

You may want to suggest a better and more reliable means of communication than emails. But you need to have a reasonable justification and a collaboration tool.

Or, you may want to determine how to create, maintain, and store project documentation. This is critical when it's digital. You'll need to explain the basic rules of cybersecurity and how to escalate problems.

STEP #23: PLAN STAKEHOLDER ENGAGEMENT

Let's be clear. You should have been managing stakeholders every step of the way up to this point. You should have spoken extensively with key stakeholders to gain a clear understanding of their expectations. Ideally, you should know their attitude towards your project already.

This is the time to develop a plan to reach the level of engagement you want from each stakeholder, just as we discussed in the stakeholder management chapters.

If you can't come up with a reasonable engagement plan ... yep, you guessed it: It's a risk.

STEP #24: PERFORM RISK MANAGEMENT ACTIVITIES

Like with stakeholder management, you perform risk management activities from your first day on the project. Then you elaborate on the high-level information with more details. In the process, you identify and analyze more and more risks.

By this point, you have a draft of the whole project management plan. You take all aspects into account and undertake a dedicated session of risk identification. Then, you want to show it to your team and stakeholders to brainstorm all possible risks.

Next is a qualitative analysis of all remaining risks and you prioritize the whole list. So, first, you need to identify the most severe risks you need to handle.

You then need to decide how to minimize the negative impact or probability of all severe risks. This should translate into additional tasks, reserves of money and time, changes to the processes and workflows. Finally, you should put it all into your project plan.

STEP #25: VALIDATE YOUR PLAN

In the previous step, you introduced quite a lot of changes to all aspects of the project plan. So, after you have corrected the plan, go back to the beginning and repeat the planning process.

You should walk through the plan and identify residual and new risks. You should also check that your plan is still realistic and within constraints.

This will inevitably lead to an expansion of your plan. That's why, when you do sanity checks on your first draft, you should allow for this extra effort and time. So, you should raise a concern not when you are already beyond constraints with your first draft but when you are at 90%.

STEP #26: CREATE BASELINES

After several iterations of risk management activities, you will have a realistic plan. If it gets the thumbs up, you need to create a scope, schedule, and cost baselines.

A baseline is just a final and approved version of your scope, budget, or schedule. They are fixed in stone and used as a reference point for your project's progress. If you deviate from the baseline too much, that's a problem you need to address.

Without establishing the baselines, you won't be able to prove that you are heading in the right direction. And you'll deprive yourself of the opportunity to improve your project management approach.

In modern project management software, you can set a baseline with one click. Check the manual to find this feature.

STEP #27: PLAN WAYS TO MEASURE PERFORMANCE

During project planning, you need to determine ways to measure cost, scope, schedule, risks, and quality performance. It is also good to know how to measure stakeholder engagement and communications.

It won't be a problem if you have project management software that allows all team members to log their time and expenses.

But, if you need to collect all this data manually, it's a considerable effort. I recommend that you write down a process for the whole team that describes how to report their progress on a task. You should create a report template where you specify the format and units of measurement. The most critical thing here is to keep the names of tasks, work packages, and deliverables in sync.

STEP #28: CREATE A CHANGE MANAGEMENT PLAN

No matter how well you plan, changes will happen.

Therefore, you need a process to log, manage, and integrate changes into your project. You also need a plan on how to prevent changes in the first place.

We'll discuss how to do this correctly in the following chapters.

STEP #29: CREATE A REWARD AND RECOGNITION SYSTEM

I often see project managers who don't take the motivation of their team seriously enough. So, they try to deal with it on the spot.

You need to develop a system in advance. There should be clear and transparent rules on how you will reward good work. People need to know how you will recognize their efforts, engagement, and initiative.

But keep in mind that you need to have the ability and budget to provide the benefits.

STEP #30: FINALIZE SUBSIDIARY PLANS AND CREATE A PROJECT PLAN

If you need to create a formal project plan, gather all the components together.

You will need to ensure that all your subsidiary plans are sufficiently detailed. Add descriptions of processes and charts of workflows. Finalize all required "how to" aspects of the plan. It's worth repeating that there's no standard here: Each company and project will require a different project management plan.

Nevertheless, you need to have a realistic plan. You and your team should have confidence in it. Key stakeholders should believe that you came up with the best possible plan. Moreover, you should convince them that you will be able to stick to it. And it doesn't matter whether you write it all out or keep it in your head, a spreadsheet, or project management software.

STEP #31: GAIN FORMAL APPROVAL OF THE PLAN

Now you need to prove that you and your plan are capable of achieving the project goals. Project owners should give formal approval. This is about sharing responsibility for the outcome and getting their commitment to help you execute the plan.

It is a good idea to review and get informal approval from key stakeholders, not only from project owners.

Quite often, this part is not mandatory. Project planning is a project manager's problem. Others are interested in the final result. However, I strongly encourage you to find a way to present your plan. It is an essential part of managing stakeholders' expectations. It's like setting rules for the game.

STEP #32: PRESENT YOUR PLAN TO THE WHOLE TEAM

The last step is to present your plan to the team.

They need to believe that this plan is feasible. Otherwise, they will not be motivated to follow it. Once you have their buy-in, you are clear to kick off the project.

CHAPTER 32
PROJECT PLANNING CONCEPTS

In the previous chapter, we discussed the science of planning. Now let's talk a bit about the art of planning. But whatever you call it, it is a challenging and complex process. A plan should be:

- feasible;
- challenging;
- usable;
- efficient; and
- optimal.

It's tricky to balance these characteristics. No one is expecting a perfect plan first time round. No one expects you to apply all the concepts and ideas that I will explain below. Planning requires experience and a bit of self-confidence. So, don't aim for perfection. Instead, aim for a realistic plan that you and your team can execute.

Most importantly, you need to prove that your plan is both **realistic** and **optimal**. You'll have to justify the decisions you made in your plan. For example, stakeholders will always question project estimates and risks reserves. They will try to minimize the importance of your concerns and assumptions. Project owners may even try to force you to commit to finishing the project faster and with a smaller budget based on their "feeling" of the project's complexity.

So, all the concepts and tips below will help you to create a realistic project plan. Moreover, they will help you protect the plan from unfounded deductions.

1. A PLAN IS NOT ONLY ABOUT SCHEDULE

Inexperienced project managers have a narrow understanding of what constitutes a project plan – for example, as a Gantt chart or simply a sprint backlog. Moreover, as you work in an environment, someone before you will have prepared a common project management approach. You might have to use specific risk register or scope statement templates. So, you take it for granted and use them as-is. Maybe you assume that all companies in the world do the same. But that's not true.

The main challenge is that all aspects of project management are interrelated:

- Proper quality and risk management require additional work, budgets, and time.
- Resource management and procurement will dictate your schedule.
- Stakeholders and communication management impact the whole project.

So, have you ever thought of what it takes to plan a project from scratch and make it all work together? Things like how to:

- identify and manage the project scope;
- assure and control quality;
- come up with a schedule;
- develop an accurate budget;
- manage stakeholders and their expectations;
- integrate risk management into all other activities;
- hire and acquire staff;

- get materials, tools, equipment;
- organize communication within the team and with stakeholders; and
- conduct serious procurement.

Today, you might be working under a Scrum or Kanban framework or within a pre-existing environment. However, sooner or later, you will manage a project where you will have to set it all up from scratch, teach your team to work, and build up a working environment. So, if you want to become a great project manager, you need to learn how to plan each aspect of a project.

You might not learn this right at the beginning of your career. Nevertheless, your goal should be to master all these areas of project management.

So, if you are using established best practices, investigate how they came about. If you are an experienced project manager, you need to review these areas and think about how you would adapt the same processes in another company.

2. PLANNING FALLACY IS UNAVOIDABLE

By default, human beings are terrible at planning. And there is nothing you can do about it. We learn to anticipate adverse events in the future only by experiencing similar problems in the past. If you are smart, you know the value of learning from the experience and mistakes of others. First, you accumulate knowledge. Then, you apply it to your projects.

On the other hand, there are too many dependencies and relations, unknown factors, and unexpected events in one project. There is no way you can take everything into consideration. So, what can you do about it?

Conceptually, there are two different types of work for which you need to plan.

First, the work that you are most sure about. You know what, how, and who will do it. You also know how long it will take and what outcome you will receive. You also know how to achieve sufficient

227

quality in the process. In general, it means that you or someone from your team have already done something similar before. The more experienced your team is, the more work becomes typical.

The second type is the work with uncertainties. At a given time, you may not be sure of who can do the job or how it will be done. It might be something no one in the organization has done before. Or you may lack confidence about the outcome until some of the work is done. Or you can't be sure about the overall quality due to the interdependencies and the nature of the work. In short, you don't know enough.

In practice, you encounter both types of work in one deliverable or work package. That's why you need to differentiate them and manage them differently. The risk management approach I explained in previous chapters helps to do exactly that.

All professional project managers agree that to manage a project you need to manage risks. The project team will do the work that they understand as fast as they can. Moreover, they'll be motivated to do it because it's feasible and tangible. There's a clear connection between their efforts and the outcome. So, now, you need to give them a clear plan to tackle the uncertainties.

Your plan is only as good as the number of unknowns that could impact it. Therefore, the better you manage uncertainties, the closer you will be to your initial plan. So you should focus planning efforts on managing risks, dealing with the unexpected, and clarifying uncertainties in a systematic and controlled way. If you take anything from this book, it should be the risk management approach that I have laid out.

3. PLANNING IS EVERYTHING, THE PLAN IS NOTHING

Planning is not about having a fixed path. The most significant benefit from planning activities is not coming up with a shiny, all-singing-and-dancing documented plan but a mental simulation of your project.

During planning, you imagine how a project will go, what can go wrong, how you will overcome problems, manage changes, etc. So, you try to identify as many uncertainties as possible.

The more "what ifs" you brainstorm and simulate, the more problems you will identify and the more prepared you will be.

I practice what I preach. For example, I sit with a Gantt chart in front of me and try to imagine how the project will proceed day after day. Then, I ask myself questions like:

"OK, that's the duration of work the team provided. But, here, we have to finish the deliverable. Did they think about pulling everything together and testing it? Most probably not. We need to add some time to brush up on external deliverables."

And:

"Here we have two holidays in the middle of the week. It'll be tempting to take a day off or vacation. So, most of the team will want to extend their weekends. I need to ask about their holiday plans ASAP. I'll definitely need to add some slack into the schedule here."

These are the types of thought processes I follow to check if we've forgotten something. Then I imagine unexpected events like sick leaves, technical problems, new risks, etc. Next, I check if there is a "Plan B" or reserves that can cover them. Finally, I also think through possible communications that we may require in case of an emergency.

4. "NO BATTLE PLAN SURVIVES CONTACT WITH THE ENEMY"

This quote by General Helmuth von Moltke can be directly applied to project management. That's why the goal of planning is to be ready for those hard punches during execution.

A plan should be flexible. You shouldn't have to change it every time something unexpected happens. You take the hit, deviate, then try to get back to the initial plan. You use the slack in the schedule, motivate the team to push a bit harder, etc. Only if nothing helps do you change the initial plan and establish a new baseline.

For example, you might need to tweak the requirements after you show some work to project owners. So your plan should include measures to handle the changes efficiently, especially if you know it's very likely to happen.

On the other hand, you need to keep track of your flexibility, which comes from risk management activities and risk reserves, undefined buffers in each task, or just slack in the schedule. Do you have enough reserves? Do you burn your buffer at the expected rate? Also, you need a reliable way to forecast how flexible your plan will be in the future.

5. ROLLING WAVE PLANNING TECHNIQUE

Lots of agile practitioners don't like waterfall or plan-driven approaches. They think that the whole plan has to be developed before you start a project and stuck to no matter what. The truth is that, even at the dawn of waterfall, managers applied progressive elaboration and rolling wave planning techniques.

Rolling wave planning allows for different levels of detail within a big project. For deliverables in the near future, we create a detailed plan. For deliverables further down the road, we make high-level estimates and predictions. As the project progresses, we put more and more details into our plan. So, there are ebbs and flows in your project planning efforts.

Right at the start of a project or when defining requirements, you'll have an idea of what you need to implement first. There might be a strict technological process that you cannot change, stakeholders may set priorities, or you need to make a decision. In any case, you need to choose what deliverables will be prioritized.

Now, you need to follow the exact step-by-step process for these first few deliverables and create a detailed plan for all aspects of the project. After that, you do the same to identify high-level information and estimates for other deliverables. These are put in the plan and become the constraints of your project going forward.

That's why you need to include all high-level information about all the project's deliverables in your plan. Even the last deliverable nine months from now should be in the project scope, budget, and schedule. Also, you need to estimate this deliverable considering all the uncertainty and risks that you have today.

When we need to estimate something on a high level, I ask the team, "How much time do we need to implement this deliverable even if clients ask something bizarre and unexpected? How much time do we need to implement almost anything in this area?"

For sure, you need to take into account your knowledge of the product and your niche, how impulsive your project owners are, the complexity of requirements, etc. You discuss it all with your team. Together you come up with the most reasonable assumption and estimate based on that assumption.

The most critical thing here is that you need to communicate these assumptions and estimates to the project owners. They may decide to adjust those last deliverables based on what they learn during the project execution. This makes your assumption invalid so they should grant you permission to adjust your estimates and change the project plan.

Don't assume that people are aware of rolling wave planning. You need to explain it every time to your project owners. Moreover, get a written agreement you can refer to further down the line.

6. PLANNING IS ITERATIVE

After explaining rolling wave planning, I need to repeat a crucial concept of project planning: You cannot and should not try to create a project plan in one iteration.

The idea is simple. When you learn something new about the project, integrate it into your project plan. Now go back to the start of the planning process. You may even need to review the project charter! Then, skip through the processes and ensure that your new input does not mess with your plan.

Let's say a big piece of work is needed. You might just include it in the schedule and carry on. However, this may result in unexpected problems.

First of all, you need to ensure that this work is aligned with the business need. Then, it may require additional quality assurance measures. Moreover, it may introduce new risks, dependencies, or even uncover hidden requirements.

The same applies to rolling wave planning. During execution, you elaborate on the requirements for the next deliverables – were your high-level estimates for those deliverables correct? Don't stop there. Check quality and risk aspects. Double-check that stakeholders understand the details of requirements in the same way. You will probably need some engagement and commitment from new stakeholders, or you might need to hire a new team member.

By the way, you might have heard about integrated change management. Keep in mind that you don't do this during the planning stages – only after you have fixed the project baselines. During planning, you simply update the plan.

7. MAKING PROMISES

If your project plan has been signed off by the customer, it is as if you have made a promise. I believe that it is your ethical duty as a professional to keep to your promises.

So, now, you need to deliver the project results within the constraints you agreed upon. The only proper way to correct the plan is by a formal change request.

This usually comes naturally when project owners ask for a change. But what if you need to make a change due to a mistake? Or due to a change request from an internal stakeholder?

For example, the team missed something during the scope definition. Yes, it's your fault. But you are worried about breaking your initial promise. That's exactly why lots of project managers fail. You can and should try to renegotiate the terms of your promise. And you must do it as early as possible. You should never delay or hide problems, even if it means your reputation takes a hit.

It may feel like you'll ruin your career if you highlight your own mistakes. But hear me out. Stakeholders will be open to such negotiations more often than not. They will help you to overcome the issue or find a solution. Why? Because they want to put things right so that the project they paid for is a success.

Project owners should be interested in a successful outcome. If not, you should quit the project as fast as you can.

You may be tempted to put the consequences of your failure on the team's shoulders. They'll have to work harder because you feel insecure about your job. Never do this! It's the fastest way to lose the team's trust and support. If that happens, nothing will help you finish the project successfully.

Keep in mind that, from time to time, someone may make a promise on the back of your promise. A lot of money and resources might be at stake. So, make sure you know about other work that depends on your project.

8. DO NOT PLAN ALONE

Engaging your team in planning activities has lots of benefits.

First of all, you can delegate part of your work to the team. If they have the relevant skills, they can do lots of planning activities far better than you because they can dedicate more time. Therefore, you will get a deeper analysis and input from different perspectives.

Second, if you delegate the activities correctly, you will also gain the team's buy-in.

Third, it will be great for team building and, most importantly, the team member will feel ownership and responsibility for the project.

If you aren't sure whether it is worth the effort, break down and analyze the Scrum framework. It's built around this concept of delegating responsibility for planning and commitments to the team. And Scrum works! You should always use the best expertise you have available. If you are the best person to do all this work and no one can help you, your project is at serious risk.

WHAT'S NEXT?

We've discussed the concepts of planning and how to plan a project step-by-step. Now, we'll take a deeper look at the most critical of those steps, one at a time.

PART SEVEN
PROJECT SCOPE OF WORK

CHAPTER 33
PROJECT SCOPE MANAGEMENT OVERVIEW

The scope of a project is all the work that's needed to achieve its objectives. On a high level, you need to identify big tangible pieces that will comprise the final product, service, or result. On the lowest level, you need to identify individual tasks that team members will perform.

Here's a career development tip for you. No matter the industry or size of a project, scope management is the most crucial aspect – you must become a professional scope manager first of all. Just think about it:

- Poorly specified requirements are the number one reason for project failure.
- To create an accurate project budget or schedule, you must identify 100% of the project scope. Otherwise, you need to guesstimate.
- Risk management depends on the clarity of the requirements and scope of work. Ambiguity in scope leads to rework and unexpected expenses.
- Quality management is simply a part of the scope.
- The WBS, RTM, and project scope statement are the central pillars of project integration.

You get the point: Scope is king. If you want to start delivering projects on time and within budget, you need to become an expert in scope management. You need to master the RTM, project scope statement, WBS, and WBS dictionary in addition to a structured scope management approach.

In this chapter, we'll discuss the overall scope management approach. Then, we'll dive deeper into each process and tool.

REQUIREMENTS VS. PROJECT SCOPE

Just to be sure we are on the same page, let's clarify the difference between requirements and scope. Here are their definitions from the *PMBOK Guide*:

> "Requirement is a condition or capability that is required to be present in a product, service or result to satisfy an agreement or other formally imposed specification."[1]

And:

> "Project scope is the work performed to deliver a product, service, or result with the specified features and functions."[2]

What does that mean? A requirement is what a product should look like, what it should be capable of, its characteristics, behavior, performance, etc., while the project scope describes what work we should perform to create the results that meet those requirements.

There's one more important definition: "Quality is the degree to which a product complies with the requirements."

You need to clarify the quality level for your project. It'll significantly impact the scope.

You see, the zero-defects approach is too costly. It requires a lot of effort to test and fix all defects. In addition, you need robust processes, workflows, and audits to achieve 100% compliance with all requirements. Therefore, in the real world, you need to reach an "acceptable" level of quality. Nevertheless, you need to include the efforts to achieve that quality level in your project scope.

HOW TO CREATE A SCOPE MANAGEMENT PLAN THAT WORKS

Your ultimate goal is to deliver what your customers believe they asked for. Read that again! Customers think that they clearly explained what they wanted from the project. You believe that you understood them correctly. However, that's seldom the truth.

Before you start defining the scope of the project, you need to imagine the project's end. How will you hand off the final deliverable to the project owners and make them accept it? Looks easy, doesn't it? But, in the real world, it's not easy at all!

What will you do if a project owner says that it's not what he expected? Of course, you can try and prove that you implemented all the requirements correctly. But it doesn't matter because your clients are unhappy and will never do business with you again.

So, you need to do more than just identifying and implementing 100% of the project scope. You need a scope management plan that helps you meet project owners' expectations.

Moreover, I believe that you need to have a written scope management plan. But I won't retype the whole template here. It's available in the supporting materials at https://itpmschool.com/materials. Feel free to use it on your projects as a starting point.

Below is a structure for all your scope management efforts. You need to describe these processes in your plan.

PROCESS #1: COLLECT PROJECT REQUIREMENTS

By this time, you already need to have a project charter. Or at least you need to collect the information that I suggest. You are looking for two things at this moment.

First, you need a business case and any high-level requirements that you captured in the project charter.

Second, you need to identify relevant stakeholders who can consider the high-level requirements.

In short, you need to communicate with all of the relevant stakeholders in order to elaborate on high-level requirements. In the process, some will also help you to identify the overall solution and any additional requirements that you might have missed initially.

Keep in mind that you may need a separate specialist trained to collect and describe business requirements by this time (a business analyst).

Likewise, you need to select appropriate tools and techniques to capture all project requirements. For bigger projects, I recommend creating an RTM.

PROCESS #2: IDENTIFY MAJOR AND MINOR DELIVERABLES

You can get creative with this step. There's no straightforward way to transform requirements into tangible results. However, we usually know what the final result should be (a house, software application, new business process, etc.). So, we need to break down this final product into bite-sized chunks. In addition, you need to identify all other tangible results from your project. All these are called "deliverables."

Next, you link requirements to these deliverables. Some requirements will require a separate deliverable. For example, project owners may require that you create a risk register and share it with them. This is a requirement of your project management approach. Therefore, this document becomes a separate deliverable.

Most of the requirements will be for the end product or service. You can create several deliverables as separate modules of the final product. Or you can create interim versions of the product that incrementally includes more and more implemented requirements.

So, a deliverable can be an interim part of the product or service that stakeholders can test, play with, or inspect. Or it can be a project document that stakeholders need. In any case, it is something important that we need to create to finish our project. To describe major deliverables, we'll create a project scope statement. This will ensure that we are on the same page with all key stakeholders on what needs to be produced.

There are several types of deliverables that we usually need on a project. For example, to track our progress, set checkpoints, and adhere to dependencies, you'll need to identify internal deliverables. You create them for internal use. You don't usually hand off internal deliverables to project owners. On the other hand, to demonstrate your progress, get feedback on your work, and manage expectations, you'll create external deliverables.

All deliverables can be interim or final. You want to get feedback from project owners continuously. That's why you provide an interim version of the final product or service.

In addition, to make your project more manageable, you may want to break down major deliverables into smaller pieces, like minor deliverables and work packages.

To identify and track all these deliverables, we'll need to create a WBS and WBS dictionary.

PROCESS #3: CREATE A SCOPE BASELINE

Here's a situation I want you to avoid at all costs!

Usually, when a project starts, you receive requirements in different forms, such as emails, PDFs, meetings, mock-ups, bug reports, etc. But you don't have a reliable system to manage those requirements. You discuss different details with project owners, stakeholders, and the project team – although project owners usually don't have enough time to review all the documentation and participate in all discussions.

Then, you create a WBS. However, you use it internally and never show it to the project owners. After that, you break down the work into tasks and estimate the project. Again, this is all behind the scenes for project owners.

Now you present estimates for the project. Can you see there's already a lack of transparency here? Project owners don't know what work you actually estimated. If the estimate is close to the sponsor's expectations, he'll not dig into the details because he's ready to spend that amount of money and time. He doesn't want to waste his precious time. So, project owners blindly approve the estimates and the work behind them. But they all assume that you read their minds somehow – that you had ultimate knowledge of their business and pain points.

Now, here comes a problem. You start project execution and create the first deliverable. You show it to the stakeholders and they are shocked. It's not what they expected at all! In the process, you also learn that they forgot about some requirements that need to be added to the project scope. Your whole project management plan is useless now. You need to make lots of changes right at the start of the project.

Why did things unravel in this way? Because you didn't walk the stakeholders through the work you had planned. Instead, you assumed that you were on the same page.

That's why you need to involve project owners as much as possible when defining requirements. Likewise, you need to talk through all the high-level deliverables. Then, if they approve it, you'll create a plan to produce those deliverables.

To get this approval on the project scope, we need to set the scope baseline. This is the approved version of the project scope statement, WBS, and WBS dictionary.

Setting a baseline is critical to protecting your plan during execution. Sometimes project owners will tell you they thought something was part of a project when it wasn't. When that happens, you can refer to the baseline they approved. As a result, you can properly integrate this additional scope into the project by requesting extra time and money.

PROCESS #3: BREAKDOWN DELIVERABLES INTO TASKS

Take work packages (groups of tasks) one by one for each separate deliverable and break them down into tasks.

If you use modern project management software, you'll end up with the following structure:

Project Result:
- Deliverable 1
- - Work Package 1.1
- - - Task #1
- - - Task #2

- - - Task #3
- - Work Package 1.2
- - - Task #1
- - - Task #2
- - - Task #3
- - Work Package 1.3 (to put everything together into a deliverable)
- - - Task #1 (to integrate all work packages)
- - - Task #2 (to test the deliverable)
- - Deliverable 2
- - Work Package 2.1
- - - Task #1
- - - Task #2
- - - Task #3
- - Work Package 2.2
- - - Task #1
- - - Task #2
- - - Task #3
- - Work Package 2.3 (to put everything together into a deliverable)
- - - Task #1 (to integrate all work packages)
- - - Task #2 (to test the deliverable)

It's a time-consuming process. You need to work with your project team and SMEs to identify all the work that the team needs to perform.

However, you should always keep in mind one critical concept: You need to identify every task needed to fully complete a work package. Likewise, all the work in all work packages should produce the parent deliverable. Finally, when a team completes all the tasks, the deliverable should be in a state where you can hand it off to project owners. Tasks should never float outside of a work package.

PROCESS #4: HOW TO CONTROL PROJECT SCOPE

It is not enough to identify 100% of the project scope in the beginning because it will change during the project's lifetime. For example:

- A requirement was not fully clear, and you needed to add new tasks.

- You didn't identify all the tasks required to finish the work package in the first place.
- You missed a requirement completely.
- The team implemented a requirement, but there are a lot of defects.
- Project owners clarify the requirements, and it's not how you understood it during planning.

The list can go on and on here. In all of these cases, you'll need to add some work to the plan. When a deliverable does not meet expectations, there will be changes. It is your responsibility to prove whether the change warrants a formal change request. If so, it should be appropriately integrated. Otherwise, it is a defect and you must make amends – sometimes at the team's own expense.

So, you need a way to monitor, control, and make changes to the scope.

The WBS helps you a lot here. First, you'll control the actual work on the work packages level. Then, you'll sum up the actual performed tasks, costs, and time. Finally, you'll compare it to the initial baseline.

Likewise, you need an efficient change management process to integrate new requirements and scope into your project plan. We'll discuss all of this in the following chapters.

PROCESS #5: VALIDATE IMPLEMENTED SCOPE CONTINUOUSLY

Once in a while, you need to get a formal sign-off that a deliverable meets stakeholders' expectations. It's crucial to do this continuously throughout the project. Even if you are leading a plan-driven project, nothing should stop you from providing product increments for review.

Why do you need this? You don't want to get all the change requests, feedback, defects, and "minor changes to the project" at the end of the project. Why? You have spent all the budget by the end of the project, and the deadline is around the corner. There's no room for negotiations and corrections. Project owners will not want to move the deadline. Therefore, they'll put more pressure on the team to get what they need. So, instead, you want to use their feedback as you implement each deliverable.

How do you actually validate scope with project owners? Just prepare a short demonstration of the deliverable. First, explain the current project status and progress. Also, point out known defects and which parts are a work in progress. After that, collect feedback from the project owners. Later, you can provide any supporting documentation and reports required by your policies.

You need to collect feedback from stakeholders continuously. But always keep in mind the project's objectives and deadlines. You need to remind stakeholders that every addition to the scope is a trade-off against deadlines and budget.

A great project manager knows that changes and corrections are inevitable. To accommodate project owners' requests and keep them happy, you need to include some reserves of time and budget to allow for an adequate number of changes. Help them understand that this is the right way to run a project.

CHAPTER 34
HOW TO COLLECT REQUIREMENTS

Full disclosure: I'm not a qualified business analyst. What I'm about to explain doesn't come from a formal education but 10 years of practical experience.

The information below should be enough for most project managers. However, if you want to combine the role of a project manager and a business analyst, you need additional training. I believe that business analysis is a full-time job. A project manager should not spend time and effort writing out specifications and user stories.

THE BIGGEST CHALLENGES WITH GATHERING REQUIREMENTS

As a project manager, I've done this various ways. I had a dedicated person responsible for defining requirements on one project. And there were projects when I had to write out requirements on my own. I can tell you that, in both cases, the challenges are the same.

First of all, you need to work with project owners and stakeholders who are always short on time.

Second, stakeholders usually do not see the value of the requirements management process. They often think that it is a part of the execution phase. That's why project owners try to keep the time spent on requirements to a minimum. And they want to "start the work" as soon as possible. So, they say, "We'll get all the details as we move forward. Let's just get started." However, they don't know that high-quality requirements streamline the development process.

Therefore, the first thing you need to do is to prove that requirements management is crucial. Moreover, stakeholders should understand the negative impact of poorly defined requirements. Also, a business "vision" has nothing to do with the specifications required by the project team. Without proper requirements management, their expectations will not be met.

Third, don't expect project owners to have skills in requirements management. You need to educate them about the overall process and their role within it. You need to help them express their needs in simple terms, while you and your team offer ways to meet these needs, again explained in layman's terms.

Fourth, project owners may not know what they want until they see it. So, once you create something tangible, stakeholders start generating new requirements at once. Here, you must control their appetites. You need to focus them on reaching the initial project objectives within the constraints they set. Or you need to persuade them to update the objectives and constraints. Otherwise, you may spiral down a rabbit hole of improvements that drags you away from the project objectives.

HIERARCHY OF REQUIREMENTS

First of all, requirements have a hierarchy. You can imagine it this way:

1. Business requirements.
2. Stakeholder requirements.
3. Solution requirements.
— 3.1 Functional requirements.
— 3.2 Non-functional requirements.

Let me explain.

BUSINESS REQUIREMENTS

These describe the overall business need. They explain why project owners decided to start a project and invest resources.

In an ideal world, project owners describe business requirements in a project charter by including a problem statement, business case, project justification, business objectives, etc. But, in the real world, project managers never see those documents or project owners never create them in the first place. In this case, you must ask project owners why they initiated the project and what they want to achieve from a business perspective. Don't force them to create those formal documents. In most cases, they don't know how to do it. Just let them explain their expectations as best they can.

Business requirements often lead us towards a specific solution or approach that we need to take. So, you should be careful here. You see, project owners identified a solution. They thought it would help them achieve the business need. Sometimes it's true, and you can accept the solution. But, sometimes, you'll need to ensure that the proposed solution is valid. In this way, business requirements dictate the boundaries and constraints of the project scope.

STAKEHOLDER REQUIREMENTS

In essence, stakeholder requirements elaborate on how to achieve the business requirements. They describe the product or service from a stakeholder perspective. In this case, it is someone who will own or use the product or service.

Usually, project owners explain what capabilities end users should have in the product or service, what action they should take, what results they'll get, etc. But keep in mind that the project owners are not the end users in most cases. Instead, they create a product or service for a broader audience.

So, there's a serious challenge here! Project owners provide requirements that they think the real users want. That's why, if you're working with an external client, you may want to help them identify the correct stakeholders' requirements. But the overall responsibility still rests with the client.

On the other hand, if you develop an in-house product, you may need to collect the stakeholder requirements yourself. Therefore, you may need to work with the end users. Or you'll work with a product manager who knows the users' pain points and analyzes their needs.

In most cases, project owners don't have the required depth of knowledge to propose an efficient solution. Therefore, ask them to provide these requirements only from a business or user perspective. Detach them from the technical aspects of implementing these requirements or the product you already have. It will give you enough space to develop the most efficient solution or generate several alternatives to choose from.

Here's another tip from practical experience: I learned that stakeholders need to see what they ask you to produce. So, visualizing the end result or product helps them a lot. Insist on creating designs, wireframes, or mock-ups right at the start of the project to help them do this. They will then find it easier to express their requirements in simple terms.

SOLUTION REQUIREMENTS

You or a business analyst will create these solution requirements based on stakeholder requirements.

They consist of functional and non-functional requirements.

Functional requirements describe what the end user will experience. It's something you can test and play with. Non-functional requirements cover other capabilities of your product or service, such as security, performance, stress tolerance, maintainability, and continuity.

Just to be clear. There's no direct connection between stakeholder requirements and solution requirements. One stakeholder requirement may generate numerous specification documents, user stories, and designs that will form functional and non-functional requirements.

Solution requirements are primarily for your project team. Therefore, they are very detailed. You need to describe, in simple language, what the project team needs to implement and how it should behave. This could be in the form of a specification document. Or you may draw on user stories to describe individual functionalities. Each industry has its best practices on how to create solution requirements. So, you need to check what works best for your project.

HOW DO REQUIREMENTS IMPACT YOUR PROJECT MANAGEMENT APPROACH?

There's a strong relationship between requirements, scope, and quality. The better you know the requirements, the better you can define the scope. The better you understand the project scope, the better quality you can achieve. And, in general, the better you identify the scope, the more accurate the project plan you'll create. On the flip side, ambiguity in requirements leads to uncertainty of scope, resulting in poor quality.

However, in the real world, requirements are never finished or settled. You may finish implementing an approved requirement. But then, you show it to the project owners and they want to tweak it a bit. Or they simply add new functionality to the product that impacts existing capabilities. So, you need to update requirements all the time. You can't change this. Instead, you need processes and tools to collect, maintain, and adjust requirements with as little extra effort as possible.

Therefore, it's a matter of selecting a proper project management approach. Should you use Scrum, Kanban, or a plan-driven approach (waterfall)? They all work well under certain circumstances, but they all have pros and cons. Consider the following.

Are you able to clearly and comprehensively define requirements in advance? If yes, it may be better to choose a plan-driven approach. You can use resources more efficiently by having a long-term plan.

If there's no efficient way to collect all requirements in advance, or they change quickly, then you're better off adopting an agile approach. You'll need to adapt quickly to the changes rather than constantly wasting time changing the plan.

But, as I said before, the industry and environment you work in have made a choice already. If you're new to the industry, you should research the best practices in requirements management.

On a practical level, it will boil down to a set of selected processes and tools. Here's a couple of examples using the approaches outlined above:

1. In an agile approach, you organize requirements through the hierarchy of epics, features, and user stories. As a result, you control the user stories implemented during an iteration. So, for example, when you implement all the user stories from one feature, you can close it.
2. In a plan-driven approach, you manage requirements in an RTM, which connects requirements to separate specifications, designs, and test cases. In addition, the RTM allows you to connect all requirements to a specific WBS element. Once finished, you can close related requirements, marking them as "finished."

HERE'S HOW I WORK WITH REQUIREMENTS

We (the project team) get a high-level draft of requirements from a customer (product owner, product team). It can be as simple as a short description of functionality. We teach our project owners to provide stakeholder requirements without attachment to any technology we use. So, they state these requirements as a "user need."

We get strange requirements from time to time. They simply don't fit into our vision of the product. In this case, we don't shy away from asking how they relate to the business need of the project and product. This way, we ensure that stakeholders align their requests with the ongoing project's goals.

Then, the business analyst and I try to expand and explain the user needs to the project team. It's a short, high-level discussion. It's up to you to decide whether you need the whole team or not. However, I recommend having at least one person from every function or department.

After a quick chat, we write down our recommended solutions, concerns, questions, and assumptions and send them to the project owners. This short meeting saves us time and effort in the long run. We show the areas where we want them to focus. Sometimes we conclude that we need to discuss requirements with SMEs or other teams. We plan those meetings at once and prepare the agenda.

Then, the business analyst works with clients and stakeholders. He collects all required details in a few days and writes out a draft specification (user stories in our case). These are our functional and non-functional solution requirements. We also get answers to all our outstanding questions and concerns.

Next, I ask the team to read and think through the draft requirements. They need to understand and discuss them among themselves. Then, we have a grooming session.

I ask one of the team members to explain a requirement to the rest of the team. The goal is to ensure that we are all on the same side. We need a shared vision of what we need to deliver.

Usually, by this time, there are quite a lot of questions. Someone might have understood it in another way. Someone might point out some dependency or a conflict with other requirements. Or possible difficulties in implementation, testing, or a flaw in the design. The business analyst takes notes and updates the user stories.

In the end, as the project manager, I ask several additional questions:

- What is the possible impact on other areas of the product?
- How complex is this requirement in general?
- Who is the best candidate to implement the requirement?
- How will we test it?
- Are there any risks here? (You should educate the team in risk management.)

The business analyst takes all this feedback and tries to clarify outstanding questions with clients and stakeholders. Then, he updates the user stories and we get the final draft of acceptance criteria. Next, he sends them for approval to the client. It all happens in our project management software. So, project owners approve requirements by setting a correct status to the user story.

TOOLS AND TECHNIQUES I USE

As you see, there are two distinct phases here. In the first phase, we need to understand business needs and stakeholder requirements.

Usually, this is purely communication between project owners, you, and the business analyst.

One technique that helps here is creating avatars (buying personas, user profiles). In this technique, you put yourself in the end user's shoes. You need to understand their pain points, needs, and wants. You may have several avatars for the product or service that you develop. These are particularly helpful when establishing stakeholders requirements, which should come in a narrative form as if from a real user.

There are several other techniques that you should be aware of. They include facilitated workshops, focus groups, nominal group techniques, mind mapping, affinity diagrams, observations, questionnaires, surveys, benchmarking, and so on.

In rare cases, you might need to conduct such information-gathering events. But not on a daily basis. Most stakeholder requirements come from project owners.

The second phase is to come up with a solution to implement stakeholder requirements and describe it in the solution requirements. This is where you mostly work with the business analyst, project team, and SMEs. You may need to clarify and adjust stakeholder requirements during this process. There are dozens of techniques. But there are four that you will need to use most of the time.

Document Analysis: One way or another, stakeholders will provide you with different documents. They may be in the form of laws, software manuals, guidelines, use cases, policies, process workflows, or business plans. As easy as it sounds, you need to read, analyze, and capture relevant requirements from them. Then, at some point, you need to discuss whether these requirements are applicable to the project's success.

Documentation can also be a source of stakeholder requirements. For example, Apple has guidelines on how all applications for iPhone should feel and look. All developers should comply with these guidelines. However, Apple does not provide the solution requirements on this matter. Therefore, you need to determine how to comply with their stakeholder requirements.

Brainstorming: You'll use good old brainstorming to develop solutions to stakeholder requirements. Thinking creatively in this way can also generate functional and non-functional requirements. First, gather relevant stakeholders or project team members. Then, let the ideas flow – you want to encourage as many as possible. You can prioritize them later.

Interviews: Talk to stakeholders directly. Record their answers. Analyze their ideas and convert them into requirements.

Prototyping: Create a working model of a future product. Your project owners can then play around with it to generate more stakeholder requirements. It's an interim stage to come up with the requirements for the final product. You can also use storyboards: A sequence of images that show how a real product will behave.

HOW SHOULD REQUIREMENTS BE WRITTEN?

You failed to hire a dedicated business analyst. Now project owners and your boss want you to write all the requirements. What should you do?

First of all, you need to be honest about your skills in business analysis. You need to communicate that you'll do your best but you can't promise it will meet industry standards because you are not qualified.

This might feel like shooting yourself in the foot. But, believe me, it's better to be upfront rather than hide the problem and get into issues later on. In most cases, project owners will accept the risk and support you. On the other hand, some projects are relatively simple. You can handle requirements management without any extra training.

Second, you need to give yourself permission to write requirements in the simplest form possible. Use narrative language as if describing a product to a friend. Also, a picture or a diagram is usually worth more than a hundred words. Use more visualizations. Your only goal is to ensure that the project team understands the solution requirements.

Likewise, you need to discuss the requirements with the team to discover any ambiguity. You should delegate writing non-functional requirements to the most knowledgeable team member. And delegating, in general, is a must. Let team members help you create initial drafts that you'll tidy up.

You can also go with user stories, which anyone can master. Search the internet for the best practices.

Overall, you need to choose a form of requirements documentation that you can handle, and that doesn't require special training. It will be a learning process. Your first requirements will likely be not very good. But take feedback from the team and improve them bit by bit. You'll get the hang of it in no time.

WHAT DOES IT MEAN TO ANALYZE REQUIREMENTS?

So, now you have documented a bunch of requirements that have come from different sources.

First of all, you need to review them all and ensure that they are aligned with the business needs of the client. Each requirement should be connected to a business case described in the project charter. Otherwise, you are planning to do something that project owners did not request. This is bad practice.

Second, you need to prioritize all requirements because your project has time, money, and scope constraints. When your plan goes beyond a constraint, the low-priority requirements should be the first to go. But you need to discuss all of this with project owners.

Third, you need to identify requirements provided by different stakeholders that contradict or conflict with each other. Keep in mind that stakeholders don't discuss requirements with each other. Therefore, you will have to resolve such conflicts.

You need to communicate or meet with all owners of contradictory demands. Then, act as in any case of conflict resolution, which we will discuss in the "How to Resolve Conflicts" chapter of the book. You can achieve the best results by collaborating and compromising. Forcing, avoiding, or smoothing the conflict in requirements usually backfires later.

Quite often, project managers are afraid to question the soundness of requirements because it always leads to a conflict with stakeholders. You need to be self-aware about such notions. You need to define all requirements and resolve all disputes. Otherwise, you'll simply delay the problem. It will appear later in any case.

HOW TO COLLECT REQUIREMENTS

Let me summarize all we have learned so far. Here are four things I want you to remember:

1. You will need to focus your efforts on managing processes to define requirements. You should act as a facilitator. Try not to get bogged down by writing specifications on your own. You should have a dedicated, trained, and experienced expert to do the work. Delegate these activities as much as possible. You need to stay at management level to see the whole picture.
2. Customers or sponsors will be interested in the project's success. So, they will be engaged in the process and motivated to provide all the information they can. Unfortunately, though, they might not have enough expertise to describe what they want in technical terms. In addition, they might not think through all the specific details. So, you need to use the right techniques and ask the right questions if they are going to provide you with business and stakeholder requirements.
3. Most key stakeholders will not provide you with requirements until you ask for them. They may know nothing about your project. They might be busy with other projects. So, you need to be proactive. Contact them as soon as possible. They may help you to define critical requirements before your planning is over. So, stakeholder management is a must. Remember, stakeholder = requirements.
4. Don't think about requirements only in terms of the product or service you need to create. You also need to consider requirements to the project management, processes of testing, getting sign-offs, rules of compliance, etc. Once you

finish working on the product itself, there might be dozens
of steps to take before it goes to the market or production
line.

In the long run, you need to strike a balance between rigid process
and no process at all.

CHAPTER 35
EXAMPLE OF GATHERING REQUIREMENTS

In general, I try to elaborate requirements bit by bit. We may work on several requirements at once. They'll still follow the same approach of a series of short meetings. I explained how this works in the previous chapter.

However, I also have to participate in several requirements-gathering events. So, I want to show you the other possible scenarios. The one below is a real story.

By the way, I'm sorry for missing out on the details, but I cannot share them due to a non-disclosure agreement (NDA). For a project manager, that's always the case. Everything you create as a part of the project is the intellectual property of the project owners.

But I can say it was a software project – a rather big one considering the fast-paced Scrum life cycle that we had. Our project owners were from a large enterprise organization and had all been in software development for many years already.

PHASE 1: WAITING FOR STAKEHOLDERS

There are many layers of stakeholders that provide requirements in the corporate world. However, product managers triage all the business needs for us. They are the champions of a product. They decide where the product's heading.

But, this time, the goal was to avoid redundant communications. So, in this case, we had to collect requirements directly from executives of a business unit that used our product.

First of all, we had to wait three weeks for an opportunity to communicate with that business unit. They had tight schedules and it was hard to find a window. That's the price of getting insights directly from executives.

I knew my project owners and their availability. That's why I had to plan this activity well in advance. Usually, I prepare for the next project while we work on the current one. So, we planned to have around five meetings spread over seven working days. We had to collect and clarify all the stakeholder requirements during this period.

PHASE 2: FOUR-HOUR MEETINGS

I have worked with many different clients from many different countries. All of them had different preferences. These stakeholders liked to solve problems in online meetings. But these could drag on for four hours, which was too much for us.

Moreover, there was a huge list of participants, including several business analysts, technical experts, some managers, and the executives. Not ideal.

So, what does it look like to collect requirements in the real world? Well, project owners just speak and share their thoughts. They don't give you "requirements" or "specifications." Instead, they describe what their problems are. In addition, they use business jargon and they get distracted easily.

This can therefore be a long drawn-out process. It's not worth recording such sessions – no one has time to review dozens of hours of footage. It's much more efficient to do it on the spot. That's why we try not to multitask and we remove all distractions. We focus on the conversation to capture requirements in the here and now.

The first requirements came from a slide deck. It was some wireframes. These explained a vision of the UI. Second, we got a bunch of stakeholder requirements in the form of:

"As an administrator, if I click here, I will see a chart ..."
"If I click on this chart, I want to see more details ... well, we are not sure in what format. You will need to come up with recommendations."
"On this screen, we should see all the information about this entity. Then, we can click on any chart to drill down further into details."

In most cases, you can't take these down as is. You need to convert them into solution requirements. Moreover, they don't cover all use cases. They are focused only on the primary case that covers a pain point or a need.

Again, business stakeholders may not understand the risks of unclear requirements. And, frankly speaking, they don't care. So, instead, they hire a whole team of experts to implement what they need into a product. It's your responsibility to lead them through a structured process – which brings me on to Phase 3.

PHASE 3: REQUIREMENTS SPECIFICATION

Keep in mind that the stakeholders had committed to helping us only for the next seven days and a certain number of hours. After that, the business unit would go on with its priorities and we could expect only sporadic involvement and communication in emails.

Usually, stakeholders think they have provided exhaustive requirements during the meeting. But the devil is in the details. Once you start digging into these requests, you will find many inconsistencies, questions, and challenges. That's precisely why we planned more touchpoints.

So, we had a half-day meeting to listen and collect high-level information. Then, we had half a day to specify what we had heard. First of all, we needed to create a structure for the requirements. We work with Scrum, so we used epics, features, and user stories. At this point, we created placeholder user stories with just a title and a few notes on what should be inside.

Second, our business analyst started to draft acceptance criteria for those user stories. This was only preliminary, but it helped to identify all unclear or conflicting requirements.

Third, we needed to provide a list of questions and discussion points to structure future meetings and run them efficiently.

Finally, we needed to check the technical feasibility, at least on a high level. We needed to identify the limitations of existing solutions. So, during this phase, many SMEs brainstormed as follows:

- Business analysts tried to break down and structure requirements.
- Technical experts came up with quick proofs of concepts.
- Designers tried to visualize the elements on a conceptual level.

PHASE 4: QUESTIONS AND ANSWERS

The vision in the stakeholder's head is usually different from what we understand. Therefore, it is important to reframe the business needs in terms of an actual tangible product. During these meetings, we showed the sketches and designs that we had created. It helped us provide better context for the questions and issues we discussed.

The worst-case scenario is to hear something like, "We didn't think about it. We don't know." Sometimes this may mean that we need to revisit the fundamental concepts behind the business need. Sometimes it means that we need another four hours to discuss it.

This time we even had to have two Q&A sessions in parallel. This way, we could focus on different aspects of the requirements in more detail.

Phases 2–4 iterated several times during the following six days. Did the work on collecting stakeholder requirements finish here? No, not even close! After these several days of intense work, we developed our own champions for the business need. Finally, our business analysts and designers had enough information to put themselves in the shoes of that business unit. They imagined the pain points and could specify requirements further without the participation of all the executives.

So, we would get in touch with the business unit several times more. But, only on some critical topics or decisions. Later in the process, product managers (not the business unit) had to read through all the specifications and acceptance criteria to verify and approve changes to the product.

PHASE 5: SOLUTION REQUIREMENTS

Another interesting fact about this case:

We analyzed all the requirements and available solutions. In the end, we concluded that it was much more cost-efficient to use a ready-made solution from a third party.

Therefore, we had to hand off this project to another team, including all the work we had done on specifying the requirements. Why? Well, for the good of the client and his business. It paid off later.

That's why it's also essential to keep requirements in good shape. There's a possibility that you'll have to give them to another team or outsource them to a vendor. If you do it well in the first place, creating a statement of work for a vendor is just a copy and paste job.

As you can see, processes in project management can have different forms. Quite often, they can be messy and unstructured. You work with real people. Some of them are busy and influential. You need to adjust to their style of work. Still, you need to explain their role in the process and let them provide the business requirements while the project team comes up with a solution.

You can scale this example either up or down. Imagine that you work with a single person. The rest of the process would stay the same:

1. The project owner describes a business need and high-level stakeholder requirements.
2. You and the project team develop possible solutions.
3. You discuss the solutions and details with the project owner.
4. The team writes detailed requirements.
5. The project owner approves the requirements, and you start planning how to implement them.

CHAPTER 36
MAKE QUALITY A PART OF PROJECT SCOPE

Project requirements and quality management are closely related. That's why you need to think about quality when you specify requirements. But, first, let's look at the definition of quality: "Quality is the level at which a product, service, or result corresponds to the requirements."

In other words, the project results should be as close to the requirements as possible. But requirements change during the process. So, you need to ensure that you comply with the latest approved version of the requirements.

This alone is not a sufficient definition. What if we complied with requirements but the product still had defects that rendered it useless? Quality also means there should be no defects.

A defect is a flaw that is not expected by the requirements. I imagine you're thinking, *"Where do these defects come from if you've met all the project requirements?"*

First, requirements are never perfect, nor do they cover all possible use cases or combinations of actions, states, and transitions. So, there will always be "grey areas" within requirements. In such cases, you'll debate whether a defect is actually a defect. Here's a rule of thumb: The fewer use cases that encounter the defect, the less severe it is.

Usually, this means that only a small percentage of end users will ever encounter this defect.

You need to educate your project stakeholders that this is part of the normal flow of any project. Then, you simply need to allocate enough time and effort to clean up such defects.

Second, there is no way you can ensure that a product is completely free of defects in practice. So, there should be an explicit agreement from the start on what kind of defects you should spend time, money, and effort putting right. Be realistic when agreeing upon the level of quality required.

It's good practice to define the severity levels of a defect to show how critical it might be to the outcome of a project – for example, low, medium, high, critical, showstopper. Of course, you can tolerate several low defects. But you can't send the product to the market with lots of high-severity defects. Moreover, you should fix critical and showstopper defects as soon as possible.

But, still, this is not an exhaustive definition of quality. We can create a product that will correspond to the requirements and have little to no defects. But that doesn't mean it will make the customer happy. So, a quality product, service, or result should always meet customers' and stakeholders' expectations. You can extend this definition further. A quality product, service, or result should be desired by the end users. What's the value of a perfect product or service if no one wants to use it? In the long run, end users are also stakeholders.

Last but not least, the grade of your product or service should fulfill the brief. Not every mobile phone should be an iPhone. Not every building should be a palace. The product can be ugly but functional and without defects. It may be cheap; still, it meets the demands of the market and corresponds to the requirements.

So, there will be results of low grade but high quality. And you need to respect the grade that project owners require.

DO I NEED TOTAL QUALITY?

Our goal is to create a product that is 100% aligned with requirements and has no defects. In addition, all stakeholders should be happy. But, unfortunately, this is often impossible. Or too expensive.

If you're developing a mobile app, you don't need total quality. But, on the other hand, if you are building software for a space shuttle and people's lives are at stake, you'll need to put more effort into fixing all possible defects. If you ever need total quality, you'll know about it right from the start.

In the real world, there's always a margin for error. You need to correspond to the requirements to a certain extent. However, there should be no critical defects that impact user experience. But where do you draw the line?

Well, that's not up to you but the project owners. It falls within the constraints of scope, time, and budget, as always. And how can you help them make the decision? By explaining the cost of quality.

THE COST OF QUALITY CONCEPT

In essence, you can pay in advance for quality when developing a product or service. Or you can pay later when you have finished the development and discovered defects and related problems.

So, there are two main types of quality costs: Cost of conformance (building a quality product) and cost of non-conformance (dealing with consequences of a poor-quality product).[1]

COSTS OF CONFORMANCE

These include:

1. Prevention costs (quality assurance)

- Proper requirements documentation
- Adequate training and skills
- Required equipment
- Enough time to do it right

2. Appraisal costs (quality control)

- Testing the results
- Inspections and audits of quality
- Destructive testing losses

COSTS OF NONCONFORMANCE

These include:
1. Internal failure costs (found by your team)

- Rework
- Scrap
- Fixing defects

2. External failure costs (found by end users)

- Liabilities
- Warranty work
- Lawsuits
- Lost business

As you can see, some of these activities are dedicated processes in project management. So, it's the work your team will do as a part of the project scope.

Your goal is to answer one question: Is it better to prevent defects or to find and fix them? For many years, the International Standardization Organization has advocated for prevention. It's cheaper to build a quality product from the start. That's why we discuss project scope management in such detail.

Nevertheless, in the real world, you'll combine the best practices from both approaches.

TAKEAWAYS

I will pause here for now. We'll talk more about quality management in the following chapters. Regarding quality and requirements, I want you to remember the following:

- It's cheaper to build a quality product rather than fixing the consequences of a poor-quality one.
- To build a quality product, you need well-defined requirements. Such requirements require proper skills (a professional business analyst) and enough time.
- Don't assume that project owners understand these concepts. You need to educate them about the cost of quality. Ideally, you need to come up with some examples or calculations relevant to your project, industry, or niche.

CHAPTER 37
REQUIREMENTS TRACEABILITY MATRIX

The requirements traceability matrix (RTM) is a document that maps requirements with other aspects of a project like business objectives, specifications, test cases, etc.

This may not be the most interesting aspect of project management but, before skipping this chapter, take note that the RTM is a powerful tool. It provides a link between project objectives, requirements, and scope of work. So, please don't use it simply to organize requirements. Instead, let it help you manage the project as a cohesive whole.

WHAT SHOULD YOU INCLUDE IN THE RTM?

Usually, the RTM is a spreadsheet. Let's review the contents. As always, you can add or omit some of the columns. And, then, I'll explain how you can use the matrix.

UNIQUE ID FOR A REQUIREMENT

First of all, we have a unique ID number for a requirement. In most cases, that's all you need.

Requirements can be broken down into smaller pieces. Therefore, you may add an "associated ID" column. In agile terms, think of it as epics and features. Or features and user stories. Or simply as main and sub-requirements.

SHORT DESCRIPTION

In the next column, give a short description of the requirement.

Don't put the full specification here. Instead, be descriptive. But be sure to be consistent with the way project owners named the feature, the title of specification, and any other related documents.

PROJECT OBJECTIVE AND STAKEHOLDER REQUIREMENT

These two columns work hand in hand.

First, we have the project objective. Ideally, you take it from the project charter. If not, you need to identify two or three measurable project objectives.

Second, we have stakeholder requirements as discussed in the previous chapters. This should be a short description that justifies the solution requirement.

They look the same. But, you'll have just a few project objectives (one, two, maybe three), yet many stakeholder requirements to reach each one.

NAME OF REQUESTER

I didn't find this column in the RTM examples I saw on the internet. But, I do recommend adding who asked for each requirement. Also, for bigger projects, you may want to have the name of a person and a department. I'll explain why you need it below.

WBS ELEMENTS, SPECIFICATIONS, DESIGNS

Then, we have a column for the WBS deliverable.

This is just the WBS element index in which the project team will implement the requirement. Usually, you fill it in after you've created a WBS.

Next, we can have columns with links to specifications and visual designs.

TEST CASES

Last but not least, we need to list related test cases. I recommend listing user acceptance test (UAT) cases or business validation test (BVT) cases. I don't think you need to list all functional test cases.

I see many examples in which people put just IDs here. But a modern project manager should link to the test cases or test suites in their test management tool or a spreadsheet.

EXTEND YOUR RTM WITH ADDITIONAL COLUMNS

Above, I've outlined the minimum information needed for a viable RTM. Feel free to extend it to meet your needs. In addition, you can map these requirements to any other aspects of the project.

I often see the **status** of a requirement and the **date of status change**.

You can add the **priority** of a requirement.

You can list the **non-functional requirements** here as well.

You can do the **release planning** here and map **releases** or **sprints**. Be creative.

HOW TO USE AN RTM

So, how do we use all of this information?

There's no point in having this fancy document if you don't use it to discover and analyze opportunities, risks, and conflicts.

1. PRIORITIZING REQUIREMENTS ON A HIGHER LEVEL

First of all, let's imagine a project with many requirements collected from different sources. And we have a limited budget.

So, we'll use the RTM to select the most critical requirements that we need to implement. This way, we can get the most from our resources and produce something that users really need.

Alternatively, we have a product that we develop continuously through several projects. Therefore, we update the list of requirements all the time. This matrix will help us to form the scope for the next project.

2. AVOID GOLD PLATING

We need to fill in the stakeholder requirement and project objective columns for each requirement. Some may not be justified.

We defer or remove these requirements because they don't bring us any closer to the current project's goal.

3. TRIAGE PROJECT SCOPE

Remember that, if a requirement doesn't support a project objective, it shouldn't be a part of that project. With project objective and stakeholder requirement columns, we can quickly triage the project scope.

4. ANALYZE THE REQUESTER

Next, let's review the connection between a requirement and its source.

First of all, you can get conflicting requirements. For example, one stakeholder will ask for a blue button on a white background. Another one will request a red button on a green background.

These stakeholders may never agree. They probably don't even know about the requirements of each other. So, you need to reach out to them to resolve the conflict. Or you can see who has more authority.

But, again, we might have a short deadline or a small budget. And different stakeholders will prioritize different requirements, but only one is possible. So, we can check whether a requirement was provided by a client/sponsor or a technical stakeholder.

At the very least, we can initiate negotiations to select one of the requirements.

5. KEEP STAKEHOLDERS ON THE SAME PAGE

RTMs also help with stakeholder integration.

Different stakeholders have different areas of expertise. Sometimes, clients are unaware of the technical needs of the project. As a result, they don't understand that they need to allocate the necessary time and budget.

So, an RTM provides transparency to all key stakeholders and their areas of responsibility.

6. AVOID SCOPE CREEP

There's a connection between a requirement and a WBS element. On the one hand, by connecting these dots, you'll ensure that you don't forget to implement some requirements. There's a saying: "What is not in the WBS is not a part of the project."

On the other hand, there won't be scope creep. Why? The project team will see that a work package or a deliverable includes a specific set of requirements. So, they'll need to ensure that any tangible results correspond to these requirements.

In addition, all stakeholders will know which deliverable to wait for, and how long they'll have to wait, if they want to test a specific piece of functionality.

7. CONTROL THE REQUIREMENTS DEFINITION PROCESS

First and foremost, having reference to specifications and designs is convenient. But it also shows you the progress on defining requirements. Are you in good shape to start the project? Do you have all the requirements? Are the designs ready?

You can color-code the cells to depict the status of a specification or design.

8. ENSURE TEST CASES COVERAGE

Now, think about having test cases in the same document.

First, it shows the coverage. Second, the project team can use this information to ensure that the product meets requirements and passes the test cases. You'll get fewer defects in the process.

9. RTMS WILL HELP YOU VALIDATE SCOPE

After the requirements definition, the RTM becomes your tool for tracking progress on the scope baseline. You'll provide deliverables and get acceptance from the client on each and every requirement.

For example, performed test cases might be a prerequisite for getting a sign-off.

As you know, it's better to get acceptance during the implementation rather than at the end of the project.

WHEN TO USE RTMS

RTMs take a lot of effort. So, I would recommend using them mainly on medium and large projects, or if you have a small team working over a long period.

In practice, you'll refer to the document several times per week throughout a project. After that, it will help you verify that you delivered on the scope requested by the project owners.

CHAPTER 38
PROJECT SCOPE STATEMENT

So far, you have collected lots of solution requirements. Then, you logged those requirements in the RTM or your project management software. Some requirements are fully specified, some are in progress, others are only a high-level draft. Overall, you have a clear understanding of what you should deliver. Now, you need to identify tangible results based on those requirements.

Unfortunately, there's no standard way to do this. First, you need to analyze a typical project life cycle and identify common deliverables in your industry. Then, you can search the internet or ask your colleagues. It shouldn't be hard to find similar deliverables. Nevertheless, each industry and niche will have specific deliverables. For example:

- In software development, the main deliverable is an application. Additionally, you may need to create a user manual, training videos, architecture documentation, etc.
- The primary deliverable for an infrastructure project is often creating and setting up network hardware.
- On a construction project, your main deliverables will be an engineering plan, a construction site, the building itself, and installing facilities.

After that, you should check the project charter. Usually, it includes expected deliverables, like the product or service you need to create, plus any supporting materials and documents. Likewise, there will be project management deliverables you need to provide.

However, don't assume that stakeholders understand typical deliverables in the same way. You need to spell out what is and is not a part of the project. You need to explain in great detail what each deliverable will look like.

For example, in software development, all interim deliverables are actually just a new version of the application that includes more and more functionality from the project scope. Then, finally, you have a version with all implemented requirements that goes to the market.

But the final deliverable includes additional work. The final version of the application, for example, should be made available on the App Store or Google Play. This requires extra effort to write descriptions and create icons for the app's page. We'll have to wait for a week or two to get through Apple's approval process. We may get rejected from the store. Then, we need to address their findings. All of those are tasks that someone needs to perform. It takes time.

Moreover, take a look at any application you use on your Mac or PC. Do you see the help menu with all those manuals and additional information? Do you need to create those documents as a part of your project?

So, through conversations with your project owners, project team, and SMEs, you need to discover exactly what they want as a result of the project.

It might seem complicated and confusing if you are new to the industry. But, with some experience, deliverables become obvious and you focus only on the details. Moreover, there are not that many typical deliverables within each industry.

Keep in mind that project owners don't have ultimate knowledge and expertise of your industry or project management. They most likely didn't participate in all the activities we have discussed so far. They won't have seen the information from a project charter transformed into requirements, which took the form of several deliverables to implement those requirements. Unfortunately, there's no transparent way for project owners to track these transformations.

So, at this point, you need to make your project owners understand what the project team needs to do and what they'll produce as a result. Then, you need to explain how difficult this will be. Moreover, you may need to explain the project and product life cycles. It's critical that you work with project owners who are inexperienced in your niche.

Based on this information, project owners need to approve the scope of work and major deliverables. Finally, you agree that you'll create a project plan to do all the required work. The project scope statement helps you to do this.

WHAT IS A PROJECT SCOPE STATEMENT?

A project scope statement is a narrative description of a product and project scope. We use it to ensure that project owners and other stakeholders understand the scope of work for the project. Moreover, we want to ensure that all key stakeholders are on the same page.

So, what's the secret here? I believe you need to use terms and language that all stakeholders understand. This document is mainly for the project owners, so here's what you need to include.

1. JUSTIFICATION OF A PROJECT

This briefly describes the needs of the business. Don't copy an entire business case here. Keep it short. If you haven't yet discussed this, make the best assumption that you can. Then, you can validate or adjust it when you show it to project owners.

2. PRODUCT SCOPE

This section describes the characteristics, traits, and functionality of the product or service you will produce.

Keep in mind that you collected requirements from different stakeholders. So, do not assume that they keep track of each requirement on your list. Also, usually, it's not clear how much work is required to deliver a requirement. So, it's the primary place to align the expectations of key stakeholders.

You need to show the amount and complexity of the work needed to meet different requirements. Therefore, this section requires the most effort. Put your writer's hat on because you need to be descriptive, and not just enumerate features and capabilities.

But, again, it should be a summary of the main features that take up most of the project's resources. You don't need to copy all requirements from the RTM here.

3. ACCEPTANCE CRITERIA

These outline the conditions that must be met before project owners accept project deliverables.

For example, you can include an acceptable number and type of defects here. Or you'll state that you need to pass all test cases through user acceptance testing. Likewise, you may have specific performance characteristics that you need to achieve. Again, you'll know if you have such requirements. They come either from the company's policies or directly from project owners.

Otherwise, describe the process of accepting interim deliverables, collecting feedback, and allocating time reserves to address these changes.

4. DELIVERABLES

List everything your project will produce – for example, the product or service itself, project documentation (WBS, list of risks, etc.), product manuals, educational materials. Project owners may also need interim deliverables for demonstration purposes.

Here you should state all the tangible results you need to hand off during the project. Project owners should agree that, once you have done so, they'll give a final sign-off to finish the project.

5. PROJECT EXCLUSIONS

Here you need to specify what falls outside of the project scope.

Quite often, some stakeholders want something specific. The others do not support it. Once this conflict is resolved, and everyone agrees to remove a requirement from the project scope, add it to this section.

Be specific and very clear about this. It saves time in the future. Firstly, you won't have to revisit these project exclusions again. Stakeholders may try to include them later during project execution. However, you should not waste time reviewing exclusions unless something dramatically changes.

Secondly, unless it's clearly stated, someone may still expect that you will deliver it. Don't underestimate people's ability to miss critical information. Overall, this will make it easier to hand off the project at the end.

6. CONSTRAINTS

Project constraints stated in the project charter could have come out of nowhere. They might be the numbers that people imagined during pre-sales bargains with zero research or justification.

In any case, you don't simply copy and paste them here. You need to establish whether it's feasible to deliver the scope within the constraints. Or you need to adjust the constraints based on your feasibility assessment. However, you do need to negotiate this change in advance.

If the constraints of time and budget are set in stone, then it's possible to justify a reduction of the project scope.

In addition to that, you may discover other constraints as well. Anything that limits your ability to deliver the product efficiently should be stated here.

7. ASSUMPTIONS

Assumptions are uncertainties that no one can clarify at the time.

You need to accept some of them during planning. However, if an assumption proves invalid, you have the right to modify the project plan.

Like with constraints, you don't just copy them from the charter. At this stage, you should have a long list of assumptions from defining requirements. In addition, you elaborated on the high-level assumptions as well.

HOW TO USE A PROJECT SCOPE STATEMENT

I want you to understand that a scope statement is just an agreement to proceed with the project within certain boundaries. It doesn't mean that you or the project owners cannot change things. Most likely, you will adjust the scope statement several times during planning as you discover more and more details.

Treat it as a short-term agreement not to change the requirements and scope of work until you finish project planning. It works as a soft restriction on requesting changes without proper consideration. And it's an agreement to integrate changes properly during project execution.

Likewise, it's an agreement on the project's most important constraints. For example, do we need to deliver the whole scope regardless of the budget? Or are we short on funds and needing to implement the most valuable requirements? If you see that clients believe that all constraints are immutable, that's a risk. You need to start managing their expectations right away. Also, notify your management about these potential risks.

So, it's a checkpoint before you start working out details of the project management plan.

CHAPTER 39
WORK BREAKDOWN STRUCTURE

You've had your project scope statement approved. Next, you need to take the major deliverables listed and put them into the Work Breakdown Structure (WBS). This is your starting point to identifying 100% of the project scope of work.

Here's the *PMBOK Guide* definition of the WBS[1]:

"Is a hierarchical decomposition of the total scope of work to be carried out by the project team to accomplish the project objectives and create the required deliverables."

Put simply, the WBS is a tool to organize and break down project scope into smaller pieces. At the very top, you have your product. Then, you have your main deliverables. Finally, you'll have smaller pieces of these major deliverables.

On any project management software, the list of tasks on the left-hand side is a WBS. However, you can organize any productivity tool to use the same concepts.

WHAT IS A WBS?

Most of the time, it will take the form of a hierarchical list like this:

1. Product
1.1 Deliverable #1
1.1.1 Work package
1.1.2 Work package
1.1.3 Work package
1.1.4 Work package
1.2. Deliverable #2
1.2.1 Work package
1.2.2 Work package
1.3. Deliverable #3
1.3.1 Work package
1.3.2 Work package
1.3.3 Work package
1.3.4 Work package
1.3.5 Work package

If you don't have project management software, you can easily create a WBS in any text editor.

Next, you can represent the same information as a hierarchical diagram visualizing your project breakdown. You can use this daily to communicate project status to your team by simply pointing to the required deliverable. For example, it'll be easier to show your expectations when you set goals for the next reporting period.

Last but not least, you can put it all into a spreadsheet. Then, you can add more columns like description, acceptance criteria, total cost, total duration, associated risks, etc. That will become your WBS dictionary. It will contain all the information about each deliverable.

BENEFITS OF USING A WBS

Why is the WBS so important? From the top of my head, here's a short list of benefits. It:

1. defines project scope;

2. defines a structure for project integration;
3. provides a foundation for estimation of resources, duration, and costs;
4. provides proof of needed resources, time, and budget;
5. helps to prevent scope creep;
6. helps to integrate changes;
7. focuses the team on what needs to be done;
8. helps to identify risks;
9. provides context for any discussion;
10. assists with managing stakeholders' expectations;
11. helps to prevent changes;
12. facilitates cooperation;
13. gets team buy-in;
14. provides ownership of a piece of the project;
15. shows the impact of each team member;
16. gives a holistic view of the role of team members in the project;
17. offers an opportunity for initial team building;
18. helps with project closure;
19. tracks project progress; and
20. acts as an accounting tool.

In theory, a WBS is an input for most project management processes like cost estimation, schedule development, risk identification, etc. It's a foundation for all communications with stakeholders. In addition, a WBS gives a framework for monitoring and controlling processes. And this list goes on and on.

You should take my word for it. If you want to finish a project on time and within budget, you need to double down on identifying the project scope – specifically, creating a quality WBS.

VALUE MANAGEMENT WITH A WBS

Based on my experience, I know of another benefit. A WBS gives you a structured way to deliver value to project owners. What does that mean?

Imagine that your project finishes abruptly within a day or a week. How can you tell how much value have you created? Can project owners send your product or service to the market as it stands? Can they get profit or any other benefits from the partial results you've provided?

Let's say you were tasked with delivering 10 different features and you start working on all of them at once but don't finish any. A feature which is 90% completed is worth nothing. So, you'll have a product that does nothing, and which you can't put on the market.

Imagine another scenario whereby you were finishing deliverables one by one and you completed five of them before the project was terminated. Imagine Facebook, but without Messenger or the ability to share videos. The other functionality works as expected, so it's a serviceable and valuable product.

In the real world, projects often experience problems when they are close to completion. Priorities change, budget runs out, a pandemic starts, and you need to wrap up the work quickly. But we manage projects as if all work is equally important. We think we should do it anyway, so it doesn't matter what we do first. As a result, we spent 80% of the planned resources and created zero value.

Even if you have never experienced such cases before, a WBS organizes the work to maximize value for the project owners. A structured approach makes controlling the project and stakeholders' engagement easier. In addition, you'll always have something to demonstrate your progress. Consequently, you can always demonstrate that your efforts led to a clearly defined result.

Keeping this in mind will instantly make you a better project manager.

1. DELIVERABLE-ORIENTED STRUCTURE

A WBS consists of deliverables. A deliverable is a tangible part of the work created by the project team to meet project objectives. Again, it can be a part of the product or service that stakeholders can test or see. Or it can be a project document or a part of the project management plan. In any case, it is something important that we need to finish our project.

Therefore, a WBS breaks down project results into tangible and finished pieces of the project scope. Adding all these pieces together should provide you with the final product, service, or results of the project.

2. DECOMPOSITION

Decomposition is a planning technique that helps divide and group the project scope and deliverables into smaller, manageable components that support your executing, monitoring, and controlling needs.

It's what you do to break down the project into smaller pieces: product/service/results → deliverables → work packages → tasks.

At the top of a WBS, there's always your product, service, or result.

On the second level, there will be major deliverables from the project charter and scope statement. Therefore, you always have at least two levels in a WBS.

On the third level, you may have either sub-deliverables or work packages.

However, a WBS is scalable to any extent. If your project is large and complex, you can start decomposition from project phases. Each phase can have a separate WBS. Likewise, you can have a portfolio, program, project, or sub-projects WBS. They all follow the same set of rules.

3. WORK PACKAGE

A work package is a small piece of a large deliverable. So, it's the result of further decomposition of a deliverable. But keep in mind, it's still a tangible and verifiable piece of work.

A work package is the lowest level of decomposition in the WBS. However, in project management software, you'll break down work packages into tasks in the same place.

My rule of thumb is to break down deliverables until a work

package fits into a reporting period – usually, one or two weeks of work.

4. PRODUCT SCOPE VS. PROJECT SCOPE

At the top of the structure, there's always the final product or result. It should represent the vision of the full scope of the project.

And, here, you need to understand the difference between project scope and product scope.

Product scope is all about features and functions that a product, service, or result should have. It defines how a product should work, what it should look like, what traits it will have. It's all about the product and its functionality.

Project scope is the work performed to create a product, service, or result with specified features and functions described by the product scope. But it's not only the work to develop the product or result. It should include efforts to analyze and research product requirements, plan the project, acquire a team, assure quality, get the product to the end users, etc. So, it includes all the work required to reach the project objectives. That's why it sits at the top of the WBS.

Next, let's talk about how to create an efficient and effective WBS.

CHAPTER 40
HOW TO CREATE A
QUALITY WBS

Here are the two most common reasons why a project fails:

1. Absence of a WBS.
2. Presence of a poorly created WBS.

Creating a poor WBS is as harmful as not having one. So, let me explain how to create a high-quality WBS. It will help you finish your project successfully.

Here's a ground rule: You should never create a WBS on your own. No matter what tools and techniques you choose, you must involve your team. After all, they are the people who will do the work.

You can create a high-level draft by moving deliverables from the scope statement and adding other things that you know. But, after that, the project team should participate in decomposition. You need to use meetings, brainstorming, and interviews.

It's a good idea to interview the most experienced SMEs and project managers to collect insights on the major deliverables. They can also suggest the best approach to break them down further. Moreover, they can provide valuable inputs on "hidden" pieces of scope that you didn't know about. Remember, you need to identify 100% of the project work.

Also, consider the internal stakeholders. They may impose additional deliverables on your project – for example, a particular report, regular meetings, or formal policy compliance.

Then, you'll have meetings with your team to discuss how to decompose the main deliverables into smaller pieces. The main questions should be, "What does it take to create this deliverable?" and, "How can we break it down into smaller pieces of work? For example, no more than a week per work package?" Finally, brainstorm what you might have missed and what is needed to complete each deliverable.

After that, you can get back to interviews with SMEs to review and validate the elements for the WBS.

KEY PRINCIPLES

Keep in mind that these principles are universal to any decomposition of work, and not just a WBS. For example, you can apply them when breaking down epics and features into user stories in Scrum.

I understand that you can't keep all these principles in your head. That's why I've sorted them in the order of the biggest impact. If you can remember and implement at least the first five principles, you should be fine.

#1. WBS elements should be defined using nouns and adjectives – not verbs.

This one is huge. If you implement only this rule, your WBS will still be twice as good. You see, nouns and adjectives describe the result – something we want to achieve. Verbs describe a process. It is hard to say when a process is fully finished and provides the desired outcome.

Let's review these titles of deliverables. "Product design creation" describes how something came to be. "Approved product design" is a tangible result, representing what you need to produce as the result of your effort. Also, it implies that you may have additional work to get an approval.

#2. A quality WBS includes internal, external, and interim deliverables.

Do you want to deliver the project successfully? Then, do not ignore your internal needs. Producing internal and interim deliverables is a part of the project life cycle. It takes time and money. Include it in the project scope.

For example, every time you need to present a deliverable externally, it needs polishing – at least a bit. You don't want your project owners to encounter defects during a vital demonstration to shareholders. That means you need to do some testing and fix all critical defects.

#3. A quality WBS includes project management deliverables: A WBS, project management plan, risk register, etc., which all take time!

Even if stakeholders don't ask for them, you need these tools to manage the project. They will require efforts from your team, not just you. So, as I said in the previous point, your WBS should include all internal deliverables.

#4. A quality WBS factors in the work to make the smaller pieces into a whole

I often see this problem, especially in software development: The main deliverable is decomposed nicely into separate work packages. They describe all the pieces that are needed. But no WBS element represents how these interim deliverables will be integrated into the finished product. Don't make the same mistake!

#5. A WBS is not a one-time endeavor.

You will progressively elaborate your WBS because you learn more about deliverables when you start working on them. You will break down the work further and clarify work packages.

However, be careful. Progressive elaboration and rolling wave planning techniques do not mean omitting parts of the scope that are unclear. On the contrary, you should add all deliverables to the WBS even if you do not know all the details.

#6. To identify 100% of the project scope, you need to include those who will perform the work.

You should also collect feedback and input from SMEs; technical, financial, and business managers; and other stakeholders.

#7. A quality WBS should contain just enough details for communicating all work – no more, no less.

Some typical deliverables may not require complete decomposition

– for example, a piece of standard hardware. Stating the model will be sufficient. On the other hand, you should describe unique deliverables in as much detail as is needed to communicate the required efforts.

#8. Match the size of your WBS elements to the level of your project.

Depending on the project complexity, you need to limit the size of a deliverable and a work package. They shouldn't be too small. Micromanagement is the last thing you need. Likewise, deliverables and work packages shouldn't be too large. Otherwise, you'll lose control of the project's progress.

The rule of thumb is to have work packages that take around a week for several team members to implement. A deliverable can take a month or two when all team members participate in different work packages. You can start with these sizes and adjust them to your needs.

#9. A quality WBS is a tool for communication.

It should clarify the work and project scope to all stakeholders (including the project team). Therefore, it should be simple and straightforward. Don't be too clever. You need to use terminology that project owners and stakeholders understand and use themselves. Moreover, everyone on the project should have access to the WBS.

#10. You should know how to deliver every work package.

Otherwise, there's uncertainty around the project scope.

If there are any ambiguities, you need to plan for design, research, and investigation of these as separate deliverables. If your project requires research and development (R&D) activities, you should plan them accordingly. Do not hide them within deliverables.

#11. A quality WBS has a coding system that clearly shows a position for each element in the hierarchy.

This applies to all representations. For example, 1.3.5 is work package #5 within deliverable #3.

It's impossible to overestimate the value of a WBS. It's such a vital tool in project management that I created a whole module dedicated to it in my Practical Project Management online course.

CHAPTER 41
HOW TO IDENTIFY TASKS

Now, I want to give a quick example of what you need to do to get from stakeholder requirements to actual tasks that your team will have to perform.

Let's assume that I'm managing a project to develop the pmbasics101.com website. It's actually my site, but let's assume someone else owns it and is giving me requirements. The project owner's name is Julie.

By the way, you can go to my site and check everything I describe below.

During one of the meetings, Julie provided me with the following (stakeholder) requirement: "We should have popups to collect emails and send out a PDF document as an incentive."

Maybe just like you, I don't have a clue what that means. So, first of all, I would do a quick search on the internet to get a basic understanding of these popups, how they work, and what they do. You can follow this process with me. Just google "popup on website" and review the first three search results.

I would ask my business analyst to do likewise. We are not taking much time yet, only about 30 to 60 minutes. We just need enough information to form a scope of work. Moreover, we don't have any solution requirements yet and these don't just miraculously appear –

the business analyst needs to write them out based on existing practices, products, and solutions, or invent a new solution.

We learned the following from our brief research:

- Common terminology of this niche, like "email service provider", forms to capture emails, incentives, automations that happen as the next step, etc.
- There are different best practices on how and when to collect emails for example, when a person visits a site or when they want to leave it. You can add a form to collect emails at the bottom of an article or in a sidebar.
- There are dozens of third parties that provide these services, which we can easily integrate into our site.

So, I come up with a rough action plan in my head that we can follow. Actually, I got it from one of the blog posts on this topic that I found during research:

1. Select an email service provider.
2. Create an account.
3. Design a form to collect emails.
4. Implement the designed form.
5. Integrate with a mailing service provider.
6. Upload the PDF document.
7. Activate the form.
8. Test the form.

However, this list of tasks is not enough. It doesn't show 100% of the scope of work. And, for sure, it's not a WBS. It is just a way to understand the scale of the stakeholder requirement at hand.

So, the business analyst will do some more research at this point. Then, he'll set up a meeting with the project owner to discuss possible solutions. As the result of this discussion, he will draft out several solution requirements:

"When a visitor decides to leave the site, a popup should appear based on the 'exit intent' technology. The popup will follow the design in this requirement (designed to be discussed later). It should happen only on blog posts of the site."

"On all blog posts, in the sidebar, there should be a button which you can click for the same popup."

"When a visitor adds their email and name to the form and clicks the subscribe button, we'll send them to a 'thank you' page containing further instructions."

"After they successfully subscribe, the visitor should get an email with a link to the incentive PDF."

This is just a draft version of functional requirements. They are not complete yet. The business analyst will describe them all in more detail. Likewise, there will be requirements for the mailing service provider. But, for the purpose of this example, we'll skip the requirements definition and get to the scope identification.

Based on the requirements and our research, I would come up with the following WBS. The email capture form will be one of the main deliverables, and it will have several work packages:

1.3 Email Capture Form
    1.3.1 Email Service Provider (ESP)
    1.3.2 Incentive PDF
    1.3.3 Integration with ESP
    1.3.4 Popup Form
    1.3.5 Incentive Email
    1.3.6 Thank You Page
    1.3.7 UAT Report

As you can see, there's nothing special here. First, I took the action items from the research and converted them into proper WBS elements. Then, I used the principles we discussed in the previous chapters. So, I described the elements with nouns. Moreover, I added a special work package – the user acceptance testing (UAT) report. This is a work package to ensure that everything works as a whole. The project owner and business analyst will finalize approved requirements with all designs required to implement this functionality in the next few days.

So, first, I would ask the team to review all of it. Then, we'll have a requirements review and scope identification meeting. Usually, it goes something like this.

Dmitriy: "Okay, we need to break all of these down into tasks. Let's start from the top. We have two main requirements for the email service provider. First, it should have this 'exit intent' capability, and it should cost under $90 per month".

John (business analyst): " Very well, I'll need to research competitors to see what people actually use. Then, I need to create a quick comparison report on features and prices for Julie [the project owner]. It will take some time to discuss it, and she needs to make a choice here. After that, she needs to create an account, pay for it, and give us the access. So, most probably, I need to record quick step-by-step instructions for her."

So, this is the list of tasks for the "1.3.1 Email Service Provider (ESP)" work package that we wrote down:

1. Competitor analysis.
2. Comparison report.
3. Approval on the selected ESP.
4. Create an instruction video to set up account.
5. Access to the activated ESP account.

Dmitriy: "Let's move on to the incentive PDF. There are no requirements here. We need to come up with a solution that the site owner will approve. Any ideas?"

Jane (content manager): "That's exciting! We have carte blanche! So, I would start by consulting a marketing expert in this area. Then, I would need to provide a list of options for vetting and get approval on the price. After that, we need to list possible options. We can put lots of different information into a PDF. But we need to decide on the strategy. So, coming up with a list of content ideas and lots of research.

After that, we'll create a draft of the text, and we need a beautiful design."

Dmitriy: "Uh-oh! That usually means coming up with several drafts. So, we actually need to create two or three versions to choose from. And let's make a note that we need a freelancer for graphic design."

Jane: "Yes, that's right. Creative staff – you know the drill. Let's make finding a graphic artist part of the first task as well. So, I'll approve them in bulk. And, yes, it will take some time to get it done. So, the last task would be to get an approval."

Boris (website developer): "Not so fast! There's a bit more to do here. We need to upload and store this file somewhere. So, I need a link. Otherwise, how do people get it from that MacBook of yours?"

Therefore, that's the list of tasks for the "1.3.2 Incentive PDF" work package that we wrote down as follows:

1. List of freelancers.
2. Budget approval.
3. List of content ideas.
4. Approved content idea.
5. Draft of the text.
6. Three versions of incentive PDF.
7. Approve version of incentive PDF.
8. Link to the incentive PDF.

Dmitriy: "Let's talk about integration."

Boris: "The issue here is that I will only know for sure once we get the approval on the ESP. They have different ways of integration. But I don't expect problems here. So, I'll need to review documentation, follow the instructions for integration, and test it. Do we want to get an email if there's an integration problem?"

Dmitriy: "No, I think that's overkill. They guarantee 99% uptime."

Boris: "Then it should be easy. But I'm not testing the designs here, only that the integration works."

So, that's the list of tasks for the "1.3.3 Integration with ESP" work package:

1. Review documentation.
2. Implement integration.
3. Integration testing.

Dmitriy: "What do we have next? The popup form."

John: "In most ESPs, you can create this popup right inside the tool. You have an interface and everything. My granny could do it!"

Jane: "Yes, but who knows what Julie will actually want. We may need to make a custom version. So, we need a designer here as well. Now, if we look at it, we have lots of things to outsource here. I feel like it would be better to make it a separate work package. So, I would separate the selection and procurement parts."

Dmitriy: "Okay, let's do it. I'll put it as a separate work package. And, I'll move the related tasks from the incentive PDF work package to this new one. "

Jane: "Yes, that will work better."

So, we updated the WBS and added the "Approved Freelance Resources" work package:

1.3 Email Capture Form.
    1.3.1 Email Service Provider (ESP).
    1.3.2 Approved Freelance Resources.
    1.3.3 Incentive PDF.
    1.3.4 Integration with ESP.
    1.3.5 Popup Form.
    1.3.6 Incentive Email.
    1.3.7 Thank You Page.
    1.3.8 UAT Report.

Jane: "Let's rename the tasks and put the following: resource list, approved budget, and resource management plan. I'll need exact dates and estimates for all these people."

So, that's the list of tasks for the new "1.3.2 Approved Freelance Resources" work package:

1. List of required resources.
2. Approved budget for freelancers.
3. Freelancers resource management plan.

KEY TAKEAWAYS

At this stage, we have broken down the tasks as follows in our project management software:

1.3 Email Capture Form
  1.3.1 Email Service Provider (ESP)

- Competitor analysis.
- Comparison report.
- Sign-off on the selected ESP.
- Create an instruction video to setup account.
- Access to the activated ESP account.

1.3.2 Approved Freelance Resources

- List of required resources.
- Approved budget for freelancers.
- Freelancers resource management plan.

1.3.3 Incentive PDF

- List of content ideas.
- Approved content idea.

- Draft of the text.
- Three versions of incentive PDF.
- Approve version of incentive PDF.
- Link to the incentive PDF.

1.3.4 Integration with ESP

- Review documentation.
- Implement integration.
- Integration testing.

1.3.5 Popup Form
1.3.6 Incentive Email
1.3.7 Thank You Page
1.3.8 UAT Report

We followed the same pattern of discussion for the rest of the work packages. But, I think you get the point.

HAVING THE RIGHT EXPERTISE

As you can see, I didn't say much during the meeting. I simply structured it around the WBS elements we identified. The team members did the bulk of the work during the discussion. They are the experts – they should identify the work. It's my job as project manager to ask follow-up questions, share ideas, and clarify any of their points.

What should you do if you don't have a team or the required expertise?

First of all, it's a risk. Second, you need to hire someone with the relevant expertise, or at least get direction from them. In most cases, there'll be such people inside your organization. You just need to find them. If you can't find them, see if you can hire a consultant or a freelancer. I appreciate there are obvious risks and costs to this approach.

If there's no one to help you, and if you don't have the budget for a consultant, start digging around on the internet, ask your friends and colleagues, etc. However, if you don't have a technical background and hands-on technical experience, you should not break down the project work yourself.

CONSIDER THE ALTERNATIVES

It may seem like there's only one way to implement a requirement. But, in most cases, that's not true. You can and should try to think about alternative solutions. At the very least, you should consider whether it's possible to make it, buy it, or outsource it.

The main idea here is to play to the strengths and expertise of your project team and environment.

CHAPTER 42
KEEP YOUR LIST OF TASKS MANAGEABLE

Let's do a bit of math. Let's assume that you have a 6-month project. That's about 126 working days. You have a team of 10 people. If you follow my advice, each person will have a task with an average duration of 2 working days. That means you'll have (126/2) x 10 = 630 tasks to manage. In reality, it would be more like 800 when you add on addressing defects and supporting activities.

On the one hand, that's 800 tasks that you need to estimate, schedule, and budget for. You need to closely manage about 10 tasks per day for all team members. And you need to keep in mind the next 10–20 tasks. In addition to that, some of the tasks will have assigned risks, outstanding questions, defects, and impediments. Likewise, you'll be getting performance data, expenses, documentation, etc.

Can you see where I'm going with this? You need to keep track of dozens of entities on the project on a daily basis, in addition to all other activities.

With proper project management software, it should be manageable. But, if you have a team of 30 people, you multiply everything by 3 and things can start to become overwhelming. In this case, you have 2 options. First, delegate this tracking to your team leads. Second, you can increase the average size of a task to 3 or 4 days.

For the same reasons, I don't recommend going below 1 working day per task. It becomes a nightmare for the project schedule. You actually need to find software that allows you to plan by the hour. If you do need to be that granular, you can bundle up small tasks into a group for tracking purposes.

So, the rule of thumb is to keep the ratio tied to the reporting period. For example, if you report each week, then a work package should not take more than 5 working days for the team. Usually, just a part of the team can work on one work package. Therefore, you'll have up to a dozen tasks every couple of days. But you'll work on several work packages in parallel.

If you report each month and the project is long and complex, you can expand your work packages up to 20 working days. But, still, you want to keep approximately the same number of tasks. At the same time, I would not make a task longer than 5 working days. Keep in mind that the bigger a task, the greater the uncertainty.

These are just my observations from my own experience. I can't give you an exact formula here. Remember that you need to keep the project and all its entities manageable. On the one hand, they shouldn't be so small that you get tied up in red tape. On the other hand, they shouldn't be so large that you notice problems too late.

You have control over the size of work packages and tasks. You need to manage how they are broken down.

CHAPTER 43
SCOPE MANAGEMENT RESOURCES

As with risk management, there's a lot to digest. And, in the case of scope management, proper implementation of processes is even more critical for the project's success. That's why I've prepared another list of resources that can help you:

- A one-page cheat sheet on scope management.
- A scope management plan template that you can use on your project.
- A requirements traceability matrix template.
- A video explaining how to implement this approach in an agile environment.

You can access these supporting materials here:
https://itpmschool.com/materials

PART EIGHT
ESTIMATION OF TASKS

CHAPTER 44
HOW TO PRODUCE ACCURATE ESTIMATES

So far, we have moved from the top to the bottom. From the project objectives, we got the main deliverables. Then, we broke them down into smaller pieces. After that, we decomposed them further into small tasks.

Let's now back up. We'll estimate each task in terms of the following:

- The HR, materials, and tools we need.
- Dependencies between tasks.
- The time and money required.
- The risks related to these tasks.
- The risk response plans we'll implement.

As a result, we'll sum up the costs to create a project budget. Also, we'll line up tasks on a calendar to create a project schedule. Finally, you'll see all the tasks that comprise a work package and all the work packages that you need to produce a deliverable. That's how the bottom-up estimate works.

The bottom-up estimate is accurate because it's easier to assess clearly defined, small tasks, which means lower risk.

1. AN ACCURATE ESTIMATE TAKES TIME

It is important to understand that estimates take time to prepare. Therefore, if stakeholders ask you to provide an estimate on the spot, always reserve the right to correct it after consulting with your team.

In practice, there are three major types of estimates[1]:

Rough order of magnitude (ROM): This is done at the project initiation. The typical range is -25% to +75% from actual value. You can estimate the whole project in a day or a few hours.

Budget estimate: This is more accurate, at around -10% to +25% of actual value, which needs to be achieved during project planning. Your rolling wave planning falls within this range. You need several days to several weeks to develop such an estimate.

Definitive estimate: After continuously refining your estimates, you get to about -10% to +10% range of accuracy, which is required for any forthcoming deliverables that you have thoroughly planned.

To obtain such estimates, you need to go all the way from requirements to defining separate tasks. Overall, it takes weeks or months of work for the entire project team to get definitive estimates for the whole project. However, in practice, you never do it in one go but progressively throughout the whole project.

Keep in mind that these ranges are not standardized. Don't assume that project owners know and understand them. You must explain that you will refine your estimates as you go.

As a project manager, you need to understand that estimates are not a wild guess. The person estimating the task should analyze the requirements, task details, etc. Then they need to investigate possible solutions. Based on their previous experience, they should compare the task with similar ones and provide you with some numbers. You need to verify that they understand the tasks, their assumptions, and what they included in the estimate.

It should be a structured process that you facilitate. This process takes time. But, again, it's a part of the project.

2. ESTIMATES SHOULD BE DONE BY THE PERSON PERFORMING THE WORK

There are several possible scenarios when it comes to estimations:

1. You have a dedicated team that will do all the estimates.
2. You need to acquire a new team. A pre-allocated SME will help with estimates.
3. You need to acquire a new team but without a pre-allocated expert. You'll start estimating once you acquire the first few team members.
4. You work with freelancers, shifts, brigades, etc. So, you don't have a settled team.

In the first case, it's simple – you allocate tasks to specific people. They do the work while team leaders may help and verify all the estimates.

In all other cases, you will need to define roles with the required skills and level of experience first. Then, assuming average productivity for a role, you will produce the estimate. And, by 'you', I still mean an expert who knows the nature of the tasks in every detail and, moreover, knows the resources required to complete similar tasks.

There are several benefits in giving a say in the estimation process to the person who'll do the work:

1. Different people perform differently when doing different tasks. There is always something a person likes to do more. Assuming an average performance introduces serious errors and risks. That's why, once you get a real person to fulfill a role, you need to go over the task estimates for this person together.
2. When a person is involved in producing an estimate, they are more committed to meeting it. They make a promise to deliver a task on their terms, so there's no excuse.
3. People will uncover lots of new risks, misunderstandings, and gaps in requirements.

3. DEFINE THE NATURE OF EACH TASK

In practice, there are two ways to estimate tasks.

The first approach is to allocate a person, assess how long it will take, then calculate costs based on that person's rate and the duration of the task.

The second approach is to more abstract: You assess the effort required to finish a task in abstract person-days, decide how many people you will assign to it, then work out the duration from that.

So, to select the most efficient approach, you need to analyze the nature of the work package or deliverable. If there's a seamless transition from one task to the next within the work package and the tasks are similar, go for the second approach because it's the most efficient use of resources.

For example, in software development, all tasks are mostly the same in nature – coding. There's little transition time and effort from one task to another because everything is digital and stored in one repository. Moreover, you can do several tasks from one package in parallel most of the time. There are not many hard dependencies. It gives you lots of flexibility during planning. If you assign one person, it takes longer than if you appoint several. There's a law of diminishing returns, but you get the point.

However, in the construction industry, this won't work. You need to assign a role to a task, assess the duration, etc. There are transitions and waiting times that are longer than the execution of a specific task. Tasks have hard dependencies – that is, one relies on another being completed. You can't build a wall unless you have a foundation, for which you need concrete to be delivered and prepared, for example.

For sure, adding more people will complete each separate task a bit faster. But you still need to wait for the concrete to set before you can start building the wall. So, double the number of people won't necessarily mean going twice as fast. Your goal here is to come up with a realistic timeline for each task based on these dependencies. Be realistic about how efficiently you can use the resources at your disposal.

Conceptually, these approaches don't change anything. Instead, they simply give you the flexibility to optimize your schedule and resources.

4. THE MATH OF EFFORT

Effort is measured in person-days, i.e., a working day for one person. So, in theory, a task requiring 10 person-days will take 10 working days for one person, or one working day for 10 people. But, in reality, neither of those scenarios will ever play out.

It may sound trivial, but I can promise you that this leads to many misunderstandings. And you need to explain it to your stakeholders all the time. After all, you can't produce a baby in one month by assigning nine women to the task.

Imagine 10 people working on one small task in a day. Communication and coordination will reduce efficiency dramatically. Again, it's the law of diminishing returns.

At the other end of the spectrum, if 1 person is working on the task, 10 working days will be more like 12, 14, or more calendar days with weekends and holidays. This isn't taken into consideration when providing estimates of effort for a deliverable, so it might take much longer than the number of person-days divided by the number of team members. The effort is an estimation of complexity, not duration.

5. WHAT DAY IS IT?!

There are different ways to measure a "day" – working, calendar, effective. For example, a *working* day is eight hours for one person. But it will be a mistake to assume that an individual can work uninterrupted for eight hours in a row on a single task. There will be meetings, coffee breaks, etc.

How many hours can a person actually work on a task? Six, at most – though, even that is too much. I would aim for a maximum of five per day. You may track all the "distractions" separately as tasks. However, in practice, this adds a huge administration overhead.

So, at some point, you need to agree in what units you will provide estimates. Also, you need to know how they will convert from effort to duration based on *effective* working hours. For example, if a task needs 24 hours of work, will it take three or four calendar days to finish? Do you allocate eight or six hours per day to the task?

There is no standardized approach here. Every organization calculates estimates in a way that suits them best. Do not assume that your clients and stakeholders understand this.

You must communicate how you will calculate estimates to each team member and each stakeholder.

6. WHAT GOES INTO THE ESTIMATE?

This is also known as the "definition of done."

- What should a person do to ensure that a task is finished?
- Should he perform testing, update documentation, or log efforts into the task tracker before work is deemed complete?
- What part of the work do you expect him to do?
- When and how should he hand off his work to another team member?

You need to explain to each team member what is required in an estimate. Moreover, it should be consistent for all tasks on the project. In some cases, estimates can differ dramatically, depending on what goes in.

Additionally, you need to explain that risk is tracked separately. Sure, you can buffer estimates by 10%–15%, that's okay. But risks that can have a greater impact on the duration or cost should go separately in risk reserves.

7. BUFFERING VS. RISK MANAGEMENT

When preparing estimates, there is always some level of uncertainty. You make assumptions. You interpret requirements, and you have constraints. You can hide all these problems in your estimates. Or you can perform proper risk management.

The idea is simple. You need to analyze the estimates and strip away any uncertainty and fears from the actual work. So, first, you need to provide realistic estimates for the work you know how to deliver. Select the most probable scenario as a foundation. Then you need to transform uncertainties into risks and related risk reserves. Moreover, you need to keep them connected to a specific work package for tracking purposes.

This way, you can control your estimates on two levels: First, the accuracy of estimates of known work; second, how many identified risks happened and their impact. If risks happen systematically, you may need to revisit all the future tasks and adjust accordingly.

On the other hand, if you hide these risks in buffers, you won't be able to carry out this analysis.

8. THREE-POINT ESTIMATE FOR PERT ANALYSIS

For most projects, a one-point estimate is enough. The only challenge is performing proper risk management activities.

However, some industries and niches require PERT analysis, or advanced estimation and scheduling techniques. So, you may need to produce three-points estimates: optimistic, pessimistic, and most probable.

I believe that this is a case of crossing a bridge when you come to it. If you know that your industry uses three-point estimates, you need to invest time to take a course or training. For the rest, you can skip this for now. Learn advanced techniques when you feel a need for professional development. In practice, you may never use them.

CHAPTER 45
HOW TO COME UP WITH NUMBERS

Corwin is a project manager on a small software development project that is about six months long. His team doesn't use an agile approach. Instead, they follow the company's custom project management methodology. Therefore, Corwin planned everything using the rolling wave technique.

His team is working on two deliverables right now. They need to start the third and last one in about two weeks. This deliverable has not been estimated yet.

In the morning, Corwin received a note to say that project owners had provided a specification and he could proceed with analysis and estimation. As always, Corwin quickly scanned the document. Everything looked relatively simple.

Next, he pinged Peter, his team leader, to check who could handle this one. They agreed that John could do it. He's new to the team, and it will be a good first task for him. Corwin sends the email with the specification to John. Then he gets in touch via Skype:

> **Corwin:** "Hi, John. I have just sent you a specification. It describes a new feature we need to implement. I talked to Peter, and he wants you to take on this task. So, as usual, please analyze the document, decom-

pose the work and provide estimates. Please also write down any questions that you have."

John: "Hi Corwin. Got the email. It is a five pages document :)). It will take some time ... about four hours."

Corwin: "Okay, take your time. We will review them together. Let me know if you need my assistance. Thanks."

Later that day, Corwin got the estimates:

1. User interface – 1w 0.5d.

1.1 Implement navigation – 1d.

1.2 Update old controllers – 3d.

1.3 Implement the view #1 – 0.5d.

1.4 Implement the view #2 – 1d.

2. Database – 4w 1d.

2.1 Read out data – 1d.

2.2 Write data in new database – 1d.

2.3 Data conflict resolution – 3w.

2.4 Error handling – 4d.

3. Update Framework – 2w.

4. Testing and Bug Fixing – 0.5d.

5. Risks – 1w1d.

5.1 Performance problems might require refactoring – 1w.

5.2 Error handling is complex and may require fine tuning – 1d.

After a quick review, a few things catch Corwin's eye: three tasks – "1.2 Update old controllers," "2.3 Data conflict resolution," and "2.3 Data conflict resolution" – are too big. So, these tasks need to be broken down further. Moreover, they stand out from the estimate of other tasks. Usually, that means uncertainty.

It's much easier to discuss estimates face to face. You can lose some nuances when using emails and text messages. So, Corwin goes to John's workplace to speak in person:

Corwin: "Hello, John. How it's going?"

John: "Hi, Corwin. Everything is fine, thanks."

Corwin: "What do you think about the new feature?"

John: "Well, it's pretty straightforward, but some aspects are not entirely clear. As far as I can tell, I think users will like it!"

Corwin: "Great. Would you please walk me through your estimates? What is included in 'Update old controllers? It sounds like a lot of work ...'"

John: "Yes. Old code, a lot of places where we need to make changes. I heard that last time we tried to deal with this, it was a mess. We need to re-write it from scratch."

Corwin: "Okay, I see. But not this time, I'm afraid. We have a short deadline to finish development. So, we can expect trouble here. Let's keep it that way. How about putting it as a risk?"

John: "Yes, I think we can do that. But don't say I didn't warn you!"

Corwin: "Yeah. I'm not happy about it either. But try to do your best with what we have today. I hope we can improve it later. What's next? 'Read-Write' looks okay to me ... but what about the 'Conflict Resolution' line?"

John: "Well, the spec says nothing about it. And I see many use cases there. So, I expect we will find them all only during testing ... So, we will be pushing the task back and forth."

Corwin: "If we get you a detailed specification, how long will it take then?"

John: "I think, seven days ... maybe."

Corwin: "Okay, we need to get the updated specification before getting to this feature. It will save us our development effort, and we still have three weeks. I will handle it. But still, it's quite a lot of work. I think you need to decompose it further. We need checkpoints of your progress. You know, to see if things start to take more time."

John: "Okay, will do. But the full spec is a must here. The next one is also scary. We need to update the framework. I have not tried it yet. But you know it's that 'third-party thing.' It is always buggy."

Corwin: "Agree. Again, let's handle it as a risk. Let's assume that everything goes well. How long will it take?"

John: "One day, I think."

Corwin: "Okay, and what if everything goes horribly wrong?"

John: "Well, I think we can implement our own framework in about nine days."

Corwin: "Let's take one day to implement, one day to debug, and say it's a medium probability risk. With an impact of up to two weeks. I will talk with technical management; maybe they know more, and we are worrying too much. So, I'll assign Peter to monitor this risk."

John: "Sounds good to me."

Corwin: "Very well. Please update the estimates and send me the final version."

John: "Okay."

Corwin: "Thanks. See you later."

Corwin received the updated estimates. He added his own notes into the comments section. He always tries to remember details about estimates and decisions he made. As John is new, Corwin feels he needs to check with Peter (the team lead). So he goes straight to him.

Corwin: "Hey, Peter."

Peter: "Good to see you, boss!"

Corwin: "I need a few minutes of your precious time. Have you seen the estimates from John?"

Peter: "Yeah, we need to explain to him our standards – a deeper level of decomposition, tasks no more than two days, and more comments. Especially for risks. But in general, he did a good estimate."

Corwin: "Yes, exactly! And do tell him more about how to describe all the problems. We should not hide them in the numbers. So, what do you think? Are the estimates valid?"

Peter: "Well, yes, in general. But I would suggest adding a bit. I believe he's underestimated the complexity of the UI implementation. I bet we will need an extra day or two. And testing. It's not enough. We will need a full day."

Corwin: "Okay, I will add this up."

Peter: "As for the risks, you need to ensure I can have some time to review that full specification you want to produce and pass back questions and corrections. I expect two or three iterations on it."

Corwin: "I see. Let me put it down here. We will need to track this activity. It will be on me."

Peter: "Super! I think we are good to show this to the project owners."

Corwin: "Thanks. I will let you know their feedback later today. See you."

Corwin spends some more time polishing the document and correcting the wording. His documents are always very professional, even small ones.

He never sends just the estimates. They are accompanied by a letter explaining that the team read, analyzed, and discussed the specification and outlining any questions or assumptions they had.

After the letter is finished, he saves it and lets it rest for half an hour. Then, he reads it again and checks grammar. His emails are always perfect. Finally, he clicks the Send button …

PART NINE
PROJECT SCHEDULE

CHAPTER 46
HOW TO CREATE
PROJECT SCHEDULE

Creating a realistic project schedule is difficult when you have the wrong mindset. Everyone expects that there's always a way to squeeze the whole project scope into the deadline project owners set. Stakeholders put a lot of pressure on you to find a solution. But, in most cases, there's no magic formula.

Therefore, the only solution is to do less, or to request more money or time. So begins a tiresome dialog with project owners and other stakeholders. Then, you need to retrace your steps in the planning process and redo a lot of work.

You can avoid some of this mental torment by having the correct expectations. Remember that planning is an ongoing process and you will have to make changes to your first draft. So, don't get too attached to it. Be ready for negotiations. Be prepared to redo your plan. Remember that the more effort you put into creating a realistic schedule, the easier it will be to execute the project.

As a result, you'll promise to deliver the project scope following a certain schedule. In addition, you may also need to provide some interim deliverables on specific dates.

STEP-BY-STEP PROCESS OF CREATING A PROJECT SCHEDULE

Below is a high-level, step-by-step process for creating an accurate schedule. Feel free to copy and paste it as an instruction.

1. Prepare a schedule management plan.
2. Set milestones for project start and end dates.
3. Add an official "holidays calendar" for each resource based on their location.
4. Add resources (or real people) and their availability.
5. Add known vacations and days off for all team members.
6. Set milestones when new resources should be available.
7. Import a list of tasks (if you didn't use a scheduling tool for decomposition).
8. Assign resources to each task.
9. Identify dependencies.
10. Set durations for each task (copy the estimates provided by the team).
11. Identify a critical path.
12. Do a sanity check. Will you meet the deadline? You should have a 10-15% buffer.
13. Move the work packages around so they are being done in parallel. Or assign more resources to do the work faster. Or negotiate to de-scope something.
14. Check workload for resources. People should not go over their daily working hours.
15. Adjust the schedule and resources until you fit into the deadline. Or prove that it's impossible. Provide the next-best alternatives.
16. Subject your project schedule to risk management activities.
17. Add new risk response plans to the overall plan.
18. Again, move the work packages around so they are being done in parallel. Or assign more resources to do the work faster. Or negotiate to de-scope something.
19. Check workload for resources. Validate the whole project schedule.

20. Repeat the process until you have a realistic project schedule that you and your team believe in.
21. Finalize the project schedule baseline.

I'll now elaborate on some of these steps.

STEP #1: SCHEDULE MANAGEMENT PLAN

The project schedule is often confused with the schedule management plan. But, it is only a part of the plan, although it's one of the most important pieces. Key stakeholders will be interested primarily in a project timeline. It answers their primary question: "When will I get the results?"

Before dragging colored bars on a Gantt chart, there are a lot of questions you need to answer. Here are the main ones:

A. What are the existing policies and processes? Your project needs to function within the environment of your organization. You'll have to get approvals, negotiate to prove the necessity of resources, and provide reports. You'll have to show your schedule to internal stakeholders. So, you need to make it look familiar to them. You need to align and integrate with all in-house processes. Otherwise, expect conflicts with internal stakeholders.

B. Define a scheduling model. Here's what that means:

Scheduling Model = (Scheduling Method + Scheduling Tool) + Project Information

The scheduling model is the critical path method in our case. But, you may need to use the PERT technique or critical chain method as an alternative.

The scheduling tool for your environment could be MS Project, OmniPlan, Merlin Project, GanttPRO, etc. Whatever the case, it should allow the implementation of the scheduling method. Therefore, we need a tool that can calculate the critical path and set a baseline for our schedule.

Project information is all the tasks, WBS elements, dependencies, constraints, etc. It's important to note that you need to provide project information in a specific format that works best with the tool. So bear that in mind when you estimate tasks without using the tool. Likewise, you need to consider whether the size of a task is manageable for the scheduling model.

C. Define units of measurement (UoM). Should the estimates be in hours or days? What UoMs does your scheduling tool use? What UoM will you use for reporting? Ideally, it should be consistent.

D. Identify variance thresholds. You don't want to micromanage your team and continually update your schedule. You need to define whether a delay of one, two, or three days warrants corrective action. It all depends on the size of the project.

E. Identify reporting format. What information will go from your scheduling model into the regular reports to the stakeholders? Again, your approach should be seamless.

I recommend that you report progress against milestones or deliverables.

F. Think through the change management process. For example, how hard is it to make a change to the schedule? How can you make it effortless and integrated?

In practice, this means that you need to set all dependencies in your project management software. This way, it will automatically shift everything around. Likewise, you want to schedule tasks in groups as they go in a work package. Don't mix random tasks from different work packages.

STEP 2: SET MILESTONES FOR PROJECT START AND END DATES

Set the project start and end dates in your project management software.

STEPS 3-6: APPLY RESOURCES CALENDAR

Up to this point, we have used working days rather than calendar ones. There are holidays, vacations, sick leaves, and unexpected delays to take into account. A resources calendar, in essence, just shows when resources are available.

And there's a whole set of problems here. First, it is really hard to be accurate. If you have a predefined team, that helps. You just need to manage vacations. But you don't know about all vacations at the start of the project. Also, you need to consider the risks of sick leaves.

I strongly recommend that you input all available information about holidays and vacations at the start. It will be tough to fix the schedule if you forget. Most probably, you'll have to start from scratch. Also, don't forget that people from different countries have different holidays.

If you need to acquire a team, you need to plan the dates when you will get a resource. So, you may need to hire a person, or you may need to wait until a person is released from another project. Mark this date. It all should go into the plan so that you don't assign tasks to people who haven't joined yet.

Moreover, you need to create a risk. What will happen if that person doesn't join the project on time? Develop a response plan.

Don't forget about the learning curve for newcomers. You may need to train them before they can reach full capacity. So, take this into account for their first few days or weeks.

On the other hand, there may also be constraints on the availability of resources. For example, people may only be available part-time. So, for example, if they only work on your team for half the day, tasks assigned to them will take twice the time. Ideally, your scheduling tool should make allowances for this.

You need to take all of this into consideration. And we are not only talking about human resources: You may need access to shared equipment and materials as well.

In any case, keep in mind that you may need to make a lot of assumptions on the availability of resources. So, first, you need to log the risks. Second, you need to be proactive to secure the resources other managers have promised you. And, of course, you need to take the final resources calendar into consideration during risk management.

As you can see, you need to keep in mind many things at this stage. Therefore, when you move tasks around, availability and holidays will impact different work packages. That's why you need project management software to help manage it all for you.

STEP 7: IMPORT TASKS AND INTEGRATE WITH THE WBS

Ideally, you should create a WBS and decompose its elements inside one tool. So, keep all the information about deliverables, work packages, and tasks in one place. And create a project schedule there as well.

Here's a critical rule: Every task should have a parent work package. A task should not float between deliverables or work packages. Otherwise, it is hidden work, which can lead to scope creep. You should be able to tie spent efforts, costs, and risks from a task to a work package.

In practice, this means you need to organize project work by deliverables. As much as is practical, you need to work on a deliverable from start to finish. You can work on two or three deliverables in parallel. In the long run, it's easier to control scope, time, and costs this way.

Also, you need to keep the names of deliverables and work packages consistent throughout all your documentation and tools. Ideally, you need to have a unique ID and a title for each WBS element and task.

STEP 8: ASSIGN RESOURCES

By the time you get to this step in the project schedule:

- You have pre-assigned resources.
- You have identified roles required for your project.
- You have acquired some team members from the in-house pool.
- You have hired some team members from the market.

If you have a predefined team, you usually just assign activities to existing team members. In practice, you allow people to assign tasks to themselves whenever practicable. Let them decide who's doing what.

However, there is a catch. If you skip the analysis of required resources, you may end up with a team not fully fit for the task at hand.

Everyone assumes that you have all the required expertise with a predefined team. However, your leadership assumed this long before you collected all the requirements and identified the project scope. Don't fall into this trap. Always analyze the scope of work with the team and verify the assumption that you really have every specialty accounted for.

STEP 9: DEPENDENCIES IN PROJECT SCHEDULE

In practice, there are four types of dependencies between tasks:

Finish-Start. An activity must finish before the successor can start. This is the most common type of relationship and should be used as a default option unless the nature of related activities requires something else.

Start-Start. An activity must start before a successor can start. For example, you must start delivering bricks before you start to build a wall.

Finish-Finish. An activity must finish before the successor can finish. For example, you can't finish clearing up until all repairs are finished.

Start-Finish. An activity must start before the successor can finish. This is so rare that it's not even worth giving an example – and they are often too confusing anyway.

In practice, 99% of the time, you'll use only finish-start dependencies. They are all you need to line up tasks.

Dependencies are also defined in another way:

- **Mandatory dependency or hard logic.** This is required by the contract, agreement, or technological process.
- **Discretionary/preferred dependency or soft logic.** A dependency you or your team chooses. In general, it is dictated by convenience or efficiency of work.

- **External dependency**. One imposed by people or organizations outside of your project.
- **Internal dependency**. This is based on the needs of the project. In other words, it is something you can control.

All you need to do is analyze all tasks and identify a predecessor for each one.

Even if activities are unrelated, you want to build a logical sequence of work. So, always use discretionary finish-start dependencies for such activities.

STEP 10: SET DURATION FOR EACH TASK

First of all, what unit of measurement are you using? Is it working days or calendar ones? Are you assuming eight hours work per day or six?

If your estimates are based on effective hours – that is, six per day – you need to adjust people's availability accordingly (so, 75% of a standard eight-hour working day). Then a task actually taking six hours will effectively equal one working day. Or you need to set your working day to six hours on your project management application. That might get complicated if you have several people with partial availability.

Always be mindful of what you estimate and what units of measurement you use in the tool – otherwise it can cause a lot of confusion.

STEP 11: IDENTIFY THE CRITICAL PATH

If you sequence all your tasks one after another in a long thread, this schedule will have the least number of risks. But it will also take a lot of time and be inefficient.

It's likely that you'll be able to implement several work packages at once because you can perform several tasks simultaneously. Accordingly, you will have parallel paths from project start to finish.

The critical path is the longest duration path through your schedule, from start to finish. It can cross different threads of activities that depend on each other. It represents the shortest possible time taken to complete a project. As a result, if you delay a task on a critical path, it will move your project's end date.

Why do you need a critical path?

- It determines the duration of the project.
- It shows you where to focus your attention. All activities on the critical path come with risks.
- Any problems with an activity on the critical path require your immediate attention.
- It shows you ways to adjust the project schedule.

USE YOUR FLOAT WISELY

Tasks not on the critical path represent what is known as your "float" or "slack." You have some leeway on the deadlines for completing these tasks before the delay compromises the successful completion of the overall project on time. So, how can you actually use this valuable management resource?

Let's say that you know that a task will take two days. However, it is not on the critical path: It has several days of float. This is an opportunity to give some work to an inexperienced member of the team without jeopardizing the schedule if it takes them more time. This frees up your most experienced people to focus on the tasks on the critical path.

The same principle applies for prioritizing anything related to the project. Must-have items should be on the critical path. We want to deliver them as soon as possible. Nice-to-haves, meanwhile, can go into parallel threads of work.

STEP 12: DO A SANITY CHECK

Now you have the end date of your project. Is it before the deadline? If so, that's good. If not, what are the trade-offs? You need to keep these to a minimum. First of all, if you're close to meeting the deadline, ask if it can be moved slightly – this is the least risky option because, otherwise, you'll need to adjust the whole project management plan.

For now, analyze the gap between the deadline and the calculated end date of the project. Can you optimize the schedule any further? How much extra time do you need beyond that? You need this information for negotiations in the next step.

Keep in mind that the project plan should be flexible. If your planned end date is too close to the deadline and you haven't left much wriggle room, that's a risk. There are also risk reserves to consider. So, allow for a 10%–15% buffer.

STEP 13: ADJUST THE PROJECT SCHEDULE

At this point, I'm assuming that you can't claw back any time from discretionary dependencies.

So, now, you need to negotiate a change in deadline. You have already optimized your schedule so it's the best option. If project owners don't want to play ball, you'll have to try and compress the project schedule further. There are only a few options here:

- Crash the schedule – spend more on extra resources.
- Fast-track the schedule by doing work on the critical path in parallel.
- Reduce the scope.

Of course, any combination of these options is also valid.

Crashing is simply adding more resources to finish the project faster. This applies to tools or machinery as well as people. So, you basically buy time. It is a less risky but more costly approach. However, it doesn't always work because of the law of diminishing returns.

Alternatively, you can try to perform tasks on the critical path in parallel. This technique is called 'fast-tracking.' It basically means that you try to start a task while its predecessor is not yet finished. So, you're juggling more balls in the air at once.

The workflow is less logical and therefore, usually, it causes rework and introduces a lot of risks. You would need to communicate a lot even if you planned these activities thoroughly. Be ready for lots of conflicts and defects. You'll have to manage them closely to keep the project running.

Also, there are long-term drawbacks. It often means taking short-cuts that, over an extended period, can cause technical issues, lower quality, poor documentation, etc. If you use this approach, make sure that you find the time afterwards to catch up and put these things right.

STEP 14: CHECK WORKLOAD FOR RESOURCES

When you are working on lots of tasks in parallel, it's easy to overload someone on a given day. If so, you need to reassign tasks or else someone will have to work overtime. By default, you should not plan for overtime unless it's explicitly requested.

STEP 15: ADJUST YOUR SCHEDULE AND RESOURCES TO THE DEADLINE. OR PROVE THAT IT'S IMPOSSIBLE

If you can't meet a deadline, you need to prove you did everything you could. So, show your current realistic schedule to project owners. Then, together, you need to decide what to do. Use the scheduling techniques we discussed in Step 13.

STEPS 16–20: ITERATE AFTER RISK MANAGEMENT

By now, you have a draft project schedule. You have managed risk continuously. You have already included some responses in your draft for the risks you identified with requirements, the environment, stake-holders, etc. But, now, you need to identify risks within your project schedule as a whole. Call them 'schedule risks.'

You want to focus on:

- When do resources become available?

- Do you have a critical person whom you assigned to all difficult tasks?
- Is seasonal flu going to be an issue?
- How much float do you have in the schedule?

It's a good idea to review the list of risk categories and brainstorm risks with your team. Each new risk you want to tackle proactively requires a risk response plan. So, it will result in an additional task or risk reserve in the schedule.

As a result, the schedule itself will change. When you finish your risk management activities, you need to revalidate the schedule once again. And don't forget to capture secondary risks.

STEP 21: FINALIZE THE SCHEDULE BASELINE

The final version of your realistic project schedule will become your schedule baseline. You'll compare your progress against this approved version.

Remember, you need to involve your project owners and other stakeholders in the process from the beginning. They should see your first drafts and help you develop a realistic schedule. This will make it easier to get your schedule baseline approved.

RESULTS OF YOUR SCHEDULING EFFORTS

In essence, a project schedule shows the start date, end date, duration, and dependencies of each activity. So, it can be a spreadsheet or a schedule in your project management software with all information and a Gantt chart.

Remember that Gantt charts, milestone charts, and network diagrams are just visualizations of your project schedule. Each of them has its own use.

- A Gantt chart is useful for tracking progress and reporting it to stakeholders.

- A milestone chart is for reporting overall project status to senior management.
- Network diagrams show how activities depend on each other.

Your main interest should be ensuring that tasks start and end on the planned dates. A Gantt chart, with its colored bars and percentage completion rate, might be misleading. It shows you that work is in progress. But, you need to track whether it's finished on time.

PART TEN
PROJECT BUDGET

CHAPTER 47
HOW TO CREATE A PROJECT BUDGET

Your budget will heavily depend on your organization, industry, and niche.

You may be working entirely independently of the organization. In this case, you may need to track all expenses, including everything from wages to materials, office rent, internet, snacks, and printer paper. However, in the real world, organizations try to provide a working environment where the project team can focus on delivering value rather than managing kitchen supplies. Moreover, it would be an administrative nightmare if every project came up with its own way of creating a budget and tracking expenses.

Therefore, you'll be working within the organization's environment most of the time. So, no matter how much theory you read, it will be completely different in practice. That's why I provide some guidance and tips below – however, the main idea is that you need to ask how to create a project budget and track expenses within your current organization.

Overall, I see three main scenarios for you:

1. **You run an in-house project**. This means that your organization already has a way to track expenses for internal projects. Ask for a template and guidelines.

2. **Your organization is a vendor, and you run a project for a client**. This means that your organization has a way to calculate a project price for the client. Note that the project's price is the costs plus profit margin. So, ask for a template and guidelines on calculating it all.

3. **You run a project in an organization without much experience of project management**. For example, a small start-up. Based on your previous experience, you'll implement the process you are familiar with. If you are new to this, it will get ugly, and you will need to grind through as best as you can. You'll use processes and tools that you create on the spot. In any case, it's a considerable risk. You need to work closely with the organization's management to develop a solution.

WHAT'S INCLUDED IN A PROJECT BUDGET?

First, you need to identify what goes into the project budget that you show to the project owners. This can be different, depending on your clients. For example:

- You simply need to calculate the cost of the dedicated project team for the project's duration.
- You may need to include hourly wages, and all the materials and tools you need to perform the work.
- You may need to reimburse all the project expenses, including office rent, wages, materials, tools, and other services.
- You may need to provide a budget only for "additional" expenses. Everything else is provided as a service to the client. Or it's an in-house project and the organization pays the wages in any case.

So, it all depends on how you interact with project owners, whether it's an in-house project, and the type of services you provide. You'll need to include all the relevant expense categories in your project budget. If you aren't given a template, here's a shortlist of possible expenses that you may need to consider:

- Salary.
- Bonuses.
- Team-building activities.
- Employee incentives.
- Outsourced labor.
- Cost of materials and equipment.
- Travel expenses.
- Risk reserves.
- Team members' training.
- Consulting fees.
- Contracted services.
- Recruitment fees.
- Office rent.
- Telephone.
- Computer lease.
- Repairs and maintenance.
- Utilities.
- Office supplies.
- Postage.
- General insurance.
- Taxes.
- Software licenses.
- Marketing materials.
- Infrastructure maintenance.

If you don't have project management software, a spreadsheet is the best alternative. So, go for Excel, Google Sheet, or Numbers.

You'll have the same list of tasks we used previously in rows. Again, I recommend that you organize this in a WBS. You should tie all expenses to a WBS element.

The primary columns of the spreadsheet are:

1. Task title.

2. Assigned to.
3. Labor.
4. Materials.
5. Training.
6. Traveling.
7. Other categories.

Your spreadsheet should include the main expense categories relevant to your project. Likewise, for each category of planned expenses, you may want to add "actual cost." It'll help you control costs by category.

Nevertheless, all accounting happens from the bottom up. First, add up work package expenses. Then, account for any variances on the deliverable level. That's why you want to keep the same hierarchy as in your WBS. If your project management software allows you to estimate the costs for tasks, keep them all in one place.

COST ESTIMATES

First of all, let's remember the ground rule: People who will perform the work should participate in the estimation process. Additionally, if you have a procurement manager, you need to involve them. Together, they should estimate the duration, efforts, and materials required, and any other additional costs. Moreover, they may give you insights on where to get the related prices.

If you don't have a project management team yet, you need to find SMEs who have expertise in similar projects. And if your company doesn't have such experts, I recommend you postpone the development of the scope and budget until you acquire these people. Then, of course, you should let your clients know, because this represents a severe feasibility risk. You, as the project manager, can't provide specific estimates yourself.

LABOR RATES

Your company should have a list of possible prices for labor you use in-house on a regular basis. In addition to that, vendors have price lists.

So, the first step is always to ask your leadership about the rates. Otherwise, you need to research the market, including freelancers, to find out average rates for the required roles. You need to make an assumption here and include the "planned rate" into your budget.

Keep in mind that the rates you use here will directly impact the hiring process. For example, it may take more time to fill the required position if you put them below the market average.

A project manager often doesn't have access to information about in-house employees' wages. In this case, the cost of their labor boils down to reporting the working hours they spent on your project.

PRICE LISTS FOR MATERIALS AND EQUIPMENT

A company should have a list of trusted vendors. Your first point of contact is a procurement manager. If you can't find such a list, you need to create one.

There's a potential risk when it comes to the cost of materials and equipment you need to be aware of. Your estimates might not be accurate by the time you come to purchase them in, say, six months' time. So you should be ready for price fluctuations. It might be a significant hit if you need a large amount of materials.

Moreover, serious procurement requires serious legal support. It's one thing to hire a freelancer on Upwork. You can do that without any help. However, it's a different story when you need materials from another country.

COLLECT HISTORICAL DATA FROM YOUR COLLEAGUES

Your company may not have a formal archive. But other project managers have tons of information. So don't be afraid to ask, especially if they've worked on similar projects.

You may identify expenses that you overlooked. In addition, these project managers may share their experience, provide you with lessons learned, and give helpful tips.

For example:

- Materials need storage. You need to rent space.
- There are transportation expenses for delivering them on time to the site.
- Machinery and tools break. They might need replacing.
- Most applications require licenses. These can be expensive for commercial use with big teams.

Remember, every project has a unique set of additional expenses.

HOW TO BUDGET VARIABLE COSTS

Costs like electricity and phone bills, file storage space on a server, etc. can vary over time. You need to budget accordingly. Again, historical data and other project managers will give you an idea of what you can expect.

RESERVES FOR UNKNOWN RISKS

When you sum up costs for all activities, you'll get a budget for work packages.

When you sum up costs for all work packages, you'll get a budget for a parent deliverable.

When you sum up costs for all deliverables, you'll get a project estimate.

When you sum up the project estimate and the total number of risk reserves, you'll get a cost baseline. Then, you need to get approval from the project owners.

When you sum up project baseline and management reserves, you'll finally get the project budget.

The management reserve is allocated for unexpected risks and events. Usually, it's an additional 5%, 10%, or 15% of the cost baseline.

But, keep in mind that you don't have direct access to these reserves. You'll need approval from clients or the steering committee to use them.

The problem is that this approach is purely theoretical. Companies rarely break down a project budget in this way. So, the takeaway here is the buffer that you need to have in your budget. Even if you performed all risk management activities, you need reserves for entirely unexpected things. And they will undoubtedly happen.

FUNDING REQUIREMENTS

And that's not all either. You need to provide a funding schedule. Don't expect that you'll get every penny on day one. Most likely, the project will be funded in installments.

You need to ensure that you have enough cash to keep the project running every day. You should pay close attention to when you need to purchase materials or pay vendors. Don't put your project on hold just because you're waiting for the next installment.

If you have cash flow constraints, you need to consider these as part of the whole project plan.

HARSH TRUTHS

Sometimes, clients and your leadership will ask you to provide a project budget when you don't have a project team. Likewise, they may not give you enough time to prepare with due diligence.

You just need to provide them with a number (total project budget). So, if you are not able to convince stakeholders to do it the right way, you need to safeguard yourself and the project team. Provide higher-level and rough estimates based on the worst-case scenario, especially for deliverables that you have little certainty about.

Yes, sometimes that means that you need to double or triple estimates. To be ethical and professional, you should be transparent about the accuracy of these estimates and offer to provide more specific estimates later in order to come up with a more accurate budget.

Project owners like to constrain the budget. And they believe that it's feasible to achieve project objectives with this budget. But don't take it for granted. Sometimes, you need to prove that the budget, stated in the project charter right at the beginning of the project, is insufficient. Again, the more you involve stakeholders in the planning process, the easier it will be to prove your point.

As a starting point, you can find a simple project budget in my supporting materials here:

https://itpmschool.com/materials

PART ELEVEN
COMMUNICATION PLAN

CHAPTER 48
PLANNING COMMUNICATIONS IN THE REAL WORLD

The project communication management plan is a classic example of the enormous gap between theory and practice. In general, I don't recommend creating a plan on how to communicate on a project. It's a waste of time. On the other hand, poor communication can cause delays and problems. This is where you should focus. Let me explain.

You have project owners and other authoritative stakeholders. They have a preferred way to communicate. You can try and enforce different methods, but I believe breaking their habits like that won't work. If they feel overwhelmed by your plan, they will quickly bin it. And, of course, your boss will be the first one to take it down.

Instead, keep your communications with stakeholders efficient. In most cases, this means the whole team adapting to the way of doing things preferred by project owners, product managers, or top stakeholders.

In rare cases, you may convince project owners to change their way of communicating. Below I've outlined what you'll need to do.

SELL THE BENEFITS OF YOUR METHODS

You and I know the value of robust project management software. However, your project owners and other stakeholders might not yet have experienced all the challenges of working with a project team. Don't assume that they chose emails as the default way to communicate for a reason. Most likely, they do it out of habit. They don't know a better way.

So, if you have project management software, you need to articulate its benefits. Here are a few points that you can use:

- All project information is in one place.
- Conversations have the context of a task, requirements, or deliverable.
- It removes bottlenecks in communication because you can reach any person on the team.
- The project manager can monitor all the conversations and prompt responses without being the bottleneck.
- Usually, it's more secure.
- It allows concurrent collaboration on a piece of documentation or requirements.
- It provides the current project status on demand.
- It gives full transparency of the team's work.

It's not enough to simply state that it is the tool that the team uses. From the stakeholders' perspective, it's just another tool they need to monitor. You need to provide compelling reasons to start using it. Remember, you have more interest in them using it than they do. If you fail to sell this idea, you'll have to manage communications both inside and outside the tool (emails).

Your organization might not even have any project management software because they don't understand the benefits. You can make a case for needing it during your existing project, while also highlighting the long-term benefits it will provide for all future projects.

Next, you need to show how to use the tool. Never assume that it's easy for project owners to embrace new project management software. Provide short instructions on logging in and the basic functionality they need to know. It should be just a dummy's guide in the form of a short instruction, quick video, or you can walk them through it. They don't need to know how the whole system works. In the beginning, they need to master only the basics.

CYBERSECURITY AND SENSITIVE INFORMATION

One thing that I learned about cybersecurity is that you can't implement it solely by technological means. It's all about people. So you need to educate people on how to be secure and safe online.

You also need to think through which team members and stakeholders should have access to different parts of the project information. For example:

- Which group has access to all the requirements and UI designs?
- Who has access to project documentation?
- Who needs access to the databases of the project?
- Who needs access to the source code?
- Who has access and privileges to assign people to these access groups?
- How does someone become a member of an access group?

Next, you need to list which communication technologies are allowed. For example: Can you:

- use Skype?
- use Zoom?
- capture the screen recordings or screenshots in any other applications?
- share all this information with the team and, if so, how?

Something that people often don't think about much is how to securely share files, particularly large ones. What tools can be used? How do you give access to those files to people outside of your organization?

I recommend that you have step-by-step instructions on how to upload, secure, and share files with anyone outside of the project team and your organization. But, of course, it all depends on the tools and technologies that you have at your disposal. So, you'll have to work out the details on your own.

I also recommend that you explicitly describe how to handle accounts and their passwords. Nowadays, your email, project management tool, file storage, etc. can all be linked through one account. Moreover, if you're in software development or similar, you will have a bunch of accounts for testing your application and product. These test accounts might have access to sensitive information. So, you need to manage and distribute them among stakeholders, clients, and other team members.

It's critical that you have rules on cybersecurity, even if they're as simple as I've described them. Why? Because sharing sensitive information is the biggest problem in this digital world. You can leak data from your clients, your team, or the product or service you create. And there is no simple way to correct such a mistake. The consequences of leaking personal and sensitive information can be terminal for a project and all the organizations involved.

COMMUNICATION WITH THIRD PARTIES

You should state any communication needs with vendors in the contract. For example, allocating a person to sit with you at a meeting to give a status report is a waste of resources for them. That's why, in the contract, you want to state that they must communicate on a certain level with the project team.

In your communication management plan, you want to articulate how you expect vendors to communicate: How often and in what form. Don't expect that the assigned person reads the contract from start to end. Highlight this part of the communication plan so they don't miss it.

So, in this section, I would describe the type, frequency, and form of communication in a simple table.

For example, you expect a weekly status report by email, or you want to have a daily sync-up meeting for 30 minutes every day via Zoom, and so on. Also, think about whether you're going to regularly visit your vendor on their site because that's also the time they need to allocate.

ACTUAL LIST OF CONTACTS

I also recommend keeping a current list of contacts, along with a short description of their responsibilities and what kind of problems each person can handle.

Again, it's a spreadsheet. At the very minimum, you want their name, title, location, time zone, preferred method of communication, and a short description of their areas of responsibility.

ESCALATION PROCESS

Last but not least, consider adding a section on how to escalate a problem. The funny thing here is that calling someone is actually the best way to convey an emergency because, in this digital era, it's becoming increasingly rare to pick up the phone.

Lots of project managers think that creating a formal, written a communication plan will boost performance. However, I think that's a myth. In a decade of practical experience, I've never gone beyond the points mentioned. The best use of your time is to convince project owners to switch from emails to a collaboration tool.

PART TWELVE
PROCUREMENT

CHAPTER 49
PROCUREMENT MANAGEMENT

This is another area where the theory is out of sync with what really goes on. That's because there is such a wide variety of business-to-business approaches. So, no matter how much theory you learn, the real-life experience will be different. Of course, you need to know the basic terminology and concepts. But, I think you have to participate in procurement management once in order to understand what you need to know. And, in each new organization, it will be a unique experience.

If you want to get in-depth knowledge of procurement management, you need a different book or a course. That's why I'll leave a curated list of resources on procurement management in this book's supporting materials. Below, I will simply keep to a few practical tips you need to be aware of.

WHAT IS PROCUREMENT MANAGEMENT?

Procurement is the process of getting the materials, equipment, and services you need. If your organization has everything in-house, you don't need to procure anything.

Conversely, you may run a project where vendors, service

providers, and contractors do all the work and produce deliverables while the project management team is simply planning and organizing. In this case, you'll have to dive deep into procurement management. Moreover, you'll need a whole team to manage all the interactions with third parties.

Most of us are somewhere in the middle of these two extremes. We need to procure something from time to time for our projects.

WHY THEORY DOESN'T HELP

Put simply, procurement needs to be planned, conducted, and controlled.

That's all very well in theory but, if you dig deeper, there's much more to it – so much so that there is a separate profession of procurement management. It's one thing when you need to buy a printer for a project, even a production-grade one. But, it's entirely another story when you need to procure 10,000 steel beams and get them delivered from overseas.

Likewise, it's easy enough to find and hire a freelancer with specific expertise to do a certain type of work. Moreover, you can manage this person as a regular team member. But, when you need to outsource something complex, you want to get some guarantees on the results. First, you need to find suitable vendors, get their prices, compare and select the most suitable option, etc. Then, you need a contract that will safeguard you from delay, poor quality, and bad conduct.

You get the point. At some point, things get complex enough that you need an experienced procurement manager or even a whole team dedicated to conducting and controlling procurement. The biggest benefit is that they don't start from scratch each time. They have running lists of selected vendors, contract templates, real-life experience, and they know all the challenges.

YOUR ROLE IN THE PROCUREMENT PROCESS

Nevertheless, the planning of procurement is on you. But that doesn't mean that all projects require procurement by default. Instead, you need to ensure that your team and organization's resources can handle everything from start to finish.

Overall, the goal is to decide what your project team can deliver and what needs to be outsourced to a vendor. Likewise, you may have the right people, but you must acquire the materials, equipment, and services to achieve project deliverables.

So, you have to create a project plan, identify the necessary resources, and by when you need them. In essence, you need to prepare requirements for these materials, equipment, and tools. After that, you ask the procurement team to plan and execute a sub-project on purchasing what you requested.

You need to treat the procurement team as a project stakeholder. They have their own expectations of you, and they have established processes, tools, and templates. Therefore, you need to follow their workflow. That means creating documentation and file requests to them in a specific format. If you already know what they need, it will save you time to complete all your project documentation using their templates. As a result, you can simply send them a part of the project's WBS or project scope statement.

The other critical aspect here is making sure that your requirements are accurate. I hope you understand that you need clearly defined requirements for procuring materials, equipment, or a deliverable. Moreover, you'll put those requirements into contracts and a scope of work (SOW) for your vendors. So, the better the requirements, the fewer issues and management overheads you'll have during execution.

For sure, you'll need to create more documentation to start the procurement process. Ask for an example or template and follow the established workflow. This all boils down to proactive communication with your procurement team. You should work hand in hand and you need to reach out to them as early as possible.

READ THE CONTRACT, SUGGEST IMPROVEMENTS

The procurement team will use standard contract templates to work with vendors. However, collaboration with third parties requires lots of communication. Moreover, you want to have control over their work. But a standard contract usually doesn't have clauses about reports, meetings, and touchpoints. Therefore, you need to ask for them. In most cases, you won't get very far, no matter how politely you ask. That's why you need your procurement and legal teams to include special clauses that will specify your requirements for communication and progress reports.

Based on your planning, if you feel like you need something extra in the contract, make sure you discuss it with the legal team. Don't accept default terms just because it's convenient for procurement. In the long run, your project success depends on these vendors.

WORKING IN A SMALL COMPANY WITHOUT A PROCUREMENT TEAM

So far, we have talked about a typical case of an organization with procurement expertise. However, you may be working for a small company without such knowledge or experience. In this case, you should be honest about your skills in procurement management. If your employee then accepts this as a risk, no problem. It's a new challenge for you! You simply promise to do your best.

First of all, you should consult with your direct manager to develop an approach. Then, you should keep them informed about your progress all the time.

Second, you may try following the lead of vendors. They have experience working with clients. So, they'll tell you what they need. For sure, they will dictate the rules, not you. But, still, you are the client. So, you may opt not to work with a vendor if something feels wrong.

Third, make sure that you read the contracts. It's boring, and it takes time. But you need to understand the primary responsibilities of both parties.

Fourth, you need to maintain formal communication. Write emails, follow up with meeting notes, ensure that both parties are on the same side.

Do what you need to do to get through your first procurement experience. The second time, it will be a bit easier but, still, it will be a different experience. Step by step, you'll get the practical skills you need.

PART THIRTEEN
HOW TO EXECUTE AND
CONTROL THE PLAN

CHAPTER 50
PROJECT EXECUTION OVERVIEW

We have discussed lots of topics in the context of project planning: Risk and stakeholder management, requirements, scope, cost, time management, communications, and procurement. Ideally, you have put your thoughts on managing all these aspects into a project plan document. So, in an ideal world, you simply need to follow the plan you've created. But, unfortunately, life isn't perfect. That's why there's always extra work when it comes to the execution of a project.

As before, first, let's start with a high-level overview. Then, we'll take a deep dive into several topics. However, note that we are getting more and more into the areas where your environment dictates the rules. So, there are not that many universal processes. You need to adapt and tailor your plan to the needs of the project and your environment. Nevertheless, I'll try to provide some examples from the trenches to help you implement what you have learned.

THE IMPORTANCE OF FOLLOWING THE PLAN

So, you put lots of effort into producing a realistic plan, even if it wasn't a formal document. Moreover, you've promised your team and stakeholders that these planning efforts will increase the chances of success. So, project owners expect to get the product or service they want, which will profit their business. Your team members will have a successful experience to add to their CVs, gaining them positive reviews and promotions. Other project stakeholders will benefit in their own way. As you can see, a lot is at stake based on your plan. So, it would be a crime not to use the results of the planning efforts.

Now, imagine that you are on a ship. You have a map with a plotted path. You follow it to get out of the port. At some point, you lose sight of the shoreline. You are fully at sea now. You regularly correct your course to stay on the plotted path. But, suddenly, you decide to toss the map away. Now, every direction looks the same. If you deviate from the initial path, you won't notice. Even a compass cannot help. You may get lucky and find a port. But, most likely, it won't be the one you planned to get to.

Believe me, it's hard to keep to the plan and keep it in good shape. Moreover, it's tempting to adjust it daily to show the "real state of affairs." However, your current progress is relevant only when compared to the initial plan.

So, the idea is simple. You collect data daily about the progress of the team on tasks. You sum it up to a deliverable level. Next, you check whether there's a variance between planned values and actual ones. You check the progress on all aspects of the project, not only schedule and costs.

However, if there's a variance, you don't adjust the plan. Instead, you work with the team to catch up and get back to the initial plan. You also have thresholds for the variance of project costs, schedule, risks, etc. Only if the deviation exceeds the threshold do you take action to correct the plan. And, even in this case, first, you may want to use management reserves to get back to the initial plan – or some other option if you see one. If nothing helps, you reach out to the project owners, explain the problem, and propose a solution to adjust the plan.

All the while, you keep constant communication with key stakeholders. And you don't hide the potential problems as they appear. Most likely, stakeholders will help you get back to the initial plan with a recommendation or a workaround. Or they simply escalate the problem and resolve it on a higher level. So, changing the initial plan should be a last resort.

ASSIGN TASKS AND TRACK PROGRESS

In practice, this means that you need to review your project schedule daily. Then, you need to communicate with assignees to ensure that they know what tasks to do, when they should be finished, and the overall expectations. Don't assume that people are proactive and will do it themselves. It will save you lots of headaches if you make it a regular practice to ensure that everyone is working on the tasks that you expect them to work on.

Tasks contain a lot of information – specifications, designs, boundaries, duration, risks, dependencies, etc. But, again, don't assume that people read all the information. They usually focus on the bare minimum to finish the task. So, if you want to point out something specific, do so. And double-check that the person has understood the information.

This becomes even more important if the person currently working on the task didn't participate in the project planning earlier. You need to articulate your expectations for the first few tasks before this person becomes more independent.

If you have a big team, you should delegate this responsibility to team leaders. If there's no official title of team leader, you need to assign this responsibility to someone with experience and soft skills to lead others. Nevertheless, you still need to closely control their work during the initial period. You need to coach the team leaders on leadership and correct their approaches.

Also, you need an effortless process to collect performance data on tasks, including efforts spent, actual costs, actual duration, risks that happened, reserves used, etc. If you have integrated project management software, you should collect all the data there. If not, create an Excel tracker or provide a template to send the daily reports in emails. On the one hand, you need to ensure that it doesn't take a lot of time for team members to report on their progress. And, on the other, it shouldn't take a lot of effort to compile all this data into a report.

ENCOURAGE PROFESSIONAL COLLABORATION

You created a project plan that describes the sequence of tasks and many other aspects. However, it doesn't explain how to do the work, or show all the interactions required to finish a task, or automatically mean that your team is committed. Team members need to communicate and collaborate with each other. They need to reach out to stakeholders for help, insights, and clarifications.

In an ideal world, this shouldn't be a problem. But, in the real world, people and organization's cultures are different. So, you need to put a lot of effort into educating your people on how to resolve issues, find necessary information, and follow your project management approach.

In practice, the best approach is to lead by example. Initially, you organize and facilitate all these interactions. You schedule meetings, invite the necessary people, facilitate the conversation. After that, you ask one of the team members to follow the same path. You encourage them to take the lead on a given challenge. Let them write emails, set up meetings, and resolve the issue. Let them decide whom to include in the conversation.

It goes without saying that you are always available to help and support them. Moreover, when you delegate responsibilities, that person should be given the necessary authority. However, there are issues that only you can resolve with your authority and title.

When dealing with less experienced teams, I often say, "Oh, look. You resolve the problem without me. I just sat there and listened to you. You did a great job! I think, next time, you don't need me looking over your shoulder."

For more experienced teams, I try to play up to their professional ego. "And why did you call a whole certified project manager to resolve this trivial issue? Seems like you solved it on your own."

By all means, follow your leadership style. But you get the point – you should help your team members become more independent of you and your management.

REMOVE IMPEDIMENTS AND ROADBLOCKS

Just as in normal life, problems appear on a project all the time:

- Work on a deliverable is due to start soon but project owners haven't provided clarifications on requirements.
- Someone joined the team but didn't get access to the project management tool with all the requirements and tasks.
- Something suddenly broke or stopped working (server, elevator, truck, subscription to file storage, etc.).
- A critical person is sick with flu.
- There's heavy traffic on the roads in your area due to repairs.

It's not enough to track today's tasks. You should be proactive and think a few steps ahead: Review your project schedule for the next few days; check your risk register for upcoming risks; be on the lookout for new threats.

In essence, you need to ask yourself, "If I disappear right now, can the team work efficiently for the next five days?"

If the answer is no, it means there are roadblocks ahead. You need to work today to remove them. Sometimes you might know about roadblocks further in the future. They should be on your to-do list as well. If you have free time now, it's better to address those issues.

However, I don't go too far beyond a few immediate deliverables being worked on at the time. Some problems will resolve themselves and some will disappear. So, you don't want to overreact.

In contrast, some problems will appear unexpectedly and block the work straightaway. In this case, you need to do whatever it takes to solve it ASAP. In most cases, you need to escalate the problem to project owners and your leadership. In any case, you need to inform project stakeholders at once.

In both cases, proactive communication is key. You should start the conversation and articulate when the problem will appear and how it will impact the work. Then, provide some solutions. Don't wait for others to do it. In most cases, you need to make a stakeholder do something to solve a problem. So, it boils down to finding the right person and good leverage to make him prioritize your problem.

MOTIVATE AND LEAD PEOPLE

So, you assigned the tasks, talked to people, and made your expectations clear. You encouraged people to work with each other to get things done. Giving a gentle push like this will work for a few days. But their enthusiasm will dwindle soon in the daily grind of project work. So, you need to find ways to motivate each and every person in your team to keep up the good work, collaborate, and simply be nice.

So, on the one hand, you'll find something that will motivate people to do the best work they are capable of. On the other, you need to lead them to a common goal. Finishing a project successfully is usually not the common goal: It's your professional goal.

An in-depth look at leadership and motivation is beyond the scope of this book, but you can learn more through my online course.

PROGRESSIVE ELABORATION

Most probably, you have some gaps in your planning – sometimes known as 'debts'. For example, if you used rolling wave planning, you need greater specification of requirements and more detail on future deliverables.

So, you'll need to have regular meetings with your team to work out these details. In essence, you'll follow the same planning process on a lower level. Once you have estimates for the next deliverable, you can integrate the details into your project management plan. Your main goal is to ensure that you fit into the initial high-level estimates.

These planning activities take time from you and the project team. Therefore, you should be honest about the effective hours team members can dedicate to implementing tasks you've already assigned to them. A rule of thumb is six effective hours for tasks and two hours of meetings per day.

MONITOR THE PROGRESS

Once the project wheels start turning, lots of data is generated. You need performance data on all aspects: Tasks, costs, time spent, risk, etc. Everything! First, you need to set up efficient processes to collect all this data.

Ideally, you should keep it all in the respective tasks within your project management software. The first thing to look for is trends in variances. If they are within the agreed thresholds, good job! Keep the focus on efficient day-to-day execution.

It makes your life easier if you keep to the WBS. This way, you don't manage one big project. Instead, you work with a series of smaller sub-projects – deliverables. Obviously, if you achieve each separate deliverable according to the project plan, then the whole project is in good shape.

Nevertheless, a great project manager knows that collecting data on motivation, engagement, conflicts, and communication is equally important. But, again, you can measure these aspects of a project only if you've created a plan in the first place.

INTEGRATE CHANGES

Changes come from two sources:

1. Project owners or other stakeholders want to make a change to the requirements or deadlines. An intermediate deliverable made them question whether something was right. Or they forgot something. Or they came up with a new idea.
2. You need to change the project plan because you deviated from the initial plan too far, and there's no way to get back on track. The plan is no longer feasible. Likewise, you may discover a new severe risk or mandatory requirement.

In both cases, you need to follow a change management process. We'll discuss this in detail later. Just keep in mind that there are no "simple" changes to a project. A change always impacts all aspects of the project.

COMMUNICATION AND STAKEHOLDER MANAGEMENT

Draw your gaze away from your team's immediate tasks and problems, and look around. You'll see a bunch of project stakeholders who need your attention.

A great project manager knows that stakeholders outside the project team also need motivation, encouragement, and leadership. In the long run, even the project sponsor who pays millions for the project is just a human being. She has fears, insecurities, and an imaginative brain that conjures up doomsday scenarios. Don't assume that project owners, executives, and your managers know everything about project management and the nature of the project.

You need to establish continuous communication with project owners. Ideally, you need to meet daily. If that's not possible, persuade them to meet as frequently as their schedule allows. Sometimes they'll assign a proxy. It can be a project manager on their side. You'll collaborate on a daily basis with this person. However, I recommend that you establish direct communication with project owners so that you can provide information firsthand.

For the rest of the key stakeholders, you'll provide project status reports regularly. Based on the size of the project and how dynamic it is, you'll need to select a reporting period. I prefer weekly or fortnightly.

Also, there are stakeholders whom you need to engage in your project. For these people, you have a plan already. Now it's time to implement those ideas and check the response. It's hard to track all social connections with dozens of people. That's why you must compare the results of your efforts with the initial plan. Moreover, there's no way to quantify these interactions. So, you need to monitor a person's behavior over time.

All the activities discussed above require communication in various forms. So, if you don't know what to do or how to proceed, remember that in 99% of cases you need to talk to someone or write an email.

It's impossible to automate all the activities on a project and make them perfect. From time to time, someone will forget to follow the process. Therefore, you need to continuously coach people to use your project management approach. You'll have to repeat your expectations and instructions over and over again.

Occasionally, brand-new challenges will appear that will require changes in the processes. You'll need to communicate these changes. And, yes, it will take several repetitions until all people remember the new process.

RESOLVE CONFLICTS

Conflicts will appear throughout a project. And I'm not just talking about personal (and emotional) ones. Conflict in requirements, conflict in priorities, conflict of visions, and conflicts between stakeholders will eat up lots of your effort and time. The good news is that all these types of conflicts can be resolved in the same way. The bad news is that you can't leave any conflict unattended. Moreover, it's hard to delegate resolution to someone else. Unresolved conflicts can escalate quickly into animosity between people.

We'll discuss conflict resolution techniques in the Chapter #58. But bear in mind that it's a big part of your daily work.

DAILY ROUTINES OF A PROJECT MANAGER

Even on a high level, there's a long list of activities that translate to a huge number of meetings, emails, conversations, documents, data management, and time spent using your project management software. It feels like each problem drags you in a different direction. So, most of the time, you are distracted rather than productive.

If you want to keep your sanity and reduce stress, you must establish daily routines as much as possible so that you can do these repeating activities on autopilot. You can refine these routines so that you only need to spend a few minutes every day on each one to maintain the project.

At the very least, you need the ones outlined below.

PROJECT HEALTH MONITORING

Every morning, I check that every team member has updated the status of the task they worked on the day before. If they didn't, I ask them to do it first thing in the morning. This way, I have an up-to-date project status at the start of the day. It helps me adjust the work and focus on the most pressing issue for the day. It also prevents the loss of performance data because it is logged into the system while it's fresh in people's heads.

Usually, I have a dashboard that shows key metrics of project progress.

DAILY SYNC UP WITH PROJECT TEAM

Every day I have a Scrum-like daily stand-up meeting. First, everyone reports on what they did yesterday and what they plan to do today. Then, we discuss roadblocks, impediments, and risks. It all takes no more than 30 minutes. This helps to ensure that people are working on the tasks that I need them to that day. Likewise, I learn about any problems in advance.

COMMUNICATION

You don't have to reply to each and every email immediately. In most cases, answering emails is not the first priority for the project unless it's specifically marked as urgent. Unless you have a policy that requires you to reply within a certain time frame, you can reply to emails when it suits you best.

I have two time slots dedicated to answering emails and clearing my inbox. This allows me to focus on other critical tasks for the day. I write emails in batches. And, as you might know, batching similar tasks is one of the most effective productivity hacks.

It doesn't mean that I don't answer emails outside these time slots. Instead, I choose to do it if I have nothing else to do that is more important. So, don't become a slave to your inbox. In my experience, only 1 in 10 emails actually helps to push your project along. The rest have little value.

DAILY SYNC UP WITH PROJECT OWNERS

Like with the project team, I try to keep project owners informed on a daily basis to minimize problems with communication and expectations. It's a 15- or 30-minute meeting. I either report on our progress and, as a result, demonstrate that the project is under control, or we discuss immediate issues that we need to resolve together. This way, the project owners always receive bad news from me framed as a challenge that we proactively try to resolve. That engages them in the process.

There's one thing I want to stress out about this communication. You do need to talk about risks. First of all, keep upcoming ones at the top of the list. But, then, don't be shy to ask whether project owners see any new risks, especially when they request a change or something new.

DAILY MOTIVATION AND ENCOURAGEMENT

People often think that leadership and motivation take a lot of dedicated time and effort. Yes, overall, on the scale of the whole project team, that's true. However, day to day, it's just about talking to people on their level.

So, rather than waiting for the perfect time or a motivational event, make these interactions part of your daily routine. For example:

- Small talks at the water cooler.
- Coffee with team members.
- Lunch with the team.
- One-on-one meetings (performance reviews).
- Playing chess, video games, table tennis, etc.
- Personal coaching.
- Saying "Thank you!" and "Good job!"
- Walking meetings outside of the office.

You need to ensure that you interact with all people in your team, not only a selected group. So, you may apply this to one, two, or three people a day. The next day it will be three other people and different activities. Try to have fun with it. Don't force activities on a person. Respect their preferences.

That's all for the overview. Next, let's discuss some important activities in more detail.

CHAPTER 51
HOW TO MONITOR THE PROJECT

What's the difference between "monitoring" and "controlling" a project in practice?

Monitoring project progress means collecting performance data from the execution of tasks. Then, you need to compare this data with the initial project plan to check for any variances.

Controlling the project means analyzing variances and deciding whether your project plan is still realistic and feasible. And, if not, requesting a change to the plan.

In practice, this means motivating your project team to log the performance data for the tasks assigned to them. They need to track things like time spent, expenses, and extra effort they didn't anticipate initially.

However, you monitor and control the project in all aspects, not only budget, schedule, and risks. Therefore, to do that efficiently, during planning you need to think through all the performance data you want to collect in advance.

So, again, the best way to make it manageable is to keep to the WBS elements and associated tasks. In essence, you collect the "actual" numbers for each aspect you estimated during planning. This way, you compare apples with apples.

As a result, there are four critical things you need to consider during planning.

1. OBTAINING DATA SHOULD BE CHEAP AND EFFORTLESS

There's little value in data that requires hours to collect and process. If you have project management software the whole team can access, you should collect all the data there. It should be built into the workflow. However, just because you have such a capability doesn't automatically mean that everyone knows how to do this, or that they will never forget to do it.

So, you need to continuously explain and teach how to report progress on a task, how to move it through the statuses, and what documents, invoices, and evidence to include. You'll have to go over this many times.

On the other hand, if you don't have integrated software, you'll need to create a simple process for reporting. Let people send an update in emails or create a shared spreadsheet to fill in. You need to keep the tasks' names in sync throughout different tools.

2. PERFORMANCE DATA SHOULD BE CONSISTENT

You need to collect the same data – estimates, reports, etc. – in the same format for all deliverables throughout a project. Otherwise, you will waste time interpreting and processing the data.

3. SET MEANINGFUL THRESHOLDS

For example, in terms of your schedule, you need to determine after how many days a delay becomes critical. There are no hard rules here. You need to assess each threshold. Let me explain.

If you have a month-long project, then a deviation of five days is quite significant. You have 19 to 22 working days per month, so five days is roughly a quarter of your schedule. If the deviation occurs at the start or in the middle of the project, there's little chance you can get back on track. So, five days is a high threshold. I would say one or two days is better in this case.

On the other hand, five days is a tiny deviation for a year-long project. Three or four weeks would be a more appropriate threshold.

This all needs to be explained to the project owners. Most of them will expect the schedule to be on track 100% of the time when, in the real world, there are daily fluctuations. So, you'll finish some tasks on time and then you'll delay other tasks. For each deliverable, these deviations may balance out in the long run. That's why trends and thresholds are important.

4. YOU SHOULD BE ABLE TO INTERPRET THE DATA

It's apparent how to collect and interpret actual costs, time spent and finished deliverables. But what about stakeholders' engagement, quality, and efficiency of risk response plans? What should be the thresholds for these?

We'll discuss this below. But the critical takeaway is that you need to think in advance about how to collect, use, and interpret the data you have. You need to plan it.

CHAPTER 52
WHAT SHOULD YOU MONITOR ON A PROJECT?

Time and money, obviously. You can compare the actual versus planned values. It's pretty straightforward.

It's more complicated with stakeholder engagement, communications, and scope. Metrics alone won't tell you the root cause of deviations. Therefore, you need to analyze them in the context of the project as a whole.

In theory, you can track hundreds of different metrics. However, in practice, you need just a few critical ones in each aspect of the project. Below are those I recommend you track.

SCOPE MANAGEMENT

Scope creep will show the amount of work you missed during planning. In practice, you need to keep an eye on what team members report. If you see that they created a new task to finish a work package, that's clearly scope creep. Same if you see that a task takes more time and a person says there are more things to do.

On a basic level, you need to control new tasks. To be transparent, you need to educate people to create new tasks for any work they didn't plan initially. They must notify you about them. It will help you to control what it really takes to finish a deliverable.

Likewise, you may identify a piece of scope that you missed in all work packages, but which is significant to the whole project. So, you may need to adjust the project plan. In most cases, scope creep should indicate issues in requirements or lack of project management efforts.

Quality of requirements may show you how much scope creep you need to anticipate. It is a qualitative and subjective metric that indicates whether the collected requirements are sufficient to define 100% of the scope.

In the real world, requirements are never fully detailed. If you feel that there's a lot of ambiguity in requirements, you should expect more scope creep. So, during planning, you need to account for this additional work. During execution, you must ensure that you finish both the planned and extra work within the allocated time and budget.

On the other hand, you may think that the requirements are in good shape. But, later, you discover that you are consistently needing to carry out extra tasks. That's an indicator that you need to adjust the project scope, which will lead to changes in all other aspects.

Percentage of accepted deliverables can show your true progress. Remember that having all deliverables 95% finished is worthless to stakeholders.

If you show a deliverable to project owners and they immediately suggest changes and find defects, it means you'll get more work. If the same happens with a few more deliverables, you can predict that you'll get more work across all of them. It will definitely impact the deadline and budget of the project.

SCHEDULE MANAGEMENT

On a high level, you always want to keep track of your schedule. However, I recommend focusing on the next important milestone, not the project deadline itself.

On a lower level, you need to know how many days you are ahead or behind schedule for each deliverable that is in progress at the time. Additionally, you want to control the time you have reserved for different risks on a deliverable level.

In schedule management, continuing deviations are more important than the current numbers. You need to be on the lookout for growing trends. They may indicate that your estimates of efforts or duration were too optimistic. So, you'll have to adjust the schedule accordingly.

BUDGET MANAGEMENT

You should track the budget the same way as the schedule. You sum up all expenses from tasks – first based on work packages, then on deliverables.

However, there may be exceptions. You need to control the estimates that you made during project planning. For example, you planned to get a software developer for $40 per hour. However, the one you found costs $60 per hour. This could be a severe impact over time.

Likewise, materials might cost more than you estimated. You need to control your price baselines, so they take account of any fluctuations in cost by the time you purchase the materials.

In most organizations, you'll need to collect and track timesheets from project team members logging their hours of work. Then, you can control wages allocation between projects.

Additionally, you may need to control the cash flow. You should always have enough money to support all planned activities between budget installments.

Last but not least, you need to collect evidence of expenses: Invoices from vendors, contractors, and other third parties in most cases. Bear in mind that you may charge different accounts for different expenses. This is all specific to the environment that you work in. None of this is universal. You must ask your management and colleagues for details.

RISK MANAGEMENT

In practice, you are trying to mitigate just a few upcoming risks on a daily basis. Each one has an owner who controls them. Therefore, you can control risks individually and check the **efficiency of the risk response plans**. It will show whether the risk is being addressed efficiently and within the limits of dedicated reserves. If not, it will create a deviation in scope, schedule, or budget. Likewise, it may introduce new risks.

On a higher level, you need to ensure an accurate qualitative analysis of risks so that you have a good idea of how many are likely to occur. In essence, you can monitor whether your probability estimates were correct.

The remaining management reserves dictate how many uncertainties and unknown risks you can absorb before impacting the project plan directly. Be careful not to drain these funds too early so you have nothing left to deal with risks near the end of the project.

STAKEHOLDER MANAGEMENT

This is subjective and qualitative. The best way to measure your progress is by comparing it with your plan. In practice, that means observing stakeholders' behavior, attitude, and willingness to collaborate. You may also try to interview them or their colleagues to get more insights into their engagement with the project. So, it's all about communication and empathy. But it's critical to write your observations down because you need to track trends, not just what someone feels like on the day.

If you strategically manage stakeholders, you need to determine their **level of engagement** (their interest and authority level) so you can work on shifting the attitudes of those who may look less favorably on the project.

Tracking **conflicts** usually identifies trends in behaviors of selected stakeholders. In addition, you might discover exciting interactions and dependencies between them.

Satisfaction is essential when providing services to a client if you want to continue doing business with them.

Controlling **expectations** will ensure that you won't fall at the last hurdle.

QUALITY MANAGEMENT

Your quality assurance team will collect many, many metrics but, as the project manager, you are mainly interested in three.

First of all, the number of **defects grouped by severity**. In essence, these are the critical defects in your deliverables that your team needs to fix as soon as possible. Otherwise, your project can't be completed.

You also need to make project owners aware of known defects that have no severe impact on the product or service. And you need to get their approval that it's okay not to fix them.

The second metric is **defects by categories or functionality**. This shows areas of the product or service that require more of your attention. It highlights the quality of work of the people who implemented the requirement.

Next, you want to track **defects reported after hand-off**. This shows you the overall efficiency of your QA efforts. If stakeholders find defects after you finish testing, that's usually a major problem because you missed a defect on a common use case of the product. You need to investigate whether the QA team understands how end users perceive and use the product. You'll need to adjust the testing of other deliverables.

You can set up a dashboard in your project management software to monitor the current status on your own. Likewise, you can set up a process whereby your QA team leader reports on the defects weekly.

HUMAN RESOURCES

Again, there are dozens of metrics related to HR management, but that doesn't mean you need to monitor them all. If possible, you need to delegate them to the HR department. In practice, I recommend using and tracking the following.

An **issue log** is a chronological list of conflicts between team members, stakeholders, and you. It helps to connect seemingly unrelated events and define patterns in people's behavior. Also, it ensures that you don't leave conflicts unresolved. Usually, it's a simple spreadsheet.

Personal development progress for every person on your project team will show you whether they are interested in getting better, taking on new responsibilities, etc. Moreover, it is a secondary metric for the overall happiness and motivation of the team. Demotivated people won't dedicate energy to professional development for the good of the project.

A **skills star map** is a chart showing the skills and experience in the different areas relevant to your project. You can also use it to track the progress of the team's development. Sometimes, it acts as a scoreboard for the team and creates a bit of gamification and competition in professional development.

The **onboarding process** is a standard workflow for a newcomer to get up to speed with a team. You need to provide access to all the tools and information as quickly as possible. The newcomer should have a simple plan to follow during the first few days at a new job. It's best to have a checklist of essential activities you need to perform.

Personal performance: During project planning, you estimated a certain level of performance for a role. Or you got estimates from a real team member. Now, you need to control whether the person in that role is meeting those expectations. If they aren't, it will impact all the work further down the schedule. So, you either need to find a way to improve their performance or adjust the project plan.

COMMUNICATION MANAGEMENT

There are no clear metrics in communications. Nevertheless, there are trends and patterns of behavior.

For example, you need to track the efficiency of your emails. So, you outline on email a problem you want to solve. How many emails does it take to come up with and implement a solution? Does it create endless threads that deviate from the initial topic? If so, you need to use a more appropriate communication method.

Then, we have **security**. You need to monitor how securely information flows between the project team and other stakeholders. Do people use secure communication channels to share sensitive data?

Also, you may want to track the actual **cost of a decision**. Take the hourly rates of everyone involved and multiply by the time they spent making a decision. It's a great indicator of the efficiency of your meetings.

PROJECT MONITORING TOOLS AND TECHNIQUES

So, how does all this happen in real life? As I mentioned above, you need a cheap and effortless way to collect all this data. Furthermore, it should be in a format that you can efficiently process and compare to the project plan.

Before you start inventing something complex, you need to ensure that you have the following simple processes.

#1: COLLECT FIRSTHAND INFORMATION

A daily sync-up meeting is an excellent way to collect high-level information. Why is it so popular and effective? Because it is simple, and there's a strict format. Every day, people answer the following:

- What did I do yesterday?
- What am I going to do today?
- What are the challenges that impede my work?

It should take no more than 30 minutes per day. If you have a large team, invite group leads only. During these meetings, you'll quickly prioritize tasks that people need to work on in accordance with your plan. In addition, you'll know about all the problems and roadblocks in advance.

But keep in mind that you don't resolve problems or capture their progress data. The team simply reports their progress and you can adjust their plans for the day. After the meeting, they need to reflect these changes in the project management software and inform their subordinates. If you need to solve urgent problems, plan a follow-up meeting.

#2: AGGREGATE DATA FROM PROJECT MANAGEMENT SOFTWARE

Ideally, you should use project management software to plan the tasks for the team. In turn, the project team should use it to log time spent, expenses, and other progress data for each task they perform. This will save time when collecting and aggregating performance data.

Modern project management software has built-in reports or capabilities to export performance data. After that, you can transfer the data into your progress report.

The key here is to educate the project team to use all available technology to report their progress. Unless you give them compelling reasons to track progress accurately and regularly, they're unlikely to keep doing it. For example, tell them that it'll ease the pressure when it comes to compiling the project progress report.

#3: DAILY WORK REPORTS

No one likes reports. Especially internal reporting to collect data. If you don't have project management software that allows the team to collaborate and track their progress, you have to do it manually. Of course, you can track everything in emails and shared spreadsheets. Whatever you choose, you need to make it effortless and valuable.

Here is a possible format:
<Work package name>
<Task name>
Initial estimate: 10h
Time spent: 6h (this is commutative time)
Remaining estimate: 1h (notice that this field shows a revised estimate for finishing the task)

Using WBS elements in these reports will make it easier to sum it all up on the deliverable level.

On larger projects, such an approach is overwhelming. Instead, you must use project management software. However, on smaller ones, it works like a charm. You can use this data to update master plans and take corrective action if needed.

WHAT SHOULD YOU DO WITH ALL THIS INFORMATION?

So, on a daily basis, you collect and analyze information on all aspects of the project. While everything is within thresholds, you keep monitoring. All daily activities need to be on track if the whole project is to be the same.

Unexpected challenges appear all the time, so it's wise to motivate the team to speed up a bit from time to time. This creates a buffer to cover up delays. But, in practice, there are no specific tools, techniques, or tricks that you can use to physically speed up the work. All you can do is to help people organize the work better. For example, you can:

- facilitate their meetings to ensure that they use the time efficiently;
- apply a bit of micromanagement to shorten delays and transitions from task to task;
- set clear priorities, trim unnecessary tasks, and remove distractions;
- brainstorm a better/faster/more efficient approach; or
- find a SME who has a solution.

So, all you can do here is increase the team's productivity. That's why I believe you should be an expert in productivity yourself. Motivation and productivity tricks are the only tools you can apply without using the project's resources.

However, you may notice that you are systematically getting behind schedule and over budget. Moreover, you use up all risk reserves, and nothing you do helps you get back on track. This means there's a systematic error in your plan. You overestimated the team's performance, underestimated the complexity, or didn't account for all the risks.

Likewise, you may discover a significant piece of scope that you missed during planning, or a severe risk that has appeared in the process. In any case, you have two options. First, negotiate to use up some of the management reserves and stick to the initial plan. Management reserves are not a part of the project baselines so they don't impact the bottom line. Second, adjust the plan to include this new information. It's bad practice to hide such things and try to handle them behind the scenes. In most cases, you'll make the situation even worse.

CHAPTER 53
HOW TO WRITE A PROJECT PROGRESS REPORT

A project progress report is an essential tool in project management. It serves many purposes. It:

- helps to build stakeholders' engagement;
- provides validation that you are on the right track;
- aligns the vision with the priorities of the project;
- helps maintain steady progress; and
- makes stakeholders feel that you are in control of the project.

It can also cover your back. But, if you treat it this way, it means that something is really wrong in your relationships with project owners or your boss.

Depending on the size, complexity, and dynamics of the project, you need to select a reporting period. Usually, it's weekly, fortnightly, or monthly. If you have daily status meetings with project owners, you may not need a progress report at all. Nevertheless, keep in mind other stakeholders who don't participate in those meetings. They may still require a regular update on your progress.

THE PURPOSE OF PROGRESS REPORTS

This may sound odd, but progress reports are not actually about progress. First of all, you try to earn trust from project owners. You need to show that you are in control of the project. Moreover, you need to prove you know how to reach the project objectives.

Once you achieve that trust, your reports serve as a reminder that everything is working well. At this point, they become a tool for problem solving. You trained project owners to do everything you needed them to do to keep the project on track. And if you highlight a problem in the report, it means you need their sign-off or even help. So, they need to take action.

Here's how it should work: You send a report and point out problems if you have any. Being a great project manager, you also provide a solution. At the very least, you start discussions to find one.

Now, project owners need to respond. Sometimes they take too long. You need to make it clear that not responding is tacit agreement with your suggested action plan. It's critical that you take the initiative to drive the project forward. Delayed responses should not be an excuse to halt progress. Sometimes, that means you need to take responsibility for a decision. Sometimes, you'll have to proceed based on your best judgment and capabilities.

In general, if there's no immediate feedback, you can assume that your progress is acceptable and proceed as planned. It's great when project owners trust your judgments. Nevertheless, I wouldn't recommend using these tacit agreements as a matter of course. Reach out to the project owners and get feedback on the project's progress. Ideally, you want to meet them personally, or at least on a video call, once a week.

PROJECT PROGRESS REPORT TEMPLATE

You need to understand that the project progress report has only one goal: To make stakeholders feel like you are in control of the project. In practice, you won't see many project owners interested in all the details of implementation. They simply want to reach the objectives. Moreover, they are paying you because they don't want to spend time on the project.

That's why I always recommend reporting the progress on a higher level than the way you manage it. You should sum it all up with deliverables and milestones. Moreover, your reports should be easy to read. Last but not least, they should engage stakeholders to take the necessary action to help you keep the project on track. That's why I suggest using the report template outlined below directly in the body of an email, not in a file. If you can replicate the same approach in your project management tool and it's always up to date, that's even better.

Here are the main sections of the report.

EXECUTIVE SUMMARY

This is the most crucial part. Here you need to summarize all the important information in the rest of the report. Treat it as if it is the only paragraph that people will read – as it probably will be!

Do I need visuals here?

I like a visual representation of the project's health. But I think they are more useful for daily updates. If you use a collaboration tool that everyone uses daily, it's better to have a dashboard there.

Do I need charts in this section?

No. Keep it as short as possible and in simple terms.

Where should defects go?

At this stage, I suggest only highlighting any outstanding known defects severe enough to impact the project progress. Others can go in the 'What Was Done' section.

The weekly status report is not the place to detail defects. So, either have a separate report or describe all the known defects in a release note related to the deliverable.

MILESTONE CHART

To reinforce the feeling that everything is on track, you should reiterate the milestone dates in every report. If you plan your project well, a slight variation of scope, costs, or time should not impact your milestones and they will stay the same for the duration of a project.

You can put it as a simple list of dates:

- Alpha build – June 23.
- PayPal enabled – July 6.
- Membership area – July 24.
- Ready for launch – August 3.

WHAT WAS DONE

It may feel like you need to highlight all completed tasks during the reporting period. However, stakeholders won't get much value from that. They don't keep everything in their heads. Moreover, they don't have time to micromanage you and your team.

Most of all, they are interested in ensuring that the team works on the right tasks and towards the required goals. So, how can you assure them? Once again, the best way is to use WBS elements. They should be familiar with these by now from the planning stages when you named deliverables using their language. So, they can relate to them.

Depending on the required level of details, you can put it this way:

Deliverable 1
– Work Package 1.1 (70% done)
– Work Package 1.2 (30% done)

Or

Deliverable 4
– Work Package 4.1.1 (3 days left)
– Work Package 4.1.2 (2 days left)

How should I state progress?
You can use one of the following approaches:

- Percentage complete e.g., 25% done.

- Remaining calendar or person-days.
- Due date for a work package.
- A complex progress report e.g., Work Package 4.1.1 (estimated: 10d, used: 7d, remaining: 5d)

In the last point, the initial estimate was 10 person-days, of which we have used 7, and we need 5 more. This implies that we are 2 days behind schedule, either because the estimate was inaccurate or additional tasks were added. You need to clarify the reasons.

Keep in mind that this information alone is not sufficient to understand whether the project is in danger or not. That's why you need an overall status in the executive summary.

There is no right or wrong format. It all depends on the preference of the stakeholders and what they see as the most informative.

WHAT YOU PLAN TO DO

Use the same structure for the items planned for the next week. You need to state how you are following the project plan. If you cannot keep to the plan, this is where you say so.

Then, list the WBS elements you plan to work on, so the weekly status report is consistent with the 'What Was Done' section in the next report. Also, it saves lots of time as you can copy most of the entries from one section to another.

RISKS

This section should include imminent risks that stakeholders should be aware of. Don't go into too much detail – just link to the risk register.

BLOCKERS AND IMPEDIMENTS

These are current problems impeding the project team's work. Why are they separate from the risks? Because they are actually happening.

Likewise, you state events and factors that are already in effect and are impeding your work, and that need to be resolved as soon as possible.

NEXT REPORT DATE

In the last section, you should state the date for the next report. This is a small thing, but it has a big psychological effect. You are promising to report back on that date that you did what you planned to do in the intervening period.

It's vital to keep to the schedule and never miss a report. So, always check for holidays and days off. It's okay if you deviate by a few days here and there. But do state the exact date by which you will provide the next report.

ENCOURAGE STAKEHOLDERS TO TAKE ACTION

In practice, you'll notice that stakeholders will carefully read the first few reports. After that, they'll relax. The very fact that the report is in their inbox will be enough to make them feel safe and secure about the project. So, most of the time, they'll review just the summary.

You'll send the report in an email below the signature. The body of the email should emphasize the most critical topic and point to the relevant section of the report. Here's an example:

Hi John and Edward,

Let's schedule a meeting tomorrow at 13:00. Unfortunately, we have a blocker that impacts our schedule during the next week. We need to resolve it as soon as possible.

Please accept my meeting invite or propose an alternative time that works for you.

The weekly progress report is below. Please review the blockers section.

Best Regards,

Dmitriy Nizhebetskiy

Project Manager, PM Basics

+38091123456789

dmitriy@pmbasics101.com

So, do not broadcast your report. Don't assume that your stakeholders are waiting with bated breath to read it. Instead, just highlight anything important.

EFFICIENT PROGRESS REPORT

You need to update your project information on a daily basis. Don't wait until the reporting date. In the previous chapter, I described the routine to collect all progress data in the mornings. It's easier to dedicate 15 minutes each day than to retrospectively collect this information for the whole week.

Moreover, I believe that you shouldn't collect the progress data on your own. Instead, it should be a little daily routine for each team member to log their efforts, expenses, and finished tasks. First, you need to establish a simple process for the whole team. After that, you need to remind everyone to follow the process rigorously.

If you don't have project management software where everyone can report their progress, you need to delegate collecting this data to group or team leaders evenly between them. Also, you need to create a template so that they can collect the data in a common format. In the long run, you should be able to simply copy and paste the information into your email and the report.

Weekly status reports are your primary tools to manage stakeholders' expectations. Your first priority is to make them valuable. These reports should help the project owners to make the right decisions without having to analyze lots of information.

If you haven't yet accessed the supporting materials, do so now. My progress report template is included:

https://itpmschool.com/materials

CHAPTER 54
HOW TO CHANGE A PROJECT PLAN

Change management is the formal and structured process by which the project management plan is altered. So, when should you start thinking about it? Right from the start and throughout planning.

Changes are inevitable. So, you need to ensure that you can incorporate them into your project plan without recreating it from scratch. Bear in mind that it needs to integrate with all the tools you used for planning like the requirements traceability matrix, WBS, project schedule, etc. When you plan each aspect of a project, you should always think about the ways it can be changed.

Nevertheless, no matter what methodology you use, you want to avoid changes as much as possible. Don't be confused by Scrum or any other agile and adaptive methodologies. They are designed to minimize the impact of quickly changing requirements. So, yes, overall, they welcome changes. However, a change of scope within an ongoing iteration is a no-no. The same applies to plan-driven projects on the deliverable level.

So, you should focus your efforts on avoiding changes in the first place. In practice, that means creating a realistic and flexible project plan that manages risks to cover uncertainties. It also needs some space for feedback and minor corrections of requirements along the way.

THE CORRECT MINDSET

There is no such thing as a small change on a project. A change in requirements obviously leads to a change in project scope. After that, the change affects the schedule and costs. However, it may introduce a conflict. It may present new risks. It will require additional effort to assure quality. It may require skills and knowledge the project team doesn't presently have. It may require changes in contracts with vendors and other third parties.

What's more important is that it will impact stakeholders' expectations. So, you need to communicate changes and control people's attitude towards them.

As the project manager, you need to understand that a change is never simple and it:

- always impacts several aspects of a project;
- always has complex interrelations with known activities and risks;
- requires systematic assessment;
- should never be included without analysis; and
- should be approved by the project owners.

Therefore, you should plan to avoid changes in the first place: If you have to accept them, never do so lightly.

WHEN DOES CHANGE MANAGEMENT BEGIN?

Change management starts only after a project management plan is approved. Therefore, you do not need to create a change request during the planning phase. Here, nothing is final and everything is a draft.

I want to ensure that you understand this. Whether you have a project management plan or a sprint backlog in Scrum, once it is signed and approved, the only way to introduce a change is by creating a formal change request.

WHO CAN REQUEST A CHANGE?

It's obvious that project owners can always request a change in requirements, schedule, budget, or any other aspect of the project. However, a project manager and other project stakeholders may also do so.

Not all stakeholders have the power and authority to enforce a change. But they can at least ask for one. Likewise, they may use their influence on fellow stakeholders to introduce a change on your project.

FOUR TYPES OF CHANGE REQUESTS

In theory, there are four types of requests, as discussed below. They all mean a change in the execution of a project, but there are subtle differences. In practice, they are not standardized, so you may only work with a generic change request.

You can use a **change request** to alter the approved plan, its baselines, a policy or procedure, etc. So, it is a primary request.

You can take **corrective action** to get back to the initial plan. Remember that you can't change the project plan at will. You must do everything possible to keep to the latest approved version. You need to resolve problems, remove impediments, and push the project further.

However, when things go really wrong, you need to get back on track. For example, you can use reserves or get an additional budget to pay for the team's overtime to catch up. If that doesn't help, you can suggest removing something from the project scope or pushing the deadline.

Preventive action is similar, but you try to take action beforehand. It applies to new and imminent challenges that you can't resolve with proper risk management. You try to prevent possible problems by including some measures in your plan.

Defect repair doesn't happen too often. It's specific to industries where a defect can lead to a severe change in scope. For example, you have a significant defect in a bridge's pylon, so you need to demolish it and build a new one.

Using these different categories will help you to differentiate and track changes.

CHANGE MANAGEMENT WORKFLOW

Ideally, stakeholders should use one workflow to request a change to the project management plan. But, in practice, they will request changes in all manner of ways. The worst are those made verbally at a meeting.

Moreover, a person may simply highlight a problem. For example, a SME finds a critical issue. He's not obliged to submit a formal change request. Instead, he simply describes the issue. But it's a real problem and, now that you know about it, you can't ignore it. So, you'll have to file a change request yourself.

In change management, the bulk of the work is on you. Your goal is to make it as simple as possible. Then, you need to educate stakeholders about the importance of this process. Therefore, let me elaborate on the critical steps for an efficient change management workflow.

STEP #1: MAINTAIN A CHANGE LOG

To make it easier down the road, it's better to have a standard form for a change request. At the very least, you need to ask stakeholders to provide one critical piece of information – how will this change help you achieve the project objectives? If it doesn't, you should reject the request.

However, in the real world, you won't have the authority to reject such requests on your own. Instead, you need to make a strong case against the change. Project owners will then have to decide based on the provided information.

You need a simple spreadsheet to track all change requests. Capture the name of the requestor, and a description and justification of the change.

When a request comes in, it doesn't always mean that it must be prioritized over all other activities. Instead, capture it in a change log. If it is not urgent, select the most appropriate time to address the request. But do communicate your plans to the relevant stakeholders.

STEP #2: ASSESS THE IMPACT

Often, the most trivial changes bring the most severe problems. Moreover, small changes have a compound effect. So, you should always assess the impact on all aspects of a project: requirements, scope, schedule, costs, risks, HR, quality, etc.

You analyze this in the context of the existing constraints and promises you have already made. You should take into consideration short- and long-term objectives.

In the long run, you need to create a new version of the project scope, schedule, and budget. So, you can use the same planning steps we discussed to incorporate the change to ensure that you don't miss how the change impacts the plan. Again, project management software can be handy here.

In any case, assessment of change requests takes time from the team. Therefore, you should discuss the priority of this activity with project owners.

STEP #3: IDENTIFY OPTIONS TO INTEGRATE THE CHANGE

Some changes may be as simple as adding a new task. Others may significantly impact the project plan or even change processes.

In either case, you need to find the best way to integrate the change into the existing project plan and baselines. You may need to develop several alternative options. This may include compressing or fast-tracking the schedule, removing or swapping parts of the scope, adding better resources or more people, etc. Each alternative will have pros and cons, and different impacts on key project metrics. The project owners need to decide what trade-off to make.

STEP #4: REVIEW A CHANGE REQUEST WITH PROJECT OWNERS

Next, you need to present the change request and available options.

You need to provide the best possible options and the project owners must choose one. In some cases, you may need to do this in front of a change control board: A group of people who will evaluate your options and make a decision. In other cases, you'll discuss it directly with the project owners via email or a meeting.

But that doesn't mean that any of the options will be suitable. Sometimes, you'll need to select a lesser evil – the best of a bad bunch. Sometimes, a change simply doesn't fit into the project's constraints. So you either need to change the baselines or to reject a good idea.

Nevertheless, a better strategy is not to discard ideas but to propose including them in the next project or subsequent product release. This way, you can collect enough scope for another project.

STEP #5: UPDATE THE CHANGE LOG

After you get a decision from the project owners, you need to update the change log.

The idea is to avoid wasting time going over and over the same change request. Believe me, I've seen stakeholders push a request several times. Unless something dramatically changes, the requests you've already rejected should not be reviewed again.

STEP #6: MAKE CHANGES TO THE PROJECT MANAGEMENT PLAN, DOCUMENTATION, OR BASELINES

If a change request is approved, you need to alter your project management plan, baselines, or processes. This new version becomes your baseline from now on. And you continue tracking progress against it.

STEP #7: MANAGE STAKEHOLDERS' EXPECTATIONS

It is critical to notify stakeholders about changes to the project plan. In the case of changes to the schedule, you need to provide an update on key milestones. Likewise, if you changed the scope, stakeholders may no longer get the specific deliverable they were expecting. Or some extra work for them appears. Any change can impact the commitments of a project stakeholder.

Don't assume that stakeholders track project progress. They don't read your progress reports carefully. So, it is worth explicitly informing stakeholders about the change in most cases. You never know whether they have some hidden expectations. This may cause additional discussions and negotiations.

SIMPLE IN THEORY, HARD IN PRACTICE

The workflow is simple. However, it requires rigorous implementation.

If you planned a project well, you will have some reserves and slack in the schedule. So, it is always possible to incorporate some additional work. Likewise, project owners may think that it's normal to provide change requests whenever they want. Therefore, it's tempting to take a shortcut and include a small change without going through the formal process. Never do that!

Your reserves are finite, and you should spend them on risks you've already identified for the scope and that the project owners have already approved. So always follow the process when you get a change request.

Poor change management is often a cause of problems, extra work, and confusion. On the one hand, you need a process to handle all change requests. On the other, you need courage and mental strength to resist assertive stakeholders and their demands. Otherwise, your project will soon become a mess. And, at the end of the day, you'll have to deal with it.

CHAPTER 55
COMMUNICATION METHODS

Your project management and leadership are entirely reliant upon how well you communicate with people, whether that's verbal, written visual, or how well you just listen. Every day, you are using emails, instant messages, meetings, voice calls, slide decks, one-on-one meetings, request tickets, etc.

It's not an exaggeration to say that a project manager spends 80%–90% of their working day communicating in one way or another, which is why you need a deep understanding of how best to do it.

HOW DOES COMMUNICATION WORK?

We use words, emotions, and body language when communicating. The person receiving our message has to try and decode it. That's where the most significant challenge lies because of personal bias. It doesn't work the same way for two given individuals. So, you need to ensure that your message is simple to decode and without unnecessary complications – for example, emotions.

When the receiver decodes the message, you will get feedback in the form of their body language, emotions, and words, which is the only way to interpret whether they understood your message correctly.

That's why active listening is such a powerful technique for a project manager. It helps you generate informative feedback.

Never assume that you send a clear, unambiguous message. You need to always verify that.

Moreover, the method you choose is a part of the equation. Even if a person is engaged and willing to help you, some methods may restrict their enthusiasm. Why? Because each method in project management implies different levels of responsibility.

DON'T GET CAUGHT IN THE COMMUNICATION LOOP

A by-product of poor communication is a communication loop. It's the worst enemy of productivity and engagement. Imagine you need assistance from a stakeholder. You write an email, describe the context, and ask one direct question needing a "Yes" or "No." Simple as could be. You send it.

Several hours later, you get the response. What the heck? It says: "Why do you need this in the first place? Give me all the details."

You explain the whole history of the matter. The next reply says: "Please send me the specification, designs, and all related communication. I'll review it later."

Oh my … You have all those in your inbox already! Why are you asking me to do that?

After several more days and useless emails, the stakeholder asks you for a meeting because he needs to clear things up.

That is the communication loop. So, to avoid it, you need to use the right communication method. You should have started with a meeting or phone call.

WHY THE CORRECT COMMUNICATION METHOD IS IMPORTANT?

Imagine you found a defect. And you know exactly who caused it. How can you communicate this information? You can:

- tap her on a shoulder and whisper, "I found a defect. Please fix it."

- send an instant message;
- send an email only to her;
- notify her and the whole team about the defect at a sync-up meeting;
- send an email about the defect to her and copy in your management (Not sure why you don't like her that much!); or
- submit a ticket in the bug-tracking system and assign it to her. The system will send her a notification.

I hope you can spot the difference in the formality of each of these methods. One will inspire trust and gratitude. Others will humiliate. Some may even harm their career. However, choosing the right one can position you as a leader and part of a team.

Do also note that each method can have merit depending on the context. You'll need to use your common sense to determine which is appropriate in the circumstances. You should understand that the response will be different in each case as well.

EVERLASTING EMAIL TRAILS

Here is an important thing you need to remember: An email lives forever. It is Connor MacLeod, the Highlander of the modern office. So even if you and the receiver delete it, the mailing server will keep a backup.

That is not all. An email can be used as evidence in court if you fail a project. Even if it doesn't go that far, your boss will use emails to establish whom to blame. People are therefore reluctant to share their thoughts and concerns in emails. They tend to keep them as formal as possible.

As a result, they are not the best way to get support and brainstorm solutions. Or, indeed, to begin escalating an issue. That will put a lot of stakeholders into defensive mode at once.

However, they are effective if you want a trail of evidence and agreements.

USE INSTANT MESSENGERS TO WARM UP ENGAGEMENT OR CLARIFY DETAILS

Many think that Skype, MS Teams, or Slack are more private – wrong! All of these tools can save the conversation history. So, they are similar to emails.

Nevertheless, they give you an option to solve a problem quickly and quietly. However, it's a good practice to follow up on any agreement made in a messenger. In most cases, you need to inform the project stakeholders about your decisions. But make sure you tell the person(s) with whom you've been messaging that that's what you're doing.

USE MEETINGS TO MAKE DECISIONS AND SELL IDEAS

Meetings can be a powerful tool to get things done. But they can also be a massive waste of time when they are misused – which they frequently are in project management.

In the two years leading up to the publication of this book, meetings evolved. With the wide adoption of remote working, they have become a quick way to do everything: Share information, resolve a problem, find a solution, etc.

But, ideally, you should not waste time describing a problem or sharing information at a meeting. Instead, you need to email all the required information in advance. At the same time, participants need to come prepared. Remember, a meeting is a tool to make a final decision when everyone is on the same page already. Yes, you can discuss some fine details or provide clarifications. However, the goal is to generate a decision, an action plan, or a solution.

However, it doesn't work this way in the real world. Instead, managers sit at online meetings the whole day. The only important variable you can control is the participants of a given meeting. So, choose wisely whose time you take from the project work.

Likewise, you can use meetings as a platform for a speech. For example, we sell ideas of project management all the time. So you need to become proficient at public speaking.

A simple technique that you can use right away is storytelling. I'm not talking about fairy tales. People relate to stories far more than business jargon and spreadsheets. So, whenever possible, try to come up with a real-life story or an example to make your point. Likewise, you can use stories to find the root cause of a problem. Stories help people visualize processes and activities. You can explain how something could happen more vividly.

PHONE CALLS GET THINGS DONE

In essence, it's a one-on-one meeting. You can use any medium available. However, in-person meetings and interviews are still the best.

Personal agreements are the most efficient way to push the project further. While at the same time, it is the riskiest one.

You can solve many delicate problems one on one. In addition, you can find out a lot of helpful information in private conversations. So, it is the best way to build engagement with stakeholders. And, while everything goes well, no one will ever blame you for managing a project this way. However, in the case of a crisis, you may not verify all agreements. So, balance the risks and the trust you can put into a stakeholder.

USE REQUEST TICKETS TO FINALIZE A DEAL

Request tickets are even more formal than emails. They are used to request someone's action, or to acquire a tool or a piece of equipment, using strict protocols. For example, companies create a ticket system to control expenses, inventory, and privileges to access sensitive information. In the long run, it's all about money. Therefore, you need to follow protocols.

It can be very bureaucratic and embroiled in internal politics. Therefore, only use a ticket to summarize an agreed-upon action. Do not solve or discuss problems here.

If you get follow-up questions in the tickets system, reach out to a responsible person with an instant message or a call. Discuss all the details and write one short and formal response in the ticket.

CHAPTER 56
HOW TO WRITE EMAILS

How many emails does a project manager write per day? I would say between 5 and 20. So, emails are still critical. You can't avoid them.

On the other hand, there are a lot of challenges with emails. Some are ignored, some replies are irrelevant, many mutate into an endless thread, and you may not even realize that there is a problem.

But, as a project manager, you need to ensure that you are an efficient communicator. So, below you'll find eight rules that will help you improve your emails.

RULE #1: MAKE SURE THE SUBJECT RINGS A BELL

Which subject is better?

Subject: Meeting notes

Or:

Subject: RE: 11/23 – Database migration meeting – Meeting Notes

Note that the second one is a reply to the initial email on the meeting, with all the information relevant to the topic.

Your subject line should trigger an instant recall of the matter you want to discuss.

In some cases, you can add "Urgent" and "Important" in the subject line. But I would recommend using these sparingly – for example, when you do want to draw the attention of all your superiors. Otherwise, it is much better to send an email first, then contact the recipient via Instant Messenger to explain why it is urgent or important.

And double-check the communication policies of your company. Such words may be limited to exceptional cases.

RULE #2: ADDRESS THE EMAIL CORRECTLY

There are three address lines in an email:

"To:" I prefer to have only one email address in this field of the person I want to take action or have a response from. If you need to ask several individuals to take action, make it clear at once. Use a special character to draw attention, like "@" or bold the names.

However, where possible, I recommend a simple approach: One email, one responsible person, one action.

"Cc:" This is where you include everyone else who needs to be informed. If you want people on this list to read your email, select them carefully for each separate message. People who are continually copied in for too long start treating such emails as spam. And what do you do with spam? Right! You ignore it.

"Bcc:" This allows you to add recipients that others won't know about. It might seem like a fantastic way to keep a third party or your boss in the loop, but you need to be very careful here not to be unethical or unprofessional.

There might be some legal and NDA cases when you need to Bcc someone, but you can always work around it by forwarding the email thread. I would suggest limiting the use of Bcc for the purpose of archiving your correspondence. This way, it can go to a separate email account or your assistant.

RULE #3: CUT TO THE CHASE

Your first sentence should state explain exactly what you want or need.

Here is an example of what not to write:

Hi John,
I want to introduce myself.
I'm Dmitriy Nizhebetskiy. I'm a software development project manager and
mentor. I help people become great project managers and fill their gaps in
knowledge and skills so that they can grow into great PMs.
Also, I want to schedule a short meeting to discuss our first steps.
Best Regards,
Dmitriy

Here is a better one:

Hi John,
I want to introduce myself and schedule a meeting today at 15:00 CET to
discuss our first steps.
I'm Dmitriy Nizhebetskiy. I'm a software development project manager and
mentor. I help people become great project managers and fill their gaps in
knowledge and skills so that they can grow into great PMs.
Best Regards,
Dmitriy

Still, this email is not good enough. It lacks a crucial component – a call to action (CTA)!

RULE #4: ARTICULATE WHAT YOU WANT WITH A CALL TO ACTION

Each and every email should end with a CTA. This should clearly state what you expect from the recipient.

In the previous example, I need John to confirm his attendance at the meeting. So, I end up with something like this:

Hi John,

I want to introduce myself and schedule a meeting today at 15:00 CET to discuss our first steps.
I'm Dmitriy Nizhebetskiy. I'm a software development project manager and mentor. I help people become great project managers and fill their gaps in knowledge and skills so they can grow into professional PMs.
Please confirm that today at 15:00 CET is a suitable time for you.
Best Regards,
Dmitriy

It may feel that some emails do not need a CTA. For example, when you provide a short answer or a document or when you don't need anything in return. That is not true. You need a CTA in all emails! You should be open to further dialogue. Therefore, you may end up with the following CTAs:

- Please let me know if you have any other questions.
- Please let me know if this answers your question.
- Feel free to contact me for any additional details.

This way you remove a barrier for clarification. Such CTAs will save you from lots of miscommunications.

RULE #5: ONE ACTION PER EMAIL

There should only be one CTA per email.

Let's say a busy person must answer several questions in the email promptly. What is the easiest workaround for them? Right! Select a simple question and give a short answer and worry about the other questions later. But that is not the result you are after.

RULE #6: PUT DETAILS IN THE MIDDLE

So, how do emails work in real life? John reads the subject and the first sentence even without opening the email. You do the same, don't you?

If the headline and the first sentence look important, you will open an email. But do you read it carefully at once? No! You just scan it first. Is it just for your information?

Then, you look for the CTA because you don't want to miss a request. After that, you check whether it is you who must answer it.

Moreover, you are trying to assess whether you can deal with it quickly or need time to prepare an answer.

Therefore, any details should not impede this natural process. Put them between your first sentence and the CTA.

RULE #7: KEEP IT SHORT. SHORTER!

The whole email should be as brief as possible. Any details should be attached or linked to if possible. Nowadays, with so much distraction, people aren't keen on reading reams of text.

For productivity reasons, lots of managers put "difficult" emails off. So, for example, if I get an email that needs a lot of time to read, investigate, and answer, I block the required time on my calendar. As a result, I have several time slots suitable for such activities per day.

Make it easier for a person to save time and prioritize the email. Only include what is important, with a headline, entry paragraph, and CTA.

Likewise, lots of managers use emails to assign a quick task. They don't require an immediate response, but you need to get back with a simple "Done" once you finish the task. One sentence and one-word emails are okay in this instance.

RULE #8: INCLUDE A PROFESSIONAL SIGNATURE

There are some rules when it comes to your signature.

Don't use images, especially of social networks. You may need to put a company's logo in your signature – that is okay.

Have different signatures for work and personal emails.

Here is the format you can use as a starting point:

<Name> <Last Name>
<Role Title>, <Company Name (can be a link to corporate site)>

<Mobile Phone>, <Office Phone>
<Instant Messengers (Skype name, corporate social network account)>

Here's how it looks when you fill it in:

Thanks in advance,
Dmitriy Nizhebetskiy
Project Manager,
Project Management Basics
+38091123456789
Skype: dmitriy@pmbasics101.com
* * *

Every email application has the functionality to create a signature. After that, it'll automatically appear at the bottom of each email you write.

1. NEVER ANSWER AN EMAIL AT ONCE

There are several reasons why:

- Don't get distracted from your current task. In most cases, people don't expect an immediate response.
- You build up certain expectations and stakeholders will expect a quick response, even out of office hours.
- The sender may sort things out without your involvement.
- Additional information may follow.

2. NEVER ANSWER AN EMAIL WHEN ANGRY

It simply never solves the problem. All you can achieve with a burst of anger is a broken relationship. If you feel that an email makes you angry or frustrated, leave it in the inbox for an hour. Then, think it through and get back with a cool head.

You are the project manager, remember? You have to resolve

conflicts, not create new ones. So, become aware of the feelings that an email or person invokes in you.

3. TREAT EMAIL AS THE LAST RESORT

If you have an option to solve a problem or deliver a message by other means, do it. Use emails to follow up on agreements and actions. It will save you a lot of time in the long run.

4. PROOFREAD EVERYTHING YOU WRITE

For me, this is a matter of professionalism and respect. I proofread any text I send. With that said, I'm not a native English speaker and I understand that there are quite a lot of mistakes that I miss. Nevertheless, I try to improve my writing skills all the time.

I use Grammarly on a daily basis. It has a free version that will eradicate 99% of your typos.

5. ADDRESS THE RIGHT PEOPLE

Don't copy everyone in just because you can. Limit the number of recipients to a minimum. Remember, it may harm your engagement with stakeholders.

6. KEEP YOUR TONE PROFESSIONAL

No matter to whom you are sending an email, your tone should be professional and calm – no jokes, no sarcasm, commanding or yelling. This leaves little room to avoid your questions or requests.

7. KEEP FORMATTING SIMPLE

By all means use formatting tools like bold type to highlight critical aspects, but remember: The less you use it, the more powerful its impact when you do. In most professional emails, anything other than bold type is just a distraction.

Also, keep in mind compatibility between different devices and systems. For instance, fancy formatting created on Mac OS may look distorted on Windows. Likewise, don't forget that many people read emails on their mobile phones. So, keep the formatting of your email as simple as possible.

CHAPTER 57
HOW TO PLAN AND RUN MEETINGS

Meetings are hungry, time-consuming monsters. Moreover, they rarely achieve much. I have worked in progressive and mindful organizations with defined rules and culture. Nevertheless, I'm still invited to pointless meetings way too often. The problem is that people don't associate time spent at a meeting with project expenses.

That's why I like the idea of giving a monetary value to a decision made at a meeting. It's a simple and effective way of illustrating the cost of a meeting in dollars. The calculations are straightforward as well. Simply multiply the hourly rates of all participants by the hours you spent to reach a decision.

Do this exercise several times, and you'll find that your team meetings are golden.

To make your meetings efficient, you need to plan the aspects outlined below. There are quite a lot of considerations but, in practice, it all happens at the back of your mind. You don't spend too much time planning every meeting. First, you'll work with the same people most of the time, and be aware of their expertise and responsibilities. Second, you can have templates ready for meetings with similar goals and agendas. As a result, you bear the fruits of your planning efforts.

You need to let these rules sink in. Then, try to follow this step-by-step process several times. Soon, you'll do it all on autopilot.

1. PREPARE AN AGENDA

There's always the temptation to just walk into the room and give a speech that mobilizes and engages all participants. Then all you need to do is reap the rewards. So, it's tempting to skip this step.

But, frankly, you're probably not a captivating public speaker. Sorry.

You need to plan before you act. Conversations tend to derail very quickly. The only way to stick to the point is to have an agenda. If a meeting is not worth an agenda, then it's not worth having in the first place.

Besides the main topic you need to discuss, there are always some additional points on the agenda. It's like scope creep. You need to identify every key activity in a meeting. All of them take time – for example, introducing new attendees, voting for the best idea, assigning action items.

2. SET A TIME LIMIT

A meeting should start and end at the scheduled times and be no longer than necessary. Otherwise, according to Parkinson's law, it will just fill whatever time you give it.

You should never delay the start of a meeting. By doing so, you are tacitly condoning latecomers. On the other hand, those who always come on time are penalized by having to wait.

Also, keep in mind that some people might have other meetings scheduled. By finishing your meeting later, you can cause them difficulties. They will have to miss the conclusion of your meeting, which is the most critical part. Or they'll have to be late for their next meeting. In the worst-case scenario, it has a knock-on effect for the rest of that day's meetings.

3. SET THE PURPOSE FOR EACH MEETING

Each meeting should have a goal – to brainstorm a list of ideas, make a decision, or sync up on the status of a project. That is something you need to achieve within the allocated time.

If you don't have a clearly defined purpose, any outcome is possible. Why waste your time?

Remember that I recommend using a meeting to make a decision, solve a problem, or sell an idea.

4. CHOOSE PARTICIPANTS WISELY

There's a limit to how many people should attend a meeting, beyond which it becomes a waste of time. The number varies depending on the purpose. But I would say no more than 10.

The main idea is to choose people who can add value to the meeting or decision. People should not wonder why they are there.

For example, don't invite management, customers, or sponsors to brainstorming meetings on a technical matter, even if they seem interested.

The same applies to your project team members. You don't need the whole team for each and every discussion. You only need people who can contribute to making a better decision. On the other hand, it's also important to include people with different expertise. This way, you'll ensure you have a range of perspectives from all departments.

That is why it's critical to define a purpose for a meeting. And it's best when you have only one goal per meeting.

5. DEFINE RESPONSIBILITIES AND YOUR EXPECTATIONS FOR EACH PARTICIPANT

Have you ever wondered how a person can decline an invitation to a meeting? It's easy when you are the boss and too busy: You just don't show up. But what about one of your peers?

You can try it yourself. Take a look at the agendas of the last 10 meetings you were invited to. I bet that there was at least one in which there was no need for you to participate. Were you invited just because someone copied you into the email thread? Or did they expect some expertise from your side?

So, explicitly state your expectations whenever you invite someone to your meeting. What do you want from that person? Why should he join the meeting? If you are not telling them your expectations, you are just bossing them around and ordering them to comply without questioning you.

On the other hand, if they decide not to come to your meeting, don't think they can help, don't want to help, or don't have time, then there's no point in them being there. Why force them to participate?

Instead, let people choose to help you.

You don't need to do this for every meeting. With most of your team members and stakeholders, you only need to discuss their responsibilities and your expectations once. You expect them to participate because you will continually need their expertise. However, when you invite a person sporadically or for the first time, spell out your expectations.

6. PROVIDE ALL RELEVANT INFORMATION BEFORE A MEETING

Whether you want to discuss something important or are looking for expertise, provide all background information beforehand. Give people enough time to analyze any documentation, ideas, your agenda, and your expectations.

The purpose of a meeting is to sync up, brainstorm, or make a decision. Do not waste time on anything that each participant can do personally. For example, reading documents out loud during meetings is unprofessional. Everyone can read.

You must make it clear that you expect participants to be prepared for the meeting, which should produce solutions, not describe a problem.

7. SCHEDULE MEETINGS BEFOREHAND

How does it feel when someone invites you to an hour-long meeting with five minutes' notice? Yep, lousy, because it disrupts your day.

"Urgent" meetings happen from time to time. But I don't think they are very efficient. You get everyone together, and the first thing you do is broadcast information and the context of the meeting. Then, you may try to discuss something on the spot.

So, if you need to mobilize your team, set up a short meeting first to introduce the problem. After people have had time to think it through, plan follow-up meetings to brainstorm the solutions.

8. DON'T BE LATE

I know I've said this before, but it's worth repeating. Always:

- come on time;
- start a meeting on time
- finish a meeting on time; and
- Be mindful of people's other commitments either side of your meeting.

9. LEAD THE MEETING, STICK TO THE AGENDA AND TIMELINE

If you don't lead and control the meeting, it will become a mess despite all your previous efforts. There should be a purpose to every minute. Take the lead and introduce newcomers. If everyone is familiar with each other, skip it. Thank everyone for coming and get to the point. Respect their time.

Quickly recap the agenda and the purpose of the meeting. State what a successful outcome should look like. It should take less than a minute. Otherwise, you've planned to discuss too much.

- Keep to the agenda.
- Drag the conversation back to the agenda.
- Track the time you allocated for each point of the agenda.

When you lead a meeting, it takes courage to keep everyone focused. It's your meeting, your plan. You need to be confident enough to restrain superiors and peers. Just be respectful. If they have some excellent ideas, propose to discuss them after the meeting.

Remember, it is crucial to have some time at the end of a meeting (see my next point).

But, what if time runs out and you have not achieved your meeting goals? Finish this one on time and schedule another one. If this happens, you have underestimated the problem. Or you've discovered something new and important. Plan again, then act.

10. ASSIGN DELIVERABLES AND DEADLINES

Even if the purpose of your meeting is a single decision, there will always be at least one deliverable – the meeting notes. Someone has to inform others about the decision and log it.

In most cases, your meetings will end up with the next steps to keep the wheels turning – the action items. Therefore:

1. Describe deliverables (meeting notes, next meeting, a report, a plan, etc.).
2. Assign one responsible person to each deliverable.
3. Set and agree on the deadlines.
4. Document deliverables in the meeting notes.

11. DOCUMENT AND PUBLISH MEETING NOTES

If you are leading the meeting, it is okay to delegate meeting notes to someone else.

Nevertheless, it is your responsibility to deliver the meeting notes.

Always invite others to add to or correct the notes. You may have missed something. Others may have understood it differently. This is an excellent way to avoid miscommunication. Just make everyone feel comfortable with correcting you.

Everyone knows the rules of an efficient meeting. Nevertheless, we still spend way too much time on them – they drag on unnecessarily, or they are held when an email would have been fine. What can you do about it? At the very least, make your own meetings useful. That would be a great start.

CHAPTER 58
HOW TO RESOLVE CONFLICTS

Conflict is a good thing and totally natural whenever people need to collaborate. However, if they remain unresolved, they can lead to animosity between people and sour working relationships. So, you should welcome conflicts but always take steps to resolve them and control the outcome.

Knowing how to effectively resolve conflicts is critical for a project manager. Learning the basics will serve you well throughout your whole career. There is a great deal of theory to be learned about conflict resolution techniques, which is outside the scope of this book. So, I recommend that you take an in-depth course on LinkedIn, Udemy, or Skillshare.

However, as with many other techniques in project management, it's hard to imagine how to implement theory in practice. That's why below I have provided a transcript of a coaching session on conflict resolution I had with a friend of mine.

EXAMPLES OF CONFLICT RESOLUTION TECHNIQUES

We are sitting in a cafe near the office. Corwin hasn't said a word or touched his coffee since we arrived.

I tried to break the ice. "Okay, buddy, what's on your mind? You are so far away from here."

Corwin snapped out of his reverie and finally sipped his coffee. He sighed and shrugged in the manner of a man resigned to his fate. "This conflict is killing me. It's been dragging on for a month. And it seems like it is just getting started."

Corwin had been managing his team for more than a year already without any problems. He had finished many small projects successfully. Then, a few months ago, the project owners extended the contract. As a result, his team grew substantially. And, finally, technical officers noticed him.

We drank our coffee and ate our complimentary cookies for a minute in silence. Corwin seemed willing and ready to share his worries. But I did not want to push.

"My team leader clashed with that technical officer. Peter is his name. You worked with him, I believe?" Corwin sat back in his chair.

"Yes, I remember the guy. He can be a bit harsh sometimes."

"They are fighting on some technical aspect of a project. It looks so insignificant to me." Corwin rubbed his tired eyes. "Yet they both believe it's this huge disaster. And now it's getting really personal."

"Yeah, unresolved conflicts can become personal. Though they rarely start like that."

He smiled knowingly, telling me I'd hit the nail on the head.

"So, what would you do in my place?"

"There's no simple answer here. Let's review your options instead." I took out a notebook and put numbers from five to one. We were going to list conflict resolution techniques, from worst to the best.

5. FORCING A SOLUTION AT THE EXPENSE OF ONE SIDE

"What is the worst approach that you can take right now?" I asked, preparing to note down Corwin's answer.

Without thinking, he said, "For sure, I can force my team leader to follow Peter's requirements. There is no way to do it the other way around. I can't force Peter to agree with our point of view. His authority and reputation are at stake already."

"That is true. You dragged this battle to the surface. Everyone's watching," I said, writing down option number five. "Anyway, that will kill your relationship with Kevin. Is that his name? Your team leader, I mean."

"Yes, Kevin. Anyway, let's move on."

4. SMOOTHING THE CONFLICT WITH EMPHASIS ON AGREEMENTS

"Next, let's talk about the 'we are all in the same boat' approach," I suggested, smiling. We both knew it would never work with our colleagues.

"That's never going to cut it. Both of them believe they are making the project better. I can see that. But that's not the point. They want to prove that their solution is better. Reputation and ego are at stake."

"Better for whom?" I asked, getting to the heart of the matter.

"That's the problem, they are challenging each other. But I doubt it's for the good of the project."

"Conflict resolution should serve the interests of the customer," I reminded him.

"So, we both agree then," Corwin summarized. "This is a non-starter."

3. WITHDRAWAL OF THE CONFLICTING PARTIES

"Have you tried to separate them for a bit?" I asked.

"Sure," Corwin smiled sadly. "That's what I did in the first place after they started yelling. I thought it was just a temporary issue. So, I told them to communicate through me so I could mediate the conflict."

"It didn't work?"

"It was a total failure," sighed Corwin. "I tried to just ignore the conflict. But that's not something a good project manager does, right?"

"You are right. It might seem like you are cooling things down to buy some time to work it out. But, in fact, you are simply dragging out the conflict. Is this when it became personal and emotional?"

Corwin spooned milky cappuccino foam from the bottom of his cup. "That was a bad move, wasn't it?" he sighed. "Okay, what's next?"

2. COMPROMISING WITH BOTH PARTIES

I wrote down point number two and the word "compromise" as a hint.

Corwin grasped the idea quickly. "So, you are suggesting finding a solution that will satisfy both of them?"

"I'm not suggesting it because I already know the answer."

"Their solutions are mutually exclusive," Corwin observed. "The only way to please them both is to let them try both approaches. But who would approve that? It puts us in a bad light in front of the project owners. They're not going to want to pay for us to resolve a major disagreement."

"Yes, it questions our expertise and professionalism." So, we came to the last and the best conflict resolution technique.

1. COLLABORATING TO FIND THE BEST SOLUTION

We both sat staring into the distance, thinking what collaboration might look like in this case.

"How about a panel discussion?" I suggested.

"Mm, panel discussion … " Corwin said, intrigued. "So you're suggesting getting other technical experts to the table? Let them all openly discuss the pros and cons of both approaches?"

"Yes, moreover, we need someone whom they both respect and see as an authority," I continued. "But these experts should not be biased."

"Someone from another department, then?"

"Yes."

"That might work," mused Corwin, cheering up a bit. "So, either Peter or Kevin may be influenced by the authority of those experts."

"And it won't look like a failure. You can just support a valid point of view from another expert. Doesn't feel like backing away."

THERE'S NO SILVER BULLET

Several days later, we had lunch together.

"How did it go?" I asked about the panel discussion.

"It did not work," Corwin groaned. "It seemed like we had a great, open discussion. I thought Peter even agreed that our solution had lots of benefits. They even shook hands. But the next day, it all started again but on another topic."

I smiled back, "So, you fixed Peter's problem. But it turns out that was not the root cause of the problem, right?"

"Now I can see that it's not a 'technical' problem at all."

Corwin was nevertheless happy that the technical part of the conflict was resolved. "My project grew rapidly. Peter and his superiors didn't contribute to that growth. They totally missed it. So, now they try to catch up."

"What are you going to do with Peter?"

Corwin thought for a moment before replying. "No matter how much we try, these techniques do not always work. But I still need to get things done and keep up with our commitments to the client. So, I'll isolate Peter as much as I can, so the team has some breathing space to finish the work. We've wasted too much time and effort on this already."

"Sounds like a plan!"

The conflict lasted for several months after that. Despite all Corwin's best efforts, nothing worked. Corwin didn't have enough authority to tackle the root cause of internal politics on a higher level. Nevertheless, his efforts helped to minimize the impact on the project and the team's morale.

CHAPTER 59
HOW TO LEARN LESSONS

Continuous improvement is at the heart of project management. All projects are unique. So, we don't assume that we can come up with a perfect approach right from the start. However, most organizations stick to the same type of projects. That's why your goal is to improve efficiency and the chances of project success within the environment of a given organization.

So how does that work?

You carry out a project and, after you complete each deliverable, you collect lessons learned based on what worked and what didn't work well. You do the same for the project as a whole at the end. Ideally, you capture all these lessons somewhere that can be accessed by all project managers.

So, this is mostly for the benefit of future projects. That's why whenever you or a new project manager starts a project in your organization, he reviews all these lessons learned to identify the same risks and avoid making the same mistakes.

As always, there's a catch. We assume that the organization has a standardized project management approach so that you can apply lessons learned from one project to another. But, in the real world, that's rarely true.

ORGANIZATIONAL CHANGES

I don't want to discourage you from collecting lessons learned. However, you need to be realistic about your ability to make organizational changes in the real world.

I know from experience how difficult this can be. I proved with measurable metrics that one policy seriously impeded performance over several years. But no one did a thing about it because it had "always worked this way." So, I couldn't do anything about it on my own until I had sufficient authority within the company to influence other stakeholders to make this change – not experience, knowledge, or qualifications, but authority.

That's why I developed a system to focus your efforts on things you can control. Your lessons learned will improve aspects of project management that don't require sign-offs or authority to be changed. And, you'll also equip authoritative stakeholders with the required information to make the change when it comes to bigger issues.

LEVEL 1: RETROSPECTIVE MEETINGS

They may not be part of a normal project management framework, but I use retrospective meetings on all projects that I lead. If it's Scrum, I hold them at the end of the iteration. If it's a plan-driven project, I hold them once every two or three weeks. And yes, you do so as Scrum suggests.

You're not trying to solve every problem at the company. Instead, you focus on collaboration, communication, and the requirements for the work at hand. Sometimes you review processes and workflows where people have encountered problems. On this level, you try to improve the tactical performance of your team. You try to reduce the number of small things that demotivate your team members on a daily basis. And, believe me, small things matter.

So how do you do this in practice? You plan a meeting. You gather your whole team in one place or on one Zoom call. You need to cover just three things:

1. What went well?
2. What went wrong?
3. What do we want to continue doing, no matter what?

You allow all team members to speak up on all three topics. However, you should focus on the past two or three weeks of work.

Next, collect all the feedback and group it by the sources of problems. After that, you need to select only three things that you will act upon to improve the work. You can vote. In the long run, you will fix these three problems.

By the way, you can use an online tool for these retrospective meetings. So people can simultaneously provide this feedback. And it saves a lot of meeting time because you will simply vote and then discuss the action plan for the selected items.

The most important thing is to do your best to resolve those selected three problems. You need to do everything possible to make it happen and show your progress. It's a good idea to report on it during daily sync-up meetings. Otherwise, your team members will see that there is no benefit in collecting lessons learned because they lead to nothing. You want to avoid that. You want to show that you care about improving their performance and your project management approach.

LEVEL 2: DELIVERABLES AND DELIVERY

You should always aim to break down your project into tangible goals. Why's that important?

You have tasks assigned to each deliverable. You have estimates of time and cost. If there are related risks, you have allocated resources. You communicated on these deliverables, and so on. So, you have metrics and measurable performance data.

If you have tangible goals and effective means to measure performance in reaching them, then it's easier to reflect on the ability of the team to deliver those results and execute the project plan. But, again, this should be a meeting held after you produce a deliverable, demo it to project owners, and get feedback.

The agenda for this meeting is a bit different because you'll be comparing the planned values with the actual values of the team. So, on this level, it's important to focus on the problems with estimations of time and cost, controlling the project scope, and resolving risks. So, in general, you collect lessons learned in the process of creating and delivering part of the project.

This is a critical checkpoint for your whole project management plan. If you deviate on one deliverable, there's a chance that you will do the same on all other deliverables. So you need to catch systematic issues and inaccuracies.

And here is the truth of the matter: At the end of a project, project owners have already spent a lot of money, effort, and time. And they still need to get the product or service to end users. So, they'll be reluctant to make changes at the end of the project. Most likely, they'll force you to finish on time. That's why it's much easier to correct the project plan at the start or in the middle of the project rather than at the end. More so, if it's a mistake on your side.

So, try to analyze the accuracy of your estimates and your project planning in general while completing the first few deliverables. Then, based on your findings, you correct the whole project plan early on so that you can deliver the rest confidently.

To make this meeting efficient, you need to collect all this project information in advance and present it to your team. Then, together, you'll analyze the performance data. If something goes wrong, you can use the Five Whys technique to identify the root cause (look it up online if you haven't heard of this). In addition, you should be on the lookout for systematic problems that may affect other deliverables.

For example, you discover extra expenses from a vendor that you didn't anticipate during planning. The same vendor is responsible for three more deliverables, so there's a good chance those will lead to similar additional expenses.

If everything went well, congratulations! You can celebrate. Think about organizing a small team-building event.

LEVEL 3: ORGANIZATIONAL CHANGES

Now we're moving on to the project overall and what lessons can be learned for the organization as a whole – for example, improvements to processes, policies, and tools.

At the end of the project, set up a meeting for a final review. Start by reviewing all the lessons learned so far. Then, you need to gather feedback on the project as a whole from the team. You should look for the following:

- Systematic and repeated issues, conflicts, and defects.
- Activities that were more complicated than they should be.
- Processes that took a lot of effort but provided little value.
- Policies and procedures that adversely affected the team's performance.
- Stakeholders who made life harder for no apparent reason.

I don't believe in capturing the lessons learned and storing them in some archive, just for the sake of good practice. You need to take action on all these findings. However, the problem here is that you don't have the authority to do so yourself.

So, you need to collect these lessons learned and present them to your leadership or PMO officers, detailing the problem, evidence, and possible solutions. This way, you'll overcome resistance on their side. In essence, you simply do the work for them.

On the other hand, it's hard to improve something without having a baseline. So, if your company doesn't have any standardized processes, tools, or templates, you don't have a way to measure their efficiency. Most likely, you'll encounter the "If it ain't broke, don't fix it" attitude. Your leadership will be reluctant to make any changes because that requires a lot of effort, and it has been working a certain way for years.

Improving project management culture in your organization is a long and complicated journey. If you are willing to start it, the first step is to get support from your boss or your leadership. You should say, "I understand that we can't improve what we can't measure. And I'm willing to take the initiative and capture some of our best practices. This way, we can compare the performance on these processes for different projects."

After that, start by documenting some of the processes. Keep in mind that you don't need to capture the whole project management approach of the company. Instead, work with one process at a time and describe it. Ideally, you need to encourage your peers to do the same.

It's critical that you don't only have the support of your boss. Another stakeholder may also get in the way because they developed the initial project management approach. That's why you need to be objective. You should do your best to follow the initial process to the letter as they see it, as it was established.

You shouldn't be critical. Instead, you should objectively measure progress, show weak spots and places for improvement. You want to collect quantitative measurements of performance. Moreover, try collecting feedback from your team members. Don't just offer your subjective opinion.

There you have it, my three-level system for learning lessons. It may seem like a lot of work and meetings. But, in practice, it's just one additional meeting for you once every two or three weeks. From my experience, the main challenge here is to make it a priority over other daily routines.

CHAPTER 60
HOW TO FINISH A PROJECT

Execution is the longest part of the project life cycle. It can span over months or even years. Nevertheless, on a high level, the process is always the same. You work towards delivering tangible parts of the project one by one.

The biggest mistake you can make is not involving project owners in the process. Ideally, you should talk about the project on a daily basis. After each deliverable is completed, you should explicitly ask the project owners if they are happy with it. You want to get their feedback all the time. All of this will make finishing the project a formality.

ACCEPTANCE OF THE FINAL DELIVERABLE

Ideally, you should never finalize the execution at the last moment before deadline, though it happens from time to time. Remember that execution is not the last phase in the project life cycle. For example, you may need to test or deploy a product or service once you have finished developing it. That's why you need to define the project life cycle at the start and include all this work in the project plan.

If you engaged project owners during execution, they need to review only the final deliverable by the end of the project. They saw and participated in the development of all other intermediate deliverables. So, they don't need to provide feedback on the full product or service you created – just the final piece of the jigsaw.

In practice, that means getting formal acceptance of the main deliverable. An email will suffice. But make sure you have it in writing – a verbal confirmation in a meeting is not enough.

FINAL SIGN-OFF

You need a sign-off on the project as a whole, not just the final deliverable. In many cases, this means handing over all the results of your project. It is all the intellectual property of the project owners. In addition, they may request a final project performance report, invoices, project documentation, etc.

Accepting the final deliverable doesn't mean that project owners won't ask for additional deliverables or make changes to the product.

The main challenge here is that you need to release people at the end of the project. Companies don't like it when resources sit idle. Therefore, in practice, you try to find a new project for your people in advance, making agreements on transfers. Likewise, a contract may expire and the contractor will leave. The same applies to you. As a result, you may need to start a new project for a new client.

So, you need to determine whether you will be starting a new project with the same team for the same project owners. Or maybe they need just an amendment to add a small piece of scope. Likewise, you should be sure that the project owners won't find a critical defect in the deliverables you've provided. This will all require last-minute changes to resource allocation across many projects.

Final sign-off means that the project owners have got everything they asked for according to the contract and agreements. Moreover, they certify that you can release the team and archive the project. If they want something extra, it will be a new project.

RELEASE PEOPLE

Depending on the type of organization and its services, people who are not assigned to a project may become a burden on the company's budget. They are paying wages instead of a client. Likewise, while a person is assigned to your project, he drains money from your budget. So, when the work is done, you need to move resources to other projects.

The workload gradually reduces closer to the end, and you need to release people whom you don't need anymore. You need to plan when is the ideal time to move a person to another project. Then, you need to work with your boss and department managers to find a project that can benefit from taking on an in-house resource rather than hiring someone new.

I believe that terminating contracts after a project ends is a terrible way to manage people. For sure, there will be people who want to leave. There will be some hired for just that project. But, in most cases, it's bad practice. During the project's lifetime, you develop and educate these people. They learn how to execute projects inside the organization. And then you simply let them go? It doesn't make sense. So, always try to keep the best people in the organization for good.

PERFORMANCE REVIEWS

These should be mandatory for every organization. But, in practice, it's rarely the case. Imagine that a person works on a project for most of his review period. Then, you released him to another project, and he asked for a performance and salary review. Who would provide feedback on all the great work he had done on your project? He will have to suffice with small achievements on the new project.

So, personally, I do two things. Firstly, I run a formal performance review according to the company's policies. I clearly communicate that this review may not result in a better salary or position. Nevertheless, I'll pass this information to the next manager.

Secondly, for those who leave the company, I write a review on their LinkedIn profile. People can decide what reviews to show on their profile page. I only write one when I can give some positive feedback. Otherwise, it's a waste of time.

DOCUMENTATION ARCHIVE

I work in an industry where everything is digital and backups are automatic. In most cases, therefore, I don't need to create explicit project archives. Nevertheless, I have a folder for each project containing all the essential documentation for my reference. And, usually, it's stored in the cloud. So, to some extent, it's backed up as well.

However, in some industries and niches, you need to archive all documentation, invoices, and emails. So, you need to ask about this at the start of a project. It's much easier to do it on the go rather than all at the end of the project. Therefore, develop a workflow to sort emails and project documentation by folders. You can also set up an automatic system to store everything in a dedicated folder.

You may need to hand off this collection to the project owners and your organization's archive for future reference.

Keep in mind that someone may require this information years after the project ends. So, be diligent in collecting everything required. On the other hand, don't forget about NDAs, which can last for many years or even a lifetime. Don't store all this information on your personal devices or cloud storage accounts. Likewise, when you leave an organization, clean up all sensitive information.

TRANSITION TO A NEW PROJECT

You will often start a new project before you finish the previous one. Therefore, project life cycles will overlap. But, if you want to improve your management approach for each successive project, you need to review lessons learned and decide what changes you'll make. While the overall approach stays the same, you need to adjust the processes and tools.

Hopefully, you follow a professional development plan. By that I mean you take courses, read articles, get certifications, etc. So, you'll have a lot of ideas for improvement. But I recommend selecting no more than three major changes per new project. You don't want to start afresh every time. You need to compare baselines so you can measure your progress.

Then, the whole cycle of project management repeats. It's important to follow the process and avoid shortcuts as much as possible. The practical project management approach described in this book is as simple as it can be. All you need to do is follow the steps. At the very least, you need to consider them all and decide whether to use them or not every time you start a new project.

CHAPTER 61
IS IT TIME FOR YOU TO BECOME A GREAT PROJECT MANAGER?

Congratulations! You made it to the end. I hope you got a lot of value out of this book.

With the knowledge you have gained, you can learn everything else you need to know to become a great project manager on your own. It's just a matter of time while you experience all the aspects of a project in real life.

Things like how to:

- integrate all these processes and tools into a cohesive whole;
- become a leader of a team of total strangers;
- rapidly build your career and reach your earning potential; and
- write the perfect CV of a project manager.

However, it's easier and faster to learn from someone's else's experience. In my online course, I explore all these aspects in depth and how they all work together. As you know, a picture is worth a thousand words. Moreover, I touch on many related topics essential for project managers, like productivity, technical skills, agile frameworks, leadership, and many more.

Check how you can benefit from the course here:
https://itpmschool.com/book-course

NOTES

8. THE LIFE CYCLE OF A LARGE PROJECT

1. Project Management Institute. 2017. *A Guide to the Project Management Body of Knowledge (PMBOK Guide)*. 6th ed. Newton Square, PA: Project Management Institute, 554

12. IMPACT OF STAKEHOLDERS

1. Project Management Institute. 2017. *A Guide to the Project Management Body of Knowledge (PMBOK Guide)*. 6th ed. Newton Square, PA: Project Management Institute, p 550

18. HOW TO BUILD ENGAGEMENT

1. Kaufman, J. (2010). *The personal MBA: Master the art of business.* Portfolio.

19. RISK MANAGEMENT OVERVIEW

1. Project Management Institute. 2017. *A Guide to the Project Management Body of Knowledge (PMBOK Guide)*. 6th ed. Newton Square, PA: Project Management Institute, chap 11 "Project Risk Management"
2. Project Management Institute. 2017. *A Guide to the Project Management Body of Knowledge (PMBOK Guide)*. 6th ed. Newton Square, PA: Project Management Institute, 667

33. PROJECT SCOPE MANAGEMENT OVERVIEW

1. Project Management Institute. 2017. A Guide to the Project Management Body of Knowledge (PMBOK Guide). 6th ed. Newton Square, PA: Project Management Institute, 131
2. Project Management Institute. 2017. A Guide to the Project Management Body of Knowledge (PMBOK Guide). 6th ed. Newton Square, PA: Project Management Institute, 131

36. MAKE QUALITY A PART OF PROJECT SCOPE

1. Project Management Institute. 2017. A Guide to the Project Management Body of Knowledge (PMBOK Guide). 6th ed. Newton Square, PA: Project Management Institute, 283

39. WORK BREAKDOWN STRUCTURE

1. Project Management Institute. 2017. A Guide to the Project Management Body of Knowledge (PMBOK Guide). 6th ed. Newton Square, PA: Project Management Institute, 157

44. HOW TO PRODUCE ACCURATE ESTIMATES

1. Project Management Institute. 2017. A Guide to the Project Management Body of Knowledge (PMBOK Guide). 6th ed. Newton Square, PA: Project Management Institute, 241

Printed in Great Britain
by Amazon

41218612R00248